JOHNNY CASH INTERNATIONAL

FANDOM & CULTURE

Paul Booth and Katherine Larsen, series editors

JOHNNY CASH
INTERNATIONAL

*How and Why Fans
Love the Man in Black*

Michael Hinds and
Jonathan Silverman

University of Iowa Press
Iowa City, Iowa

University of Iowa Press, Iowa City 52242

Copyright © 2020 by the University of Iowa Press

www.uipress.uiowa.edu

Printed in the United States of America

Text design by Ashley Muehlbauer

Printed on acid-free paper

Library of Congress Cataloging-in-Publication Data

Names: Hinds, Michael, author. | Silverman, Jonathan, 1965– author.

Title: Johnny Cash international: how and why fans love the man in black / Michael Hinds and Jonathan Silverman.

Description: Iowa City: University of Iowa Press, 2020. | Series: Fandom and culture | Includes bibliographical references and index.

Identifiers: LCCN 2019047807 (print) | LCCN 2019047808 (ebook) |

ISBN 9781609387013 (paperback) | ISBN 9781609387020 (ebook)

Subjects: LCSH: Cash, Johnny—Appreciation. | Country music fans. | Popular music fans.

Classification: LCC ML420.C265 H52 2020 (print) | LCC ML420.

C265 (ebook) | DDC 782.421642092—dc23

LC record available at https://lccn.loc.gov/2019047807

LC ebook record available at https://lccn.loc.gov/2019047808

CONTENTS

Part 1: Histories and Contexts of International Cash Fandom

Part 2: A Year in the Life of Cash Fans around the World

ACKNOWLEDGMENTS

We would like to thank many people. First, we thank our editors at the University of Iowa Press: Catherine Cocks, who initiated a discussion about a Cash book; Ranjit Arab, who shepherded the book through much of the publication process; and Meredith Stabel, who saw it through its completion.

Silverman received institutional and collegial support at the University of Massachusetts Lowell, including from Diana Archibald, Todd Avery, Luis Falcon, Natalie Houston, Sue Kim, Jacky Ledoux, Bridget Marshall, Keith Mitchell, Beth Mitchneck, Anthony Szczesiul, and Todd Tietchen. Librarians Deborah Friedman and Rose Patton were invaluable getting all sorts of materials through interlibrary loan. Kathleen Campbell from the Country Music Hall of Fame and Library was invaluable in aiding Silverman to research Cash's fandom through fan club newsletters and other materials.

Hinds was given logistical and financial support from the School of English at Dublin City University for the trip to Groningen, for which he would like to thank his head of school, Derek Hand. Other colleagues provided all manner of support and anecdotal material for the research, thanks to Noel Jackson, Gearoid O'Flaherty, Will Murphy, Leeann Lane, Paula Murphy, Jean-Philippe Imbert, Kit Fryatt, Ian Leask, and Joe Rivera. Friends and family also provided an intrepid team of auxiliary fieldworkers, witnessing Cash happenings and incidents around the world. Apologies if your name does not appear here, but people who spring to mind immediately are Franc Myles (for his intrepid companionship on the road in Alabama and Tennessee), Stan Erraught, Philip Coleman, Niamh NicGhabhann, Jane Clare, Geraldine Hall, Maria Stuart, Tom Conaty, and Ellen Dillon, as well as all relevant Wests, Ryans, and Mulveens. Thanks too to Karen in Memphis and the organizers of Nomadikon at Muscle Shoals, as well as those who facilitated the trip to Coimbra.

Many stories came our way from or about Cash fans in the course of this work, and some had to remain untold. Thanks to all who allowed us to be party to their Cash fandom. We particularly want to thank our interview subjects, particularly Elvira van Poelgeest, who made so much happen, and the Black Suspenders, Albert Visser, Theunis Lourens, and Kees van der Lay. Readers are about to see how Finbarr "Barry" Winters and Charlie Taggart were powerful figures of inspiration for the Irish dimension of the project. Thanks too to Aaron Prociuk, the wonderful Marco, and all in Coimbra, especially Alexandra, Hugh, Pedro, Paolo, and Steve.

We did not know anybody, save for Barry and Elvira, who posted all their videos and comments on YouTube, and only a few people who filled out our survey. But we would still like to thank the laconic Norwegians, Half Man Half Biscuit, Deborah from Nowhere, and all the rest.

Silverman would like to thank his mom, Beverly Silverman, his brothers, Jason and Joel, his sister, Alba, and his nephews, Noah and Theo, for their support, and he would like to thank the Hinds family for their infinite patience; they hosted Silverman for almost two months during the construction of this book.

Michael Hinds knows more about their patience than most, and he would like to thank them all in turn. His mother, Kathleen, was vital in keeping up communications with Charlie Taggart in Omagh, and she was an observant research participant at Johnny Cash tribute shows in Tyrone and Dublin. She read an embryonic version of this book with an aptly critical eye, as did others; thanks to all for that. Hector and Henry Hinds were irrepressible in all sorts of ways, providing unanticipated perspectives on the work and not letting the work entirely spoil their enjoyment of the 2018 World Cup. Christine presided over everything with stoicism, wit, and love, despite having to endure the ordeal of coming home from a twelve-hour workday as a corporate lawyer to find a houseful of man-children spouting about people posting videos of Johnny Cash. How she did that, only she knows.

PREFACE

Jonathan Silverman first met Michael Hinds in 2010 when he presented a seminar on Johnny Cash's song "A Boy Named Sue" at Mater Dei Institute, where Hinds was in the English department. They then taught UMass Lowell's study abroad program together in Dublin, finding they had an extensive list of common interests. Johnny Cash appeared somewhere on that list, and they had exchanged stories about him and his fans, so when Silverman ventured an idea about writing a book on Johnny Cash's international fans, they knew each other well enough to know it might work.

Partnering on a cross-cultural subject between two scholars from different countries proved necessarily advantageous and challenging. Silverman comes from the field of American studies and Hinds is a literary scholar, but both focus on the text/subject and work toward its context as a way of trying to understand it. The sense of relevant context might vary, whether because of discipline or, critically, a geocritical perspective; but both were committed to the idea of international Cash fandom as a kind of text, as was each different fan or fan performance, significant both individually and collectively. Negotiating these texts was the lifeblood of the project, and the Cash fan material was always compelling, never monotonous, always retaining an element of necessary intrigue.

To the degree we succeeded in this work, it was because of our ability to work together, the abundance of material, and the cooperation and often encouragement from our subjects, who invited us to follow them as they pursued their fan dreams. It was also because of the presence of Johnny Cash—no longer among the living, but very much alive through his fans.

INTRODUCTION

At a former prison on an island off the coast of Ireland in June 2018, an Irish Johnny Cash tribute band finished a concert celebrating the fiftieth anniversary of Cash's seminal album, *At Folsom Prison* (Columbia, 1968). To close the concert, the band was joined on stage with a Dutch rockabilly band for "Will the Circle Be Unbroken?," the famous Carter Family song that Cash often played with his wife, June Carter Cash. Before 2017, the two bands had never met, and a concert had never been held at the prison before.

These performers were first and foremost fans of Johnny Cash. They came together out of a love for him as well as a desire to do well by him. Putting on a concert required effort and organizational and promotional skills, as well as the ability to communicate with other fans and the general public. While the prison concert is perhaps an extreme example of Cash fandom at work, these Cash superfans did what they have always done: they used the technologies available to them and their own ingenuity to demonstrate their love of Johnny Cash.

Such fans are just part of what constitutes international Cash fandom today. The long story of the phenomenon begins in the early stages of his fame, when Cash first plays Canada in 1957 and his records begin to arrive at destinations in Europe. His fandom grew during his lifetime principally because of a relentless touring schedule, a vast recording catalog, his presence in American and international popular culture, and devoted fan stewardship. That fandom has continued to grow since his death in 2003, fueled by the growth of the internet, which has aided fan communication and travel, and his continued presence in popular culture through releases of posthumous albums and placement in movie and television soundtracks.

Yet fans are really the ones who create other fans. They do so through their divergent activities, which range from the intensive to the passive. Travel is an intrinsic mode of international fandom, as when fans ventured to see Cash in concert in his lifetime, both at home and abroad. Now fans tour the places where he lived, recorded, and performed—experiences that they either design for themselves or follow according to what the tourist industry offers. Others express their fandom at home by incorporating Cash into their daily lives and sharing those activities with others. These forms of fandom are enabled and intensified by digital fan culture; new forms of creative collaboration and communication have flowered online, and that includes the world on YouTube. Cash videos there can generate millions of views and tens of thousands of comments. Not all of those viewers and posters are classifiable as fans in a traditional sense, yet if a commentator posting about Cash has to withstand the abuse of online trolls, that is fleetingly as heroic an endeavor as the transatlantic journeyings of others.

They have much material to discuss. Over his fifty-year performing and recording career, fans have found their way to Cash first as the singer of songs such as "I Walk the Line," "Folsom Prison Blues," and "Ring of Fire" in the first phases of his recording career, then "Hurt" and "The Man Comes Around" in a later period. Alternatively, they may have first heard his two live prison albums in the 1960s, or of his status as the Man in Black, or seen him as the star of his own television show. They could have witnessed his appearances in many forms of popular culture or become intrigued by his tumultuous life, with drug and alcohol addiction, two marriages, and his frequent (if minor) clashes with the law in the 1960s.

Twenty-first-century fans might have come to him through the well-received biopic, *Walk the Line* (2005), starring Joaquin Phoenix and Reese Witherspoon, or the frequent use of his music in films and television shows in the last few decades, including *Logan* (2017) and *Dawn of the Dead* (2004). They also derive fascination from the more subtle aspects of his life: his stint in the army, where he both learned how to play guitar and was the first American to find out about Joseph Stalin's death; his political work on behalf of prisoners and Native Americans; and his intimacy with audiences over the years.[1]

After his first trip to Canada, he never stopped going abroad, even when his star dimmed in the United States. The gig archive of the Johnny Cash Infocenter records that he visited Australia in April 1959, then played his first European show at a festival in Germany on September 20 of the same year. Five days later, he appeared solo on a British television show, *Boy Meet Girls*. Later that year, he played at American military bases in Europe. He made his first Asia tour in early 1962, playing dozens of dates in Korea and Japan. In the 1960s, he regularly played in Europe and occasionally in the Far East, where he played on military bases as well as in clubs. He continued to tour Europe until 1997, playing his last shows there in Scandinavia and Germany. Historically, touring has been critical in building a following and a reputation, and Cash was on the road constantly, playing in hundreds, if not thousands, of places, and fan newsletters record how he would often meet fan club members backstage.

Aside from its impact in gate receipts and record sales, touring was vital for the bonds it fostered between performer and fan. Cash's career-long commitment to international touring meant that he kept on offering fans the feeling of having shared a space with him. Every show ended with an audience member being able to say, "I saw Johnny Cash." Critically, however, it also enabled them to say it to one another. Fans often encountered each other for the first time at Cash's gigs. The first waves of international Cash fandom can be traced directly to the goodwill generated by his shows. It was fortified by the idea that Cash was a particularly hardworking artist, one bound to the road. Fans appreciated Cash's labor in coming to play for them, and they reciprocated by traveling to see him whenever they had the opportunity—and not just when he came to a city close to them.

Cash was (and is) disseminated around the world through radio, television, and movies as both a singer and actor. He appeared as a guest star in popular dramas; a surprising number of people we interviewed in Europe referenced Cash's appearance as a homicidal preacher on *Columbo* (1971–2003) in 1974, an episode that was screened and rerun across the continent. His great late burst of creativity with the American Recordings albums gave him another international life, and his 2002 video for "Hurt" dominated global airplay on MTV. The song then found yet greater popularity with the emergence of YouTube and became a global text, one that millions recognize.

"Hurt" on YouTube also demonstrates how Cash increasingly caught the attention of fans for whom English was not their primary language, communicating profoundly to them regardless. For his reemergence into popular music that came with the release of the first American Recordings album in 1994, his managers booked him into locales seemingly meant for rock stars, including Emo's, a famed punk club in Austin. In the same year, at the storied Glastonbury Festival in England, he shared the bill with Oasis, Orbital, and Bjork, assuring his introduction to younger fans as a simultaneously canonical and contemporary figure. He was able to powerfully renew attention over a long period of time, and since his death in 2003, fans worldwide have continued to remake him all over again.[2]

This book focuses on how the original mark that Cash made on the world was transformed by the fans who sought to perpetuate his legacy. They do this radically, veering between the hyperstrategic and the anarchic, working in communities or individually. Some are defined by restless progress in their fan activity; others are entirely settled. There are two worlds at work here: one organized by traditional Johnny Cash fandom, clearly circumscribed, and another beyond its borders, in which Johnny Cash is a vital cultural phenomenon and of real interest to a lot of people.

Over time, the question of Johnny Cash's place in the world is posed and then reiterated by his performances, his handlers, and his fans. What Cash stands for is complex and indefinite, but that might be because he stands for complexity itself; his contradictions resonate powerfully with fans, enhancing his integrity, and he seems even more popular and present in the years since his death. A fandom so large and diverse cannot be controlled by just a few people. Cash's original fandom is based in the race-troubled American South, which can lead to unexpected and unwanted affiliations, as when a neo-Nazi wearing a Cash T-shirt appeared in media footage of the 2017 Charlottesville riots. The Cash family has had to become increasingly dedicated to preventing the theft of that integrity by political groups, notably those of the alt-right. His popularity is so radical that it has become a problem.

For us, contemplating international Cash fandom began by exploring our independent encounters with it. Hinds had met a Northern Irish shopkeeper, Charlie Taggart, who played only Cash as he worked. Silverman worked as a Fulbright scholar in Norway, providing a selection of seminar topics to educators and students across the country, from which they repeatedly requested seminars on two things: the United States elections and Johnny Cash. Charlie was clearly a fan; what was singularly interesting and instructive about him was that he was from Northern Ireland, and he brought his fandom into his world of work. Cash led international fans to America and Americana, but it also brought them home. The Norwegian audience proved Cash's transgenerational popularity as an educational subject and cultural icon.

With a Johnny Cash fan who is not from the United States, inevitably the question arises of how the fan came to learn of Cash in the first place. We began our research with a survey that asked fans about their own origin stories as well as their ideas about where Cash's nationality fits into their own views on the United States. This project was useful, but it also generated a sense of ambiguity about the significance of Cash's Americanness that persisted throughout the entire project.

As globalization has diminished the significance of national discourse (ironically thereby creating hypernationalisms that had long been thought consigned to the great ideology dump), the value of a figure like Cash is that he at once seems American and universal. The fans in this study show that his international status is a given, his Americanness more contingent.

Fans understandably resist the idea that their fandom might be explained in the crude terms of cultural imperialism, as if they have no say in deciding what they like. Bertha Chin and Lisa Hitchcock Morimoto call this transcultural fandom, when "fans become fans of border-crossing texts or objects not necessarily because of *where* they are produced, but because they may recognise a subjective moment of affinity regardless of origin" (2013, 99). Cash appeals across nationalities and age groups as a mysterious, deep-voiced performer of music, as well as a visually arresting icon and artist who empathizes with the marginalized. His fans feel recognized by him, wherever they come from.

Thinking about Cash internationally also means thinking about him visually. Fans from all over the world use Cash's image, whether online or on their bodies, whether through tattoos or T-shirts, in a show of global popularity. The extent of that popularity is demonstrated by the Johnny Cash Project, a remarkable online collaboration between fans to construct pieces of video art designed to accompany Cash's "Ain't No Grave." This is an explicitly international project, with contributors identifying their specific location (usually a town or city of origin, but sometimes just a state), showing that his fans map themselves in ways that cut against the broad strokes of nationality.

If this location activity demonstrates how contemporary fandom maximizes the power of an available technology into creativity, then we can venture a comparable point about the role that newsletters and fan clubs played before the digital era. English fans did a lot of the work on those early newsletters, fashioning a gateway between Europe and American fans. Indeed, Cash has a particular resonance in England, where the construction of fandom has a thorough foundation in sport culture. Sport and Cash fandom often share the same complicated relationships with class, language, and affiliation. We demonstrate this in a reading of a series of English cultural texts while we also address Cash's presence across media. All of these English fans claim him as part of their world, as part of their cultural property, thereby bringing him into their clubhouses.

The opening chapters of this book provide context for interpreting Cash fandom as an intriguing international phenomenon; they also provide direction for the second part of the book, which engages the activities of international Cash fans from June 2017 to June 2018, along with what was happening on YouTube at the same time. These chapters regard online activity and traces its movements over land and sea, beginning with a trip to Groningen, the Netherlands, to visit Elvira van Poelgeest, founder of the Johnny Cash Infocenter (http://www.johnny-cash-infocenter.com). She spoke to us about creating an international network but then also generated another field of activity around our project as it evolved, inviting others to participate, including her band, the Black Suspenders. Through her Facebook call for participants, Finbarr "Barry" Winters, an Irish fan and a member of a band called Strictly Cash, flew in to be interviewed as well, acting on an impulse to be seen and heard that over the next few months took him to remarkable places.

Elvira and Barry's multifaceted fandom became a vital strand of the project, not least because of their evident interest in how their fan work was being studied. They are simultaneously impassioned and organized, generous with their time, and open to scrutiny. They are also ready to travel in the pursuit of their fandom, both around Europe and to the United States, providing a model of international superfandom—a strategic and progressive activity that is always looking to grow. Barry and Elvira were looking for experiences, audiences, and other fans through Johnny Cash. Their activities increasingly lead them to places where Cash fandom has become an international business, with cultural entrepreneurs looking to build heritage and tourist resorts based on Cash's legacy.

The unruly commons of YouTube is the counter to such organization. Cash's international presence is tangible in the comments sections beneath various postings of Cash videos amid an anarchy of discourse: literary, first-ism, movie referrals, philosophy, sympathy, bigotry, racism. More than ever, questions emerge here about whether a comment on a YouTube video represents a gesture of fandom. YouTube has also spawned a superabundance of international Cash performances, in particular his massive hit "Ring of Fire" (1963). Its power as a song lies in its simplicity, which helps demonstrate the way Cash appeals. He is someone who invites emulation; he is a player who gets people to play. Fans often cover their subjects, but not all cover artists are fans, as a taxonomy of types of performance and their attendant motivations demonstrates.

Hinds went to France to seek out Marco Rockmilhaud, the maverick owner of a fan-oriented Johnny Cash Facebook page. Marco is passionate about Cash, but on his own independent terms—a reflection of the singular way Cash's music had come to him during his childhood in Nigeria. Marco was adamant about the leftist orientation of the Cash fandom he knew, an assumption that was radically challenged a week after he was interviewed, when the Cash family spoke out about Charlottesville. This dramatically showed how Cash is a phenomenon of history as well as popular culture; it further indicates the value of framing the study of his fandom temporally. The year of Cash fandom under scrutiny had to take account of this extraordinary intervention, even as some fans were unwilling to discuss it.

Fandom has been transformed by the internet, but some intrepid international fans have also traveled to experience or sample more of Johnny Cash, thus demonstrating the types of fandom that money can buy, and that the internet can help arrange. Silverman observed this firsthand on two occasions in the course of the year's work. The first occurred when he was embedded in a fan pilgrimage to the mid-South being undertaken by Barry Winters and his Austrian friends, Brigitte and Walter Ringhofer. Barry traveled to follow Cash's footsteps as a historical figure but also as a performer. His trip was planned around looking to get on stages that Cash had once inhabited. Ringhofer was there to observe and collect, taking over eight thousand photos and videos—a hoard enabled by the cheapness of digital storage. His particular motive was to gather material and garner publicity for a Cash museum he has opened at home in Austria, where he has inaugurated a European Johnny Cash Festival.

Silverman followed Elvira and her Dutch friends a few months afterward, on a trip broader in conception than that of Barry. It engaged race and class as contexts for thinking about Cash—something his fandom often avoids. Elvira's profile as an international promoter of Cash fandom also translated into privileged access to the emerging map of Johnny Cash tourism and its related economy. She was offered experiences that are not public (yet), and may never be, like sleeping in his bedroom and trying on his clothes.

Using Cash experimentally as a basis for all interactions in a non-American environment, Hinds went in May 2018 to the Portuguese university town of Coimbra, exploring the degree to which a city might be experienced as if it were a Cash fan. Despite his not having an obvious profile in Portugal, it quickly became apparent that Cash intergenerationally permeated cultural and political discourse, representing an alternative vision of the past to a country still reflecting on its postrevolutionary situation.

The year of observation closes by looking at Cork, Ireland, Barry Winters's native city and where he reunited with Elvira's band in June 2018 to perform at a former prison. This seems a fitting conclusion to a year of following superfans, but there is no obvious terminal point for international Cash fandom. It is a relentless organism that never stops evolving. The last word in the book is left to yet another Cash fan, one born in Pakistan, who proves the radical extent to which Cash inspires affection and hope, a figure of decency to summon in the direst of circumstances.

In the end, international Cash fandom tests the limits of geography and identity. A more discriminating vocabulary thus has to evolve to properly describe all the different impulses and identifications that might exist within it. Within its internationalism, Cash fandom is also transnational, meaning that fans connect in ways that minimize the importance of national identity. This sometimes takes the form of stressing relationships to regional or even more intimate identities, which can be seen as translocal, a term defined by Brickell and Datta as "simultaneous situatedness across different locales" (2011, 4). This suggests that specific locations mean less than the connections between them, but in practice, Cash fandom paradoxically intensifies a sense of place. As fans respond powerfully to the imaginary geography of Cash's songs and the actual geography of his life, they also express a strong sense of relationship, if not always affiliation, to their home locality. "Country" is an all-important designation here: it represents a musical genre as well as a political or geographic way of describing a person's relationship to a place, whether a town, region, or nation. In his autobiography, Cash shows that he had quickly figured out that "country" fandom was becoming a curious business—a way of embracing a style that is not necessarily a native inheritance:

> I was talking with a friend of mine about this the other day: that country life as I knew it might really be a thing of the past and when music people today, performers and fans alike, talk about being "country," they don't mean they know or even care about the land and the life it sustains and regulates. They're talking more about choices—a way to look, a group to belong to, a kind of music to call their own. Which begs a question: Is there anything behind the symbols of modern "country," or are the symbols themselves the whole story? Are the hats, the boots, the pickup trucks, and the honky-tonking poses all that's left of a disintegrating culture? Back in Arkansas, a way of life produced a certain kind of music. Does a certain kind of music now produce a way of life? Maybe that's okay. I don't know. (1997, 13–14)

As Cash writes in the next paragraph, "Perhaps I'm just alienated, feeling the cold wind of exclusion blowing my way" (14), but he is also listening acutely to the pulse of our mediated reality. In the same way that he is both a country music artist and more than that, Cash fans think problematically about the meaning of "country," and their intensely creative and transgenerational fandom has emerged out of that. Fans respect the sense of connection to Arkansas that Cash expresses, and they undoubtedly want to partake of it, but it also generates a desire in them to realize connectedness to their own countries, wherever or whatever they might be.

PART ONE

HISTORIES AND CONTEXTS OF INTERNATIONAL CASH FANDOM

1 FIRST ENCOUNTERS WITH INTERNATIONAL CASH FANDOM

The Irish Shopkeeper and the Norwegians

Two fans from two countries provided the primary inspiration for this study. One was a Norwegian schoolboy, who lifted his trouser leg to Silverman to reveal a tattoo of Johnny Cash just after Silverman had delivered a lecture as part of his Fulbright program in 2007. The other was Charlie Taggart, a shopkeeper in the Northern Irish town of Omagh, County Tyrone, whom Hinds met in 2013 when he went to buy a newspaper. The student was part of a class group that had requested the seminar on Cash, but it was not possible to know just how many of his classmates were Cash fans as such. In contrast, Charlie was playing Cash on a cassette player in his shop; it turned out that Cash was all he played, every day, noting, "It's always a good day for Johnny."

It turned out that Charlie was locally renowned for his devotion to Cash, and in the days after Cash's death, people had taken time to visit the shop and express their condolences. The love for Cash shaped and framed Charlie's own experience, as well as that of his family, and gave him a singular standing in his community. The Norwegian student bore his love on his body, but it undoubtedly was a manifestation of stronger feelings generated by his fandom. Both fans exemplify the international reach of Cash, but their cases also indicate how he connects transgenerationally and how fandom can become intimate. Tattoos are for life, and Charlie's life in his hometown was defined by his fandom, with locals greeting him by saying, "How's Johnny Cash?"

These stories act as a prologue to the work of this entire study by engaging with Cash fans at home and abroad. These stories set Cash fans' work against the particularities of their local histories and the conditions in which they occurred. Hinds met Charlie by chance, and they fell into speaking a language they shared. Silverman was at the boy's school at the behest of two governments; discussion proved challenging, so the tattoo had to do all the talking. Taken together, Charlie and the Norwegians demonstrate the complicated ways that international Cash fandom might, and often does, work.

Context is everything. Silverman and the student were in the classroom because of decisions made far away, as well as in the class's electing to have him deliver a session on Cash. The job was more about talking than listening, so there wasn't much time for hearing from people about why they liked Johnny Cash. Indeed, Cash was in many ways a relief from the other topic that was continually requested: the George W. Bush administration and the 2008 presidential election.

International fandom is inevitably complicated by the range of tensions that are at work in how fans understand their own national identity and what it means to align oneself with cultural objects from another country. A Norwegian fan of Johnny Cash is not simply rejecting Norwegian culture in favor of American culture. It is a far more intimate and precise business than that. For a fan like this to attach himself to a cultural phenomenon from outside his own nationality is surely significant; it indicates that nationality is not uppermost in his hierarchy of desire and identification.

Similarly, with Charlie Taggart, understanding his Cash fandom requires a contextual approach, starting with a knowledge of what Irish people mean when they talk about country music—something complicated by the national passion for country and Irish, a local adaptation of the country genre. In talking about how others in his town feel about Cash, Charlie says, "Well, you know, they like country and Irish." This Irish-produced fusion music joins Nashville conventions to those of traditional Irish culture, and its artists typically perform a lot of cover versions of American standards and traditional Irish balladry. Their own compositions tend to apply a generic country music framing to lyrical content that describes rural Irish experience, forming a country hybrid. "Four Country Roads" (Denver Records, 1981) by Big Tom and the Mainliners (once Ireland's Kings of Country) describes a County Galway landscape against a Tennessee soundscape.[1]

Julian Vignoles (1984, 70–72) describes country and Irish as a form of expression that is as truly Irish as anything else the country has produced, not least because it has the authority of being what people actually like. Its invariably clean-cut performers also appeal across dividing lines of class and religion, thereby unifying Irish people in cultural conservatism—a significant achievement in a country often defined by such divisions. The heartland of country and Irish is the northwestern frontier between Northern Ireland and the Republic of Ireland, and many of its most celebrated performers have come from towns and villages within fifty miles of either side of the dividing line—places like Charlie's hometown, Omagh. In his well-known passion for Cash, Charlie cleared significant space between himself and others in his locality. He was emphatic in saying that *those* people primarily liked country and Irish, whereas he liked Cash. Country and Irish was "for dancing," Charlie said, and he did not dance.

The self-conscious singularity of Charlie's fandom was a response to a peculiar environment wherein relationships to America were culturally dominant. Omagh is home to the Ulster-American Folk Park, a history park that recreates the experience of emigration to the United States, with Irish buildings relocated from their original sites, then restored; a reconstruction of a ship used in the passage from Ireland to America; and recreations of American buildings from Pennsylvania. All of this is built next to the actual Irish homestead of the Mellon banking family of Philadelphia. The area also claims the families of Davy Crockett and US presidents Grant and Wilson as part of its heritage. Cultural migration is a two-way street. You might visit an Irish bar in Nashville, but around Omagh, you drink in the Golden Nugget or the El Paso. Northern Ireland is also rich in temperance preachers, gospel halls, and line dancers. Omagh produced Ireland's most famous Elvis tribute performer, Frankie "Frank" Chisum. In this part of the world, it is not unusual to engage with America; what matters more is how distinctively one engages with it.

Significantly, one of Cash's few successes in the Irish singles chart came by recording with a popular country and Irish performer, Sandy Kelly, who lent him some of her confirmed marketability with "Woodcarver" (KTel Records, 1990). So Johnny Cash has a place in the Irish love of country and Cash tribute acts perform all over Ireland, but he is not "country" as many

Irish people choose to understand it. It should be added that country and Irish fans also really like Cash—just not as much as Taggart. In particular, they like Cash's song "Forty Shades of Green," which has become a mainstay in the country and Irish canon. The joke is that only a few people seem to realize that Cash wrote it, assuming instead that it is homegrown because it matches the country and Irish formula so closely. In rejecting country and Irish's imagination of a shared life between the old and new countries, Taggart is way out of this local trend, casting himself as an outsider.

According to record sales, Cash has never been a massive hit in Ireland, yet people have always liked him and watched his TV show on the national television channel of the Irish Republic, RTE—indeed, the only television channel there for many in the 1970s. Cash toured the country many times and enjoyed tremendous name recognition, which generated seriously committed Cash fans in lots of different Irish places, even though they do not organize themselves en masse. Cash here is international in that he bridges Ireland and the United States, but he is also transnational in that he allows his fans to express ambivalence about national identity. Charlie Taggart is Irish, but in his liking for somebody as thoroughly American (or un-Irish) as Cash, he steps outside the common tastes of both his country and his local region with a deliberate gesture of self-assertion.

Charlie has been listening to Cash's music since the 1950s, and his fandom can be traced through music technologies, from analog to digitalization. He first heard Cash on the radio, bought singles, then albums on vinyl, eight-track tapes, and cassettes. He began buying CDs when they effectively became his only option after other technologies became obsolete. For years he made mixtapes on cassette to play in the shop, then in 2018 moved to using USB sticks and a media player.

The mixtapes meant that he was continually renewing his relationship to Cash through a curation process. He had also begun generating long playlists on his computer, given the capacity that digital technology afforded him. He incorporated material by Cash as well as American country artists whom he deemed worthy of association with Cash, usually centering each mixtape on a particular theme. In June 2018, his current project was based on the concept of borders—a live subject both in an American and a Irish–British context, given the immediate pressures of Trump, the unforgotten Troubles, and Brexit (which threatens to restore a militarized border between the north and south of Ireland).

Charlie Taggart and his wife, Bridget, in his store in Omagh in Northern Ireland.

Fans have to operate in many networks, even domestic ones, and Charlie's wife, Bridget, provided a cooler and comic perspective on life with him (and Johnny). A central anecdote in their life history was about how Charlie was playing Cash's "Lost on the Desert" in their kitchen as Bridget gave birth to their son in an upstairs bedroom: "I was up there in the desert by myself. The nurse said to keep the music going, but if he had come in the room, he would have got the tape player round his head."

They had once gone to Dublin, where Cash was playing two shows a day over a three-day period, and saw all six performances. Charlie spoke animatedly about the subtle distinctions in pacing and mood that could be appreciated between these performances—matters of seconds in changes of rhythm. Bridget's silence was eloquent. She recounted seeing a bad show in the Hippodrome Theatre in Birmingham, England, where they had lived and worked for a substantial period in the 1970s and 1980s, when Cash could barely communicate with his audience. Now Charlie said very little, only adding, "He never hid his feelings." The Cash life was very much a life shared, although Bridget said she had not realized on her wedding day that she was marrying both Charlie and Johnny. She said a woman had once asked her in the shop what Charlie was like at home, and Bridget said that it would take an awful lot to annoy him—definitely a form of compliment.

Beyond his family, Charlie does not seek out other Cash fans for society and has never been in a fan club. He subscribed briefly to an English newsletter about Cash in the 1970s, but he evidently preferred to do his listening and thinking for himself. It was nothing personal, he said; he was just content being his own kind of Cash fan, emulating how Cash projected his individualism. When he talked about the many times he saw Cash in concert, there was barely a reference to the crowd that might have been there on a particular evening or how they affected the event. Charlie was too intent on looking at Cash to think about them.

He was alert to whatever traces of Cash that he himself might pick up from the street. He remarked that he had recently been in Belfast (the capital of Northern Ireland), where he heard student buskers playing "The Long Black Veil." He went over and started chatting, and they said they had just learned it. This microhappening is evidently a source of pleasure to Charlie, a man who loves stories and storytelling. Cash was a great storyteller too, but beyond that, he also occasions some great stories for Charlie. When working as a bus conductor in Birmingham, Charlie took fares and maintained order on a double-decker bus, but he found a space for his fandom. He spoke about an evening when the bus was rolling into Witton Square in the city center, at the end of a long route, and Charlie had been singing "Dark as the Dungeon" for he did not know how long. As the bus came to a stop, a passenger took hold of his arm and enquired: "Do you *have* to do that?" No need to answer.

Charlie's interest in storytelling was not only a hobby but his very definition. In discussion, he referenced writers such as P. G. Wodehouse, Raymond Chandler, and Dennis Wheatley, then moved into movies and spoke of his love for the Marx Brothers and Laurel and Hardy. This confirmed his appetite for mischief—a trait that he also identified in Cash, and that he thought of in culturally specific terms. Charlie said that "people do not get the American humor" (as in most people in his locality), but he clearly felt secure in his own ability to decode it.

Charlie talked knowledgeably about all of Cash's niche activities and manifestations, both inside and outside of music, but refrained from choosing between them. He was especially reluctant to talk about favorite songs or performances. He preferred to embrace the work of Cash as a complex comedy, a story with a positive vision of human possibility. He said that he liked almost everything Cash produced, expressing only a qualified dislike (after being pressed) for the spoken-word sections of Cash's travelogue album, *The Rambler* (Columbia, 1977), because it seemed "somewhat self-indulgent"—a refined piece of criticism on a Cash recording that comparatively few people listen to. In this respect, Charlie was a genuine expert, a self-appointed chair in Cash studies at an imaginary Irish university. His job is to listen to Cash and to encourage others to do the same; he does not want to be Johnny Cash, just admire him through contemplation.

Charlie is particularly sensitive to Cash's dualism, nailing it in a phrase: "Johnny is a nice guy, Cash a contrary stubborn individual." Charlie returned to this idea over and over again in discussion. He expressed this by answering questions about Cash in ways that stressed contradiction, if not evasion: "I wouldn't separate his public life from his private life. . . . He was a good guy and a bad guy."

When asked to identify Cash politically in a single phrase, he chose "dove with claws," Cash's famous response to a reporter's questioning in 1969 about the significance of his performance before troops in Vietnam, and one he later disavowed (Silverman 2010, 131). Cash's self-representation here was Whitmanesque and problematic; it adopted the role of appalled witness and compassionate healer, a wound dresser: "If you watch the helicopters bring in the wounded boys, and then you go into the wards and sing for 'em and try and do your best to cheer 'em up, so they can get back home, it might make you a dove with claws." That Charlie should have selected this particular self-representation of Cash is given further significance by the fact that he is an inhabitant of a small town in a small country, one that is best known for being eviscerated by a car bomb in 1998, the last grotesque flourish of the thirty-year conflict euphemized as the Troubles (*Irish Times* 2018).

The reverberations of that conflict centered in Northern Ireland but were felt in the United Kingdom and across the Irish diaspora. Violence occurred at the national level with the IRA's armed struggle against the British state, but it took an even more vicious form locally, with depressingly frequent conflict between Catholics and Protestants, and with car bombs devastating the social fabric. Cash's expression of a paradoxically violent impulse for peace makes a lot of sense for someone like Charlie.

Charlie is (and appears to have always been) adept at walking a line between the polarities of the Northern Irish conflict. He has two shops, one in the determinedly Protestant part of his town named Campsie, the other in the determinedly Catholic section called Gallows Hill. The question of his own religious faith was not broached in initial conversations, although it is usually Cash's gospel providing his shop's soundtrack. In Northern Irish social intercourse, to ask people whether they are Protestant or Catholic can lead to violence. (It also has little or nothing to do with religion in terms of faith commitment; instead, it signifies a political stance regarding the identity politics of Irishness and Britishness.) People often infer from each other's names and living situations whether they are Catholic or Protestant—an unreliable mechanism at best. It's better not to ask.

Although Charlie's liking for Cash's gospel music indicated an inclination toward evangelical Protestantism, his surname is commonly a Catholic one. He eventually clarified that he was christened a Catholic, but that there had been intermarriage in his family between Catholic and Protestant—not uncommon in most parts of Northern Ireland. Rather than any particular religious affiliation, he stressed the value that his father found in meeting other people and learning from them, and in particular he emphasizes the value of listening. He also remembered his mother singing gospel songs in his youth. The gospel according to Cash is more than an expression of a particular strain of Christianity for Charlie; it reaches back to the tolerantly spiritual culture of his upbringing.

Charlie's commitment to Cash became a way of transcending the mess of Irish identity politics and enabled him to project an image of himself to his entire community as somebody on a different cultural path. He did not think of the religious divide as being particularly grievous in his hometown ("Omagh doesn't have a problem, really"), yet his awareness of the reality of political division was also evident, demonstrated not least by how he talked about his "Borders" playlist: "People have been narrow-minded about things. The music I picked hasn't got borders. . . . I have no borders in here."

Similar impulses were at work in Norwegian attitudes about Cash. As a roving Fulbright scholar, Silverman traveled around Norway talking about American culture in high schools. Teachers were asked to choose from a list of ten topics. Because it was a US election year, elections were naturally the most popular choice (not least because it was part of Norway's national curriculum). Johnny Cash came in a clear second, however, which led to Silverman's giving thirty-nine lectures about Cash all over the country.

His presentations combined Cash's musical history with his biography, focusing on how a song would tell a story about a part of his life or career. For example, "Five Feet High and Rising," a song about the 1937 flooding of the Mississippi River in Arkansas, facilitated discussion of Cash's early life in Dyess, Arkansas. "It Was Jesus" introduced Cash's religious faith and why he moved from Sun Records to Columbia in the late 1950s. Silverman played "Ring of Fire" after playing a snippet of Anita Carter's version, "Love's Ring of Fire," to talk about the process of song construction and the uncertainty of authorial history. Then came two versions of "Folsom Prison Blues," the early bluesy version and the more wide-open rock 'n' roll version from the prison album. "Jackson" facilitated discussion of the importance of June Carter in Cash's life text, and "Last Night I Had the Strangest Dream" allowed for consideration of Cash's confusing stance on the Vietnam War. The presentation ended with the video of "Hurt," as part of a discussion about authenticity and aging.

The idea behind this was to give Norwegians a sense of the scope of history and culture behind Johnny Cash, to give them a sense of how Cash might fit into their ideas about the United States—and vice versa. Cash's life covered more than seventy years, and his engagement with politics, commerce, history, and music was one way of understanding the United States. Given the range and depth of all that experience, a challenge was to find a way of doing justice to Cash in the time allotted for the presentation. One teacher gave Silverman nine minutes, another two hours. The nine-minute version came as a postscript to a lecture on the American presidential election, and it consisted of "Folsom Prison Blues" and "Hurt"—in some ways the two most crucial songs for understanding Cash.

The response to the presentation was positive from both teachers and students, but their questions on politics were much more provocative than what they offered about Cash, probably because Silverman invited participation in the presidential lecture in a way he could not with Cash. When there were questions, they often seemed to come from either students who had seen

Walk the Line or teachers who had seen Cash in Norway.[2] For example, two girls in a small group peppered Silverman with questions about Cash directly from the movie: "Didn't he have a bad relationship with his father?" "Didn't he feel responsible for his brother's death?" "Didn't he have a drug problem?" They had ingested the plot points and transformed them into knowledge; they were asking questions to which they thought they already had answers. Teachers told Silverman about the times they had seen Johnny Cash in concert. One teacher from outside Oslo related that Cash had played only a few miles from the school, as if his presence still lingered. The brain's chemical reactions, the retrieving of memory, put Johnny Cash in that very room.

Silverman did not know how many fans he was actually reaching in these classes. Even the teachers who chose his presentation might not be fans; they may have chosen Cash because they thought the topic educational or diverting. Yet they were also offering up their own knowledge about him; they asserted a relationship with Cash—a move that is a vital strand in the DNA of fandom. They had seen the movie; they had gone to the concert. Cash was thus something that they thought they owned, at least to some degree. The seminar gave context to their experience and possibly enriched it. Yet in the psychology of fandom, fans want to find things out for themselves rather than being taught by someone else. If the Norwegian girls were Cash fans, then they were not going to be Cash fans because some American professor had told them to do it.

An old joke in Northern Irish culture is about a man being brutishly asked in Belfast about whether he is a Protestant or a Catholic, to which the man replies, "I'm Jewish." The prompt reply comes: "Are you a Protestant Jew or a Catholic Jew?" Charlie Taggart has apparently managed to beat this question by being so much of a Johnny Cash devotee that it never occurs to anyone to ask whether he is a Protestant Cashite or a Catholic Cashite. His total commitment to Cash has become his signifier. Fond but teasing greetings from those who know him are not "How are you?" or "How's it going Charlie?," but "How's Johnny Cash?"

Charlie's creation story with regard to his Cash fandom provided the basis for this analysis. He described being in his early teens in the late 1950s, living in the tiny village of Mullaghmore, just outside of Omagh, and listening avidly to the radio, seeking out whatever he could find. Radio in the 1950s was not exactly a medium for diversity in Northern Ireland. There were a few BBC stations but no independent ones, and for people close to the Irish border, there was also the option of tuning in to Radio Éireann, the state broadcaster of the Irish Republic. Charlie was in the habit of listening to that station early every morning because it played only music for a sustained period at that time of day. Often the music was classical or traditional Irish melodies. But one summer morning (as Charlie tells it), the anonymous DJ put on Johnny Cash's "If the Good Lord's Willing and the Creeks Don't Rise." Cash then appeared on the playlist for three or so weeks, and Charlie's fandom was born.

After this moment, his own life story became enmeshed with Cash's, even if Cash could not know it. According to his survey response, "As Johnny's music evolved to changing circumstances, he brought me with him." In this way, Charlie conceives of himself as intimately connected to Johnny (the nice man) while remaining in awe of the tricky phenomenon called Cash. For better or for worse, as Bridget notes, this was another form of marriage. Charlie's mission was to travel through and experience as much of this duality as he can. Within (and sometimes beyond) his budget, he saw Cash perform in the United States, Canada, and Europe, in Liverpool, London, Branson, Ballyconnell, Dublin, Birmingham, Bristol, and Madison Square Garden. Charlie's venue text is an "I've Been Everywhere" to complement that of his idol. He is not only a follower of Cash but also a collector of his own attendance at Cash performances.

Most curious of all is the night that Cash actually played in Omagh, May 1, 1989, which Charlie described as "the most wonderful experience ever," not least because he could incorporate more loved ones than was usually possible into the experience: "Our family had the whole front row." Charlie did not meet with Cash that night, as some of his fellow townspeople did, but he was philosophical about it: "People who met him went out a different exit." He also took pleasure in recounting anecdotes he heard from others who were in the hotel where Cash was staying after the show—although yet again, he was not there. So in some respects, Charlie's pleasure at this hometown gig was for the experience it offered the town rather than himself, because he already had a reservoir of fan experiences to process as his own. It also meant that his town could better approximate the pleasure that had sustained him throughout his whole life.

Charlie says that he does not own much by way of Cash memorabilia because he does not do hero worship; he has only has a couple of photographs up on the wall that people have given him. Then he conceded that he does have the giant poster that was put up around Omagh to advertise the Cash gig, which hangs proudly at home. He was pleased for his town, and in turn pleased for himself. To quote Charlie's own words, "The public and the private cannot be separated"—not for Cash, and not for him.

When asked about tribute artists, Charlie said that he had little interest in them, for the most fundamental of reasons: "Not as good as the real thing." He said that he went to one tribute concert in the local arts center, where he saw "a small man with a good voice . . . but he was very small." This led to a further series of thoughts about Cash and his particular aura, which makes clear the fact that this was the real reason he did not go to these shows: "What makes a good performer? The charisma. You can feel it when you are in the back of the hall. . . . Cash had it in abundance." No matter how well someone might perform, Charlie said, "Cash does it better."

That concert had been sold out. Yet the competently performing man in the theater could only appear small to Charlie—"very small." Because Cash was defined for Charlie by his aura, nobody else could have that. Charlie could not pretend to like the tribute in the same way that others could. He said that Cash was not just words and music for him but an alchemist: "Take 'Ballad of a Teenage Queen,' there is really nothing in that song . . . but Cash made it into something." Other people could admire the tribute act because they were reminded of songs they had heard Cash sing, and they were content with that. Charlie could only be reminded of the feet and inches (and genius) that were missing.

The dailiness of Charlie's fandom, his opening of the shop and his almost immediate pressing of the play button, confirms his sense of ritual. Visitors to his shop, like Charlie himself, were not expected to stop and listen to the music but instead were asked to admit it into their own dailiness, to acknowledge its companionability. Charlie compellingly reflected on the relationship between his work and his fandom. In the shop, he sees the same people every day. "Every customer has a story," he notes. "I don't talk much. I listen." One customer, fearing the onset of Alzheimer's, has asked that Charlie write his story down before he forgets it himself. This directly relates to what Charlie found by listening to Cash's songs, whether he wrote them, chose them, or had them chosen for him: "A lot of them are about people's lives."

Charlie had clearly given much thought to the question of his favorite song, and he declared that this moment's favorite Cash is "The Diplomat," which powerfully reflected on old age, as Charlie was doing on behalf of himself and his elderly clientele. The song's title also artfully referred to the role that Charlie himself performed, mediating Cash's work and using that work to interpret experience.

When Charlie was asked about the Charlottesville controversy of August 2017, his answer brought a kind of relativity to the question. First he brought up the coat worn by Melania Trump in the week before the interview, when she was visiting immigrant children; it read, "I really don't care. Do U?" (*Guardian* 2018). No deconstruction of what this might mean follows. But then he said, "I see a lot of people wearing different clothes, and I don't think they always know what it means." People can wear Johnny Cash, thereby bearing his name, but such people can still be thugs and ignoramuses. Who knows how and why people wear a particular garment? "It might be the only T-shirt he's got." This was too forgiving, but it typified Charlie's refusal to judge absolutely. It showed a wariness of what the truth of a situation might hold, a quality that Cash, the dove with claws, himself possessed—he who played for both Democratic and Republican presidents.

This open-mindedness recalls the account of Charlie's upbringing, with its broad and worldly point of view. He remembered how his grandfather would read aloud to them about world affairs from the *Irish Times,* traditionally the paper of the Southern Protestant establishment in the Republic, and an unusual choice of newspaper in Northern Ireland. Out of that, Charlie duly acquired a sense of the world and its dynamics. When asked about what he thought of the United States during his childhood, he provided a striking answer: he "was more worried about Suez." When twice given the chance in interview to make connections among the United States, Ireland, and Johnny Cash, Charlie declined. Instead, he indicated that his path to Cash came from a particular worldview, one that comes out of a particular sanity and knowledge. Charlie found his singular way to the worldliness and wit of Johnny Cash, his tools for living through conflict and division.

Like Charlie, the American poet Wallace Stevens famously lived according to a routine. He would go to work at the Hartford Accident and Indemnity Company, then return home. After dinner, he would retire to his study and write poems. In that poetry, Stevens immersed himself in what he called his *mundo,* an alternative universe of imaginative license and possibility, a world of leisure rather than business. This idea of creating a space within which one can really explore what one wants to be, outside of a world of work and social responsibility, is useful to reflect on when considering how fandom operates, especially for people who have an abundance of other responsibilities in their everyday lives.

Charlie has gone further, however. He made a *mundo* Cash at work, enfolding business and leisure. He was with Cash in the shop as much as he was with him at home, generating his own aura of living in two worlds at once. There was something serene, perhaps even saintly, about Charlie. He had no apparent need for exchange with other Cash fans; he was more or less free of the demands of a conventional fan economy; he did not express his fandom through performance or the collection of objects. Everyone is welcome in his shop, yet whatever satisfaction and pleasure were derived from his fandom remained his own business.

In contrast, moving around Norway on a Fulbright means that your business is everyone's business. This took dramatic form when a student drew up his trouser leg to show his Cash tattoo. It was at a Christian school in the portentous-sounding Tomb, a small farming community south of Oslo. The teacher had allocated two hours for talking about Cash—a half hour longer than any other presentation—and practically the entire school was in attendance. Silverman was introduced as a real American. The length of the presentation permitted songs to be played in full and gave enough time to talk expansively about Cash.

Once it was over, the student approached Silverman, saying he had something to show him. Cash was etched on the upper part of his calf, with Elvis Presley nestled underneath. The student might have been seeking an endorsement, or he might have been signaling that he did not need one. Questions could proliferate here about the extent of Cash's influence in Norway, about the fact that this school was a Christian academy, and as such might have been especially responsive to a performer as devout as Cash. This student could have been affirming Christian values, or he might have been rebelling against them. The tropes and identities attached to Cash explained plenty of it: Cash is rebellious, independent, dark, thoughtful, and religious. Subsequent discussions will also show that tattoos of Cash are relatively popular, and every culture has its tattoo parlors. At the time, Silverman did not think of actually interviewing the student, because it had nothing to do with the book on Cash he was then working on. Yet he did take a picture of the tattooed leg, and he used it as a symbol of the unknowingness of fan

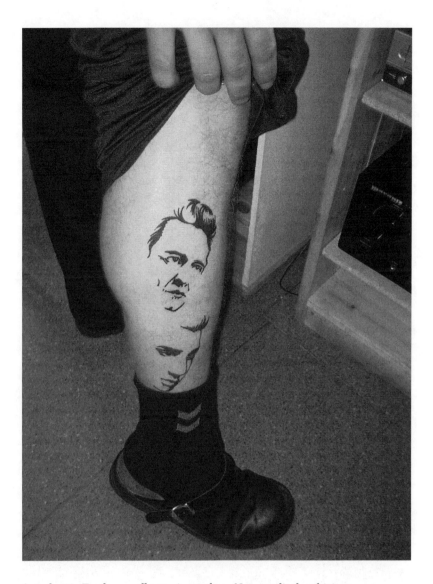

A student in Tomb, a small town in southern Norway, displays his tattoo.

desire to close his book. The student and Silverman were part of the same cultural ecosystem, one that brought them together in the same place but by different paths.

Cash is an apt icon for someone who was a maverick and Christian at the same time. Cash's presence in a small Christian school in a farming community was thus not really surprising. Charlie Taggart came from a small town as well. That Cash appeared in juxtaposition with Elvis might indicate that the boy was working his way through music icons, one at a time, or that he saw them as a complementary pair, Cash a tragic mask beside Elvis's comic one (or maybe it was the other way around). As to why he got the tattoos, the story of the boy from the Tomb remains a matter of speculation. Yet it is a productive enigma, one that has prompted this study into ensuring it hears such stories, teasing out their potential significance, both local and international. Above all, the boy was saying, definitively, that he was a fan.

2

I AM CASH,
WE ARE CASH

Thinking about Cash as a Visual Icon

As the Norwegian student from Tomb shows, to put another person's image on one's body is to fuse oneself to that person for life. The student chose Cash and Elvis, both dead white men from the American South. The understandable impulse is to think about how extraordinary a decision that is, a decision only highlighted by where it was made. Yet an important part of the work of this study is to reverse that perception, to see that within international Cash fandom, this is exactly what happens: people in diverse locations make gestures of commitment. In their peculiarly visual commerce, Cash-tattooed fans signify their connectedness to one another even as they are standing out from their local communities.

Tattoos, T-shirts, and posters of Cash begin with images mostly drawn from a twenty-year period of a fifty-year career. There is a young, thoughtful Johnny Cash (1950s); Johnny with his chin on his hand, smoking (1950s); Johnny with a Western tie (1950s); drug-shrunken Johnny (1960s); Johnny giving the bird at the San Quentin concert (1960s); and Cash walking with a guitar (1980s). After *Walk the Line* was released, there is Johnny as movie-poster outline (2000s), then variations based on those original images, like the increasingly popular zombie Johnny, or images of Johnny with writing added. The Norwegian teenager's tattoo looked to be in the 1950s range, with Johnny's hair slicked back. Images from this era are among the most troubled and therefore romantic of his career—the part where he becomes successful, struggles with drug and alcohol addiction, and becomes politically active with the prison concerts and the recording of the "Man in Black."

In early Christianity, icons were images of worship and often focused on the representation of a figure or figures; they also performed the critical function of providing a common visual language for worshippers across a complex geography. By bearing Cash's image on their bodies, or on their clothing or on their walls, fans make gestures of commitment. They also reinforce the most resonant images; indeed, the Cash image collection is created by professional photographers, then curated by users. If Johnny Cash is conceived of as a series of defined images over time, then it follows that Johnny Cash comes to fans as a visual presence, and that fans take those images and put them to use regardless of where they came from. As Nancy K. Baym notes, fans "exploit intellectual property by transforming it into their own work" (2018, 123). The visually creative work that fans commission or create is independent of the images presented to them, even as their work is limited by their own perceptions of who Johnny Cash is.

The Cash images that people wear around the world indicate how Cash exists in the collective imagination of fandom. Yet it is significant that a Norwegian teenager might make the same decision as an American or Italian one; it is significant that Cash is the figure they have decided to bear for perpetuity. The images might just be images in the virtual space of the web, but those arms and legs are real. If the Cash image has become a globally recognized one, then the local nature of the decision to etch him onto skin demands respect. Cash fans around the world want each other to know that they love him, but they also want to tell people where they come from and who they are. Choosing a particular image from a particular moment need not imply that fans revere only that version of Cash. Yet most people like their heroes to look good. Most media coverage of Cash's death chose to show images taken years before he died. In the aftermath of Cash's death, Cash's aging body in the "Hurt" video has become iconic in its own right—but not as a repeatable icon for wearing.

Like all texts put out in the world, Cash's images are at the mercy of audience interpretation and use. Getting a tattoo, wearing a T-shirt, or displaying a poster is an act whose consequences seem confined to one's immediate community. Its internationality comes from its wide use as a symbol of American cool. However, the viral nature of an associated image can attract users who do not share the same values. In the case of the Cash family intervening in the wake of an alt-right member wearing a Cash T-shirt at the Charlottesville Unite the Right rally, they serve to inoculate fellow users and wearers—but that work can only last so long. The Johnny Cash Project, where users help construct a video for Cash's "Ain't No Grave," operates as a partially closed system of fandom, where users from around the world choose to work on the project. Both tattoo wearers and amateur video makers share a desire to work with the Cash image as a way of showing their connectedness to Johnny Cash.

Charlottesville

There are dangers in being so inspirational as you cannot predict who will want to borrow some of your integrity. This is evident in the Charlottesville riots of 2017, where an American neo-Nazi appeared on news media wearing a Cash T-shirt. Cash's family quickly moved to deplore the action: "To any who claim supremacy over other human beings, to any who believe in racial or religious hierarchy: we are not you. Our father, as a person, icon, or symbol, is not you. We ask that the Cash name be kept far away from destructive and hateful ideology" (Cash 2017).[1] Wearing a T-shirt is a way of showing that one is a fan; it is a commodity purchased to show affiliation, if not outright loyalty. The Charlottesville man, regardless of the specific intent of wearing the T-shirt that day, was saying that you can be a white supremacist and a Johnny Cash fan. In response, the family was saying, no, you cannot. It subsequently transpired that the white nationalist radio station, Stormfront, had also been using Cash's cover version of Tom Petty's "I Won't Back Down" as a theme song, prompting a cease-and-desist order from the American Recordings and Universal Music Group music labels. Affiliations matter; they cannot be preemptively controlled. It was not enough to ask that such an ideology keep away from the Cash name. The allure of Cash's aura meant that it had to be enforced by threat of legal proceedings. Asking Cash fans what they thought of these incidents proved to be revelatory, not least because it showed that Cash fandom could be affected by the politics of the cultural moment to an unanticipated degree. Cash's moral authority and influence are things that many seek to claim, but these capacities make him a compelling figure—not just in the cultural history of America but also in that of the world. Something is at stake in Johnny Cash's legacy, his fans seem to say, and it is worth fighting for.

In this context, it is not surprising that YouTube webcaster Hip Hughes (July 25, 2014) self-consciously declares that he is (literally) putting on a Cash T-shirt to "explain" the Israeli–Palestinian conflict: "A summary of Palestine and Israel. I'm putting my Johnny Cash on, looking at Israel and the Gaza Strip with a short history of what has brought us to where we are today." Cash is the signifier of sanity; it suggests that even the most intractable situations in the world can be Cash explained. Cash is not a deus ex machina; he does not solve the problem. Rather, he allows us to see it for what it is. Cash, something of a conundrum himself, allows us to see the conundrum of Palestine and Israel. He transcends history and its complex expression. Either way, he matters to the world.

Both contexts operate within the standard transactional nature of fan-related clothing: association through wearing an image. They also share the gaze of a spectator who wants to combine situation, person, and Cash's image as a way to make meaning. The Cash family knows the way fans might make those connections. Presumably the Charlottesville Nazi was trying to be some variation on "alt-" in wearing the shirt, signifying some combination of independent, rebellious, or cool. This interpretation requires speculation. Hughes goes a bit further, as he actively uses a positive interpretation of who Cash is and what he stands for in order to shine a positive light on his own virtue—or at least his equanimity. Both Hughes and the Charlottesville Nazi trade on the understanding that viewers have an idea in mind of who Cash is in order for their use of the T-shirt to make any sense. However, the choice is still left up to the viewer to repudiate the terms of the deal, whether that is the Cash family or a spectator on YouTube.

Decorating Cash on DeviantArt

As with tattoo artists, contributors to the DeviantArt website rarely depart from the fundamental restatement of a familiar Cash image. Where they differ is in how they find variation in framing devices and color choices, then disclosing their place of origin on the site and quoting a price for their work. As such, DeviantArt is an international marketplace as well as a showcase; it confirms the contemporary apprehension of visual art as something inevitably framed by the laws of the market. A further contrast with tattooing is that tattoo images are commissioned by the person who will bear them, whereas DeviantArt artists generate images in hopes of finding a buyer. They might be making the image out of their own fandom, but the cash motive means that they are trying to appeal to somebody else's.

The sheer range of DeviantArt contributors who have worked with Cash's image confirms him as a canonical part of a transglobal repertoire and one with crossover marketability. A quick survey sees artists from Spain, Costa Rica, the Netherlands, Venice, London, Germany, Romania, and Brazil. They depict and redepict Cash across boundaries in the same way that others paint nudes or bowls of fruit.

Cash's image is adaptable to art, with its contoured outlines of quiff and guitar flowing one into another. He looks like an exemplary shape that artists might generate on a drawing board, with all the economy and resolution of international style, as recognizable as a Bauhaus chair. Contributions to DeviantArt affirm this resolution through play, often showing familiar tropes and images working in concert. Bokula (2009) from Serbia offers a kind of crossover Cash, using the classic cigarette-in-mouth picture, then combining it with JOHNNY CASH in a punkish font, with "The real rock'n'rolla" in an antique cursive font. Bokula proclaims, "Johnny Cash—The Real RocknRolla, the real American gangsta . . . my idol . . . True great." Bokula's Cash is a mash-up of classic, punk, and hip-hop values while being firmly identified as American. The comments below Bokula's work (in both Serbo-Croat and English) focus in particular on his choice of font. This reminds us that if this is a piece of art, it is also a piece of writing. The image of Cash is inviolable; the artist can only attach further value to it with slogans.

Two contributions, from Caffeinegoddess (2003; USA) and Aprilgriffin (2012; Canada), rebuild classic Cash images entirely out of text, the first using cut-up newspaper while the second shapes and reforms a portrait of Cash from his own words: "You've got to know your limitations. I don't know what your limitations are. I found out what mine were when I was twelve. I found out that there weren't too many limitations, if I did it my way." A cheerful English student, SigmaOctanus (2010), presents "Yet another zombie, Johnny Cash!," acknowledging that he is perpetuating a cliché. His materials are aptly modest: "Just biros [a type of pen] and water." The image of the zombified Cash is in itself a signification of his recognition value; Cash is zombie worthy because he is genuinely iconic. It also indicates an apprehension of an ambivalence about life and death that Cash presents.

There are images of him from the 1960s when he is so emaciated from drug use that he actually looks like a zombie. Yet a zombified image is funny; most Cash zombies bear a grin that indicates a defeat of mortality. The zombified Cash giving the bird is a riotously triumphant figure, one that has become canonical in its own right. It is the avatar on the home page of the French Johnny Cash fan club.

German graphic novelist Reinhard Kleist's *Johnny Cash: I See a Darkness* (2009) presents some of the DeviantArt tropes with remarkable confidence: Cash's image is a steadfast presence in almost every frame, the assemblage of black lines around which all the rest of reality is organized. Some tattoos of Cash take on a similarly angular, almost cubist quality, focusing on the remarkably confident geometry of his face and abstracting his representation into a few angular lines. Indeed, the quiffed hair of footballers in the 2018 World Cup tournament is a kind of Johnny Cash hair. His hairlines might connect millions.[2]

Creative Community

The abiding issue hinted at when considering tattoos and DeviantArt artwork through fandom is one of definition: Do they count as an expression of fandom, and to what degree? In addition, it is impossible to consider these disparate images together thanks to their vast quantity; we can only be aware that they exist and are associated with only occasionally identifiable locations. However, there is one Johnny Cash art enterprise that is an exception: the Johnny Cash Project (http://www.thejohnnycashproject .com/), a crowdsourced collaboration that permits fans to write or draw on preexisting frames for a video reel to accompany "Ain't No Grave," the title track from Cash's last album. The project is the conception of Chris Milk (Chris Milk, YouTube, September 29, 2010), who describes it as a "global collective art project":

> Through this website, we invite you to share your vision of Johnny Cash, as he lives on in your mind's eye. Working with a single image as a template, and using a custom drawing tool, you'll create a unique and personal portrait of Johnny. Your work will then be combined with art from participants around the world, and integrated into a collective whole: a music video for "Ain't No Grave," rising from a sea of one-of-a-kind portraits.

The video itself is a postmodern image mash-up, what Milk calls "a moving, ever evolving homage to this beloved musical icon." The project aspires to create something organic and responsive that evolves in communication with Cash's fandom, as is noted on the website: "This living portrait will continue to transform and grow, so it's virtually never the same video twice."

The guidelines for contributors do not say whether the image should be representational or abstract. There is no need. Unlike with T-shirts and tattoos, the images operate within a single locale of the Johnny Cash universe, albeit one with a global ambition to bring together as many Cash fans from around the world as possible. The interpretation must come from within that context. The project thus relies on collaboration in a different way than wearing a T-shirt. It forces the fan to take concrete action, but it does nevertheless operate with images in the Cash canon, as well as ones created or altered by fans. Importantly, it simultaneously values independent and collective fan contributions; it recognizes individual fans even as it shows them that they are part of a global community.

In the "Explore" section of the website, the frames chosen for the completed video run at the top of the page, evidently to catch our attention, but that horizontal stream of singular frames is just as compelling as the fascination engendered by the individual contributions submitted for each frame, which tug our attention down a vertical plane and add a dimension to the apprehension of the project, not least because it gives us a sense of what this collaborative enterprise represents as well as the infinite variables for the never-completed video that all these frames potentialize. Hovering a cursor over each thumbnail brings up the contributor's name and location. Users can thus not only broadly appreciate the project as international but also see it as translocal. Contributors are asked to identify themselves by location, and they do so by city, town, or state, but not necessarily nation, so the site ends up creating a map of a dynamic, highly local, creative Cash-world. Contributions reiterate key motifs in the Cash image lexicon. These motifs also tend to be key motifs in rock hieroglyphics: wings are attached to Cash; drawings of June Carter and Jesus Christ emerge, then disappear; a whole range of graffiti is etched in various places. There are stars and stripes, crucifixes, roses, and many, many skulls. These contributions decorate images of Cash chosen by the project directors, which operate in the same range of portraits (they depict Cash in early middle age) that appear in most of the tattoos. Images' variation and continuity are both remarkable.

In the shadow of Charlottesville, however, a swastika might be thrown into the image stream, or a Confederate flag—images that a quick glance may have not noticed.

Chris Milk posted an update on the project on YouTube in 2010, noting, "Over 250,000 people from 172 countries have participated" (2010). A quick glance at the various contributions (up to a hundred alternative versions) for the first seventy-eight frames of the video (out of 1,370 total) indicates that there are contributors from thirty-six European countries, eight Middle Eastern countries, twelve in the Americas (not including the United States), thirteen from Asia, and three from Africa, as well as contributors from Australia, New Zealand, and the island of Pitcairn. Of course, this is only a small representation of Johnny Cash fans. Yet it is perhaps surprising because the places listed indicate that one person (or sometimes many) chose to contribute to a highly specialized online project. Each had to do the labor of accessing the project, then committing to the idea of contributing to it—something that is not as easy as it looks. Some contributors would simply write a message on the frame rather than creating an image, perhaps inscribing a quote from a song, writing a note of thanks, or, most frequently, noting, "RIP."

No other comparable Cashworld project is visible online. This hints at the thorough iconicity of Cash in our time; it also indicates that Cash fandom finds extraordinary expression. We should also think seriously here about the sheer iconicity of Cash's face. If Roland Barthes were to today rewrite his *Mythologies* (1972), his famous symbol-oriented examination of culture, perhaps instead of writing about the face of Greta Garbo, the famed actress of the 1920s and 1930s, he would write about the face of Cash.

Cash inspires tribute, as all idols do, especially dead ones, but he also inspires contributory tribute. He makes the kind of art, and he constructs the kind of image and life text, that in turn inspire others to make art—an art readable mostly as translation or citation of Cash's exemplarity. His gestures are met by other gestures in response. His in-performance hollers, his stance, his stare—all demand an echo. This in turn suggests that Cash fans do not only admire him or stand in awe of him but also act with him. Liking Johnny Cash is a performative phenomenon. This might well be because Cash demystifies the mechanics of making art; he exhibits a proto-punk do-it-yourself aesthetic. Making fans active also creates the possibility of bringing them close together as a community, however precarious. People cite Cash's integrity, humility, and authenticity, both in their comments online and in conversations we undertook during this project. People trust Cash to a remarkable degree—a product of how Cash so thoroughly and dedicatedly lays bare his means of production. In the Johnny Cash Project, people willingly learn how to contribute, framing their fandom and Cash's example within a culture of work. The list of places elicited by the Johnny Cash Project shows this particularly participatory expression of Cash fandom to be both hi-tech and lo-fi, both global and local, and both metropolitan and rural; the fandom moves across languages and types of community.

By responding respectfully to Cash's own somber religiosity, his fans make a truly broad church of collaboration. Each image in the Johnny Cash Project is like a frame in an enormous stained-glass window, albeit in monochrome. Out of all the frames we scrutinized, one stood out for its peculiar clarity of gesture. This was not to do with the image generated but in how the contributor identified herself: "Deborah from Nowhere." In the sense that she had contributed in cyberspace, this was true; but it also could be an existential proclamation, a sense of philosophical dislocation. Yet now she is well and truly mapped into Cashworld, which has room for any amount of people, from any amount of nowheres.

3

ON AUTHENTICITY AND AMERICANA

Cash as Representative Icon Abroad

Cash fans have opinions. A Belgian writes that Johnny Cash is connected to the United States through his patriotism: "He was an ardent patriot, like many Americans seem to be. He did not care for party or political affiliation but for what was right and wrong in his mind. He loved his country and all its people." A Dubliner adds that Johnny Cash was "a great American but he had a broader vision of the World." Martin from Argentina opens up another world altogether: "He is the emptyness in every one of us. The void in you when you sit at de border of your bed asking why you have to get up."[1]

The first two responses suggest Cash's qualities as a positive political actor; the other categorizes him as anything from melancholic to nihilistic. Such division is typical of the many responses to the survey on Cash fandom that we administered since we began working on this project in 2016. While many of the answers coincided, irrespective of the respondent's country of origin, questioning about the relationship between Johnny Cash and the United States veered into unanticipated areas. This suggests that the question itself had its problems—or more productively that it caused problems that demanded more complicated answers. It also suggests that the question of Cash's relationship to his country of origin, despite a legacy of rarely diluted patriotism, does not matter much in the 2010s, despite—or perhaps because of—

the cultural influence the United States wields. Overall, the results of our survey suggest that the respondents agree on the broad outlines of Cash's appeal: his iconicity, the qualities of his voice and the subjects of songs, his affiliated performers, his empathy. Where they differ seems to be in the way individuals *feel* his appeal; this does not seem to be geographically based. On the subject of Cash's appeal as an American, the responses are universally divergent, perhaps because of the contested nature of what the United States means.

More than fifty people volunteered to answer the survey. They came from seventeen different countries, largely in Europe and including the United States. Some had primary or secondary personal connections to us in Ireland and Norway; others responded to posts requesting survey responses on Facebook and at the Johnny Cash Infocenter. Considered as a group, these Johnny Cash fans nearly all agreed on the following: they prioritize their personal relationship to him over their connection to other fans; they mostly cite Bob Dylan, Elvis Presley, and Bruce Springsteen as complementary artists; they came to Cash mostly before the movie *Walk the Line* was released and are interested in most aspects of his career; they were only rarely performers of his music; and only a few had seen him live in performance. Keywords like "honest," "authentic," and "real," as well as "great" and "legend," provide the coordinates to his appeal. People everywhere understand Cash as someone who can be clearly recognized—especially in his contradictions. These contradictions also abounded, however, in responses to the question we posed about whether Cash modeled American ideas and values. The answers reflect the understanding that the question itself contained assumptions that demand further exploration. Importantly, determining what it means to be an American was challenging, because the term itself is inherently undefinable. Although the term "American" technically describes two continents, it commonly means someone from the United States. More importantly, it contains too many associations to be meaningful—associations that are often under dispute.[2]

A more interesting question relates to the fact that fandom in many ways transcends nationality or even internationality. Some of the material relating to Cash fandom is not particularly international, in the sense that much fandom expression looks the same wherever you are: tattoos, cover versions of Cash songs, contributions to the Johnny Cash Project. Even YouTube comments, themselves a form of fandom expression, often cannot be traced to a particular place. Yet Cash is a powerful symbol that connects everything, regardless of borders, real or imagined. As such, Cash fandom is transnational.[3] In this way, there is no difference between a Cash T-shirt on the body of a twenty-year-old in Manila and a Cash T-shirt on the body of a sixty-year-old man in Dublin. A T-shirt is a T-shirt, a song is a song, and a commodity is a commodity.

Yet even if the material is the same, the people are different. A cover version of a Cash song might be sung with a slight accent; the body is in Manila; a tattooist served in the military during the Balkan war; an Argentinian deliberates whether to bother filling in the survey. He does not decide to do so because he is Argentinian and Cash is American; yet he is Argentinian and he loves Johnny Cash. The Johnny Cash fans whom we surveyed think less about national identification than their identification with Cash and what they think he means to them. These stories of origin provide a context for moving into Cashworld. Cashworld is an authentic place, if not a physical one. It is based on the feeling that Cash has what real life lacks. Yet for Cash fans, their day-to-day existence is their real life. The authentic Johnny is a notion mutually constructed by Cash and his fans.

Theodor Adorno (2002) argues against the enshrining of the authentic in modern culture, in part because it was used as a way of tacitly justifying violence and tyranny. From the perspective of authenticity meaning everything, inauthenticity is typically regarded as "where something broken is implied, an expression which is not immediately appropriate to what is expressed" (5). In a radical piece of counterthink, Adorno suggests that inauthenticity can be looked at otherwise, that it is where critical distance can be achieved. In this way, Cash embodies a question about the perception of authenticity, not authenticity itself, and querying the truth of a situation is a thoroughly international phenomenon.

If you cannot stand your everyday life, like Martin from Argentina, that loathing is authentic. Cash helps Martin face apparent misery and enables him to share something he loves. We constructed the survey in an attempt to elicit responses that would tell us something about what made Johnny Cash fans Johnny Cash fans. We sought to write questions that would prompt those who responded to reflect on their own experiences with Johnny Cash, as well as to address what Cash might mean more broadly. As such, the questions were deliberately brief, the idea being that the fans' words would take over:

When did you become a fan?

Why do you love Johnny Cash?

In what ways do you think of Johnny Cash as an American?

Are there other musicians you feel similarly about?

What are some words that you would use to describe Johnny Cash?

Are you aware of other fans of Cash? Do you perceive of yourself as a part of a group? Or is your relationship with Johnny Cash more personal?

Have you seen him perform live? Or on TV? Or is your relationship with his music through records, tapes, and CDs alone?

Do you like all of his music equally? Or are there particular albums or phases of Cash's career that you love?

Are there parts of his music or career that you don't like?

How do you view the way in which Cash has been represented after his death?

Have you ever performed a Johnny Cash song as an artist? Did you record any such performances?

Is there anything you would like to add?

Where do you live?

What is your country of origin?

Cash fans from seventeen countries responded, giving the survey geographic diversity even when the answers broadly expressed similarity. Not all fans provided precise locations, but those who did are from the following places: twelve people responded from Ireland (six from Cork, others from Dublin and Waterford); six from the United States (California, Kansas, Missouri, Maryland, Massachusetts, Tennessee, West Virginia); five from the Netherlands (Limburg, Eindhoven, Terneuzen, Rotterdam); five from Norway (Oslo, Sandefjord, Eastern Norway, Northern Norway, a small farm in a rural part in the North of Norway); four from the United Kingdom (a farm in England); three from Sweden (Uppsala); and one each from Argentina (Del Mar Plata), Australia (Brisbane), Austria, Belgium, Bosnia Herzegovina, Finland, France, Germany, Italy, Spain (Valencia), and Switzerland.

Looking at how fans responded to the question about Cash and America, they can be sorted in a few categories: history and culture, music, region, identity, universalism, and patriotism. Patriotism was perhaps the least expected, but given the contemporary context, it isn't surprising. The majority of the responses were posted in 2017, a few months into Donald Trump's presidency.

History and Culture

Cash means history. One respondent notes, "He's rooted in the land, history, and culture of America." Another writes, "He represents a branch of the very important country/r&b music genre," noting, "To me he represents the core of American values; honesty, down to earth, shows respect to everyone; he represents 'the old West.'" These responses reflect ideas that seem to come from an uncomplicated view of the United States—a type of past generated from popular culture images made familiar through media like cinema.

In part because of the exertions of American soft power (through cinema in particular) during the 1950s and 1960s, the very framing of the related questions in the survey might have acknowledged this possibility. As Victoria de Grazia (1989) notes, American cinema, for a variety of cultural, political, and capital reasons, became dominant in Europe after World War II. She notes that Americans exhibit a type of individualistic freedom that people used to institutional dominance find appealing and perhaps a potential model for change. The genre of the western was especially popular in this period; indeed, Charlie Taggart described an elaborate theory about *The Searchers* (1956), a product of growing up with the genre.

In what also might indicate the unique pressures of an election-conscious environment in the post-Trump moment, Cash is being constructed as a candidate, a third-party representative. This is both politically aspirational (in many ways, he would be the ideal candidate) and evasive about real options to the point of being nihilistic. A vote for Johnny Cash is a vote wasted. As a dead hero, Cash nevertheless allows expression for the disaffected, as one respondent noted: "He's like Abraham Lincoln a man with karisma and who other people respect."

Music

Only a few responses tie Cash's music to American identity. One wrote that Cash "covered a range of 'American' genres, influenced countless American artists, encapsulated Americana in his songs," positing that Cash's real American connection is actually through his development of American music. It is also interesting to see the term "Americana" in play; this term was used by several respondents. Cash may stand for progress in terms of prompting and influencing others, but he also communicates nostalgia, which unsurprisingly emerges from the fans who have liked him the longest.

Americana became recognized as a formal genre category in the 1990s (Shriver 2009; Rau 2016). John Carter Cash (2011) claims that it was fostered by Cash's American Recordings albums in the 1990s, but it clearly names a type of music that had been around since the 1960s—a type of contemporary folk music that allowed drums and sometimes distorted guitars. The term hints at a form of rebellion, as well as a concession to genre confusion that Cash himself embodies. Cash has worked in multiple genres, including country, rockabilly, and folk, and his performance in the prison concerts can be counted as rock 'n' roll. He is really sui generis. "Americana" just names something that cannot be named—which accounts for how those surveyed might hesitate when asked about Americanness.

Personal Identity

Some survey respondents took his roles as a singer and actor as his American connection. One saw Cash "as an outlaw and a rebel and a preacher." Another described him as a "prisoner, tough denim guy." "Denim guy" is particularly funny because Cash really did wear denim when posing for album covers, even though he is thought of as the Man in Black. Denim is a renowned American fabric, and jeans remain a particularly American commodity. Yet denim for Cash was a multidecade concession toward modernity—a concession that did not really work. The move from black to denim corresponds with his worsening chart performance and waning cultural relevance, save for a few albums in the mid-1960s.

The "prisoner" comment directly engages Cash's identity through the prison albums, perhaps capturing the popular misconception that Cash himself served time (and prisoners often wear denim). Some visitors to Folsom Prison cannot believe that he was never a prisoner there, as Cash inhabited the role of jailbird so successfully. Similarly, outlaw, rebel, and preacher match up with roles he played on his albums and in popular culture. He played a preacher on the internationally popular TV shows *Little House on the Prairie* (1974–82) and *Columbo* (1971–2003), even as he recorded religious albums and the entire New Testament.

Region

Cash's identity as a Southerner comes through in only a few responses. Another region respondents cited was the West; one cited Cash's "Stetson/country appeal." Others thought his American identity came through "his roots in American country music primarily." Cash is rarely referred to as Southern despite his roots, reflecting a strategy he deliberately undertook as an artist. His folk albums are all geared toward the West, and his prison albums were recorded in California. He lived in Nashville, but that was largely for convenience. It is a curiosity that fans did not write about his accent, despite its being such a vital part of his sound. The implications of Cash's rendering of Tom Petty's "Southern Accents" do not seem to have penetrated the consciousness of fans too deeply.

Patriot

One fan comically fused the idea of Cash's patriotism with other aspects of his identity: "Critical patriot and christian junkie." Another was particularly measured about Cash's patriotism: "He did not care for party or political affiliation but for what was right and wrong in his mind. He loved his country and all its people." This was echoed by another respondent: "He loved America. His songs were about everyone from the down and out to the top and well to do."

Cash's patriotic output includes a spoken song called "Ragged Old Flag," which is about a presumably fictitious meeting between the narrator, who is visiting a small town, and a local inhabitant, who tells a long story about where the flag has been. Presumably this is not what the respondents are referring to; they mean something less tangible. Cash was a visitor to many countries, a type of cultural ambassador. As someone who met many presidents before he died (and whose wife, June Carter, was a distant relation to former president Jimmy Carter), "patriot" seems an appropriate cultural identity.

Social Critic

Despite the "patriot" label, some saw him as a critic of the United States. One respondent wrote, "He endorsed and held high the original idea of what America is all about, dared to criticize but always supported the president in office." Another noted, "He was a great American . . . one of the best . . . he seemed to love his country but he didn't like some of his country's ways and he had that right as an American just like many other Americans." This probably comes from "The Man in Black," the prison albums, and his work on *Bitter Tears* (Columbia, 1964), his Native American folk album. The first two are both widely available in Europe, and the last secured Cash the attention of the BBC for the first time.

Related to his patriotism was Cash's affinity for the downtrodden: "I think of Johnny Cash as a representative for Americans that no one else cared about." Another respondent wrote, "He is a voice for those who had/has none, a father for the country he grew up in. He is the best example of an American i know of." And finally: "He was for everyone and the American way of life."

Bigger than America

Some fans prefer to think of Cash as being outside of the United States altogether—that he was "A great American but he had a broader vision of the World." Others flatly rejected this notion. One said that Cash isn't American but "universal." Another thought he's "much more." Another thought of him as American only "in the literal sense" of the word.

A few respondents had nuanced takes that deserve more attention. One accumulated American signifiers to give a complicated idea of what Cash represents: "Outlaw music, images of the west, American fundamentalist Christianity, links with Billy Graham + Dylan + Vietnam War, TV appearances, rugged conservatism." In other words, Johnny Cash can only be described through a bricolage of Americanness. Another respondent composed another patchwork Cash: he "embodies a certain idea of America, from the Frontier myths to the railways, from the fight of the Native Americans to his own past as a cotton picking boy." One respondent got at the heart of the problem by asserting that the word "American" communicates "a sort of 'doing-my-own-thing'-freedom and spirit that's supposed to be typically American (even if that might be a legend or a myth)."

Counterreading

While the responses to the survey do some work in getting us to parts of Johnny Cash's appeal as well as confirming some of them, they also indicate that Johnny

Cash is an interpretable text, and like all texts, it becomes open to interpretation once released into the world. The same happens to the questions about Johnny Cash; they can lead to an associative exploration.

The question about American identity may have been problematic, but it becomes productive once we turn away from exceptionalist assumptions about America and perceptions of Americanness as a dominant subject. Once an acknowledgment of the singular circumstances of each international respondent becomes active, different possibilities come into play. We know what unites a Cash fan from Wichita with one from Stockholm—it is Cash—but it is also vital to know what differentiates them.

Survey responses from Norwegians indicated that some had seen Cash live, others came to him through different means, and they all shared a dislike of his 1980s-era music. There were seven respondents in total—three women, three men, and one with sex unspecified. They came from the very poles of the country, something they keenly communicated: one came from eastern Norway, another from "a small farm in the rural part of north Norway," one from Sandefjord in the very south. One just said he was from Norway, but he left the best answer of all when asked whether he had ever performed a Johnny Cash song: "Better not."

In terms of Cash's Americanness, one respondent wrote: "To me he represents the core of American values; honesty, down to earth, shows respect to everyone; he represents 'the old West.'" Another wrote, "I think of Johnny Cash as a representative for Americans that no one else care about." Another left that question blank. Too few responded for us to draw conclusions about Norwegians from that survey, or even from Silverman's read-only Norway trip. Nevertheless, we venture that these Norwegians in one respect seem to be like many fans in the rest of this study. They were less interested in Cash's Americanness than we perhaps assumed, yet they were interested in how he spoke for core values of honesty and unpretentiousness (although such values are ones that any culture would aspire to cherish), and how he spoke for people who might otherwise go unremembered and unremarked. Cash let them announce who they were and where they were from. Transnational fandom—fandom that crosses and queries boundaries—does not mean that Cash's origin is immaterial. Rather, he does not necessarily carry the burden of Americanness.

Another counterreading is performed by Martin from Argentina (the sole Argentinian respondent to our survey), whom we previously quoted as saying,

"He is the emptyness in every one of us. The void in you when you sit at de border of your bed asking why you have to get up." This is only existentialism if read out of context; but if Martin's disaffection is particularized, it becomes a matter of material history rather than philosophy. Martin lives in Mar del Plata, south of Buenos Aires, a city that dramatically illustrates the nation's income inequality. The charity SOS Children's Village reports that poverty there "is around three times higher than the national average" (SOS, n.d.). Some online searching reveals that Cash had worked for the charity there. The forum where this information appeared (GreaseSpot Cafe; http://www .greasespot.care) was mostly dominated by evangelical Christians. On this site, an inaccurate and defamatory claim about Cash's singing of a racist song is used to fashion a born-again narrative:

> God first
> Did you know that Johnny Cash play a song that was Racism?
> 4–26–2010
> In about 1960 Johnny Cash play a song that was racism but after he got into the Lord he changed. His life was from February 26, 1932— September 12, 2003 where did good works in SOS Children's Village in Mar del Plata, Argentina and other places.
> His life change from a man of hate to a man of love he was know has a man for the poor and all people black and white. So he did one bad thing but measure the love brought to the world in his songs.
> We all do things we are sorry for later Johnny Cash was recorded for the world to show error in judgment does not make the man. Thank you and Johnny Cash thanks you with love and a holy kiss Roy and Johnny Cash.

Another poster (HAPe4me) intervenes to set the matter straight:

> If you are referring to a song called "ship those ni———s back" it was not Johnny Cash. The story has been making its way around the Internet for a long time, and recently went viral with a youtube or something. Cash never recorded that song. Most likely it was Johnny Rebel (aka Clifford Joseph Trahan) a white supremest country singer, but it most certainly was NOT Johnny Cash.

This dialogue has a tangential relationship to what Martin wrote; it relates to beliefs he does not appear to share ("I don't like gospel that much"). Nevertheless, it serves to show that the relationship of Cash to this particular place is informatively complex. Of all the towns in Argentina, Mar de Plata has a heightened Cash awareness owing to his work there. A local recording studio, Salas de Ensayo y Estudio de Grabación, has a Sala Johnny Cash as one of its rooms. Martin is a part of this larger context, no matter how isolated he might feel.

There is also a question of language here, and what happens to English when a non-Anglophone Cash fan essays it exogamously. Looked at from an Anglo-normative perspective, the following answers seem limited and strange, but when they are regarded as the personal testimony of a respondent from Valencia, Spain, they acquire historicity and poetry in equal measure. This fan, Francisco Javier Mota (a Cash fan for twenty-five years) replied to the question "Why did you become a fan?" with canonical force: "Cause is God." To what had proved elsewhere to be an unanswerable question of Cash as American, Mota responds, "All the ways." In our survey's invitation to list other musicians, his personal canon is both American and Latin, thereby revealing an individualistic and nuanced contextual system for his Cash construction: "Jerry Lee Lewis, Edmundo Rivero, Rosando."

Edmundo Rivero was an Argentinian tango singer, and Mota's citation opens up a fascinating comparative potential between the sex and death rhythms of this Latin form with Cash's own stylings, thus enabling a re-interpretation of "Ring of Fire" as a tango on amphetamines ("Edmond Rivero," n.d.). Rosendo Mercado (whose surname generates another link to Cash through its monetary aspect) is a foundational Spanish rock musician, one who emerged as Spain itself emerged from forty years of fascist rule in the mid-1970s.

Cash is therefore part of a signifying chain of resistance; this in turn might allow for a reappraisal of the American question. For Mota, Cash is the right kind of American, one who does not comply or acquiesce, as Leslie Fiedler (1960) puts it (after Herman Melville)—one who says "*No! In Thunder.*" To this Spanish fan, Cash is a figure of cultural authority, a benign boss who wipes away the memory of the dictators of the past. For Mota, Cash-related keywords are "Godelleta, Boss, Master." "Boss" and "Master" are unmistakably deific terms, but Godelleta is also the name of a small town outside Valencia, and it is unclear whether Mota put the word in this part of the form by mistake. If not, it intriguingly maps the idea of Cash onto the very idea of home—not displacing a Spanish reality with an American one but rather fusing them.

Technologically, Mota has experienced Cash through "only tapes," yet at the same time, he is sufficiently internet savvy to have participated in the survey. As to the questions about not liking parts of the music, or with regard to his postmortem representation, there was a flat "no," then, "Igualmente don't knowno." This small detail also serves as a reminder that we are reading English in which somebody is working hard to express himself satisfactorily; the smoother stylings of some other respondents inevitably come with a sense that they are using arguments that they in part have read or heard elsewhere. Yet Mota's language is free of such mannerisms and has the integrity and force of error. When asked if there is anything he wished to add, he wrote, "Johnny Cash make me Happy, I have her Facebook tattooed."

Wrestling with a foreign medium, Mota's last word was to communicate his commitment of Cash to his flesh (assuming that "Facebook" should read "face"). In this we get the rush that comes with historicity. By contrast, the YouTube video that shows "50 Johnny Cash tattoos for Men" can only be of general interest because it only shows limbs with Cash tattoos, and therefore only indicates a broad culture of commitment across white maleness, as the limbs are all white (Next Luxury, YouTube, March 9, 2017). After Tomb, we now get an answer to the question, "What sort of person gets a Johnny Cash tattoo?" Such a person is Francisco Javier Mota from Valencia—not a type but a singularity.

The more that you look, the more you find. In such an economy, the most apparently disinterested and to-the-point responses acquire a peculiar mystique, as with the following responses from Deborah in Italy:

When did you become a fan?

6 years ago.

Why do you love Johnny Cash?

His voice evoce emotions.

In what ways do you think of Johnny Cash as an American?

His southern accent.

Are there other musicians you feel similarly about?

No.

What are some words that you would use to describe Johnny Cash?

Emotional

Are you aware of other fans of Cash, do you perceive of yourself as a part of a group? Or is your relationship with Johnny Cash more personal?

It's more personal

Have you seen him perform live? Or on TV? Or is your relationship with his music through records, tapes and CDs alone?

I became a fan only after his death

Do you like all of his music equally? Or are there particular albums or phases of Cash's career that you love?

Of course I prefer some songs instead

Are there parts of his music or career that you don't like?

When he was stoned

How do you view the way in which Cash has been represented after his death?

A way to represent what he deserved

Have you ever performed a Johnny Cash song as an artist? Did you record such performance?

No, I'm not an artist

Is there anything you would like to add?

No

Where do you live?

Italy

What is your country of origin?

In Italy

In surveying the Johnny Cash Project, the mysterious figure of Deborah from Nowhere emerged, apparently unmappable and therefore stateless. In this sense, she was the perfect figure of the Cash fan whose main identification is online; she had a certain abstracted cool. Another (the same?) respondent is Deborah was from Italy, who showed her own disdain for the questions being asked. It was hard not to respect the impatience of "Of course I prefer some songs instead." Deborah's cool might be read within a peculiarly Italian sense of style, an indifference *di moda italiana*—or maybe it should be called the word from *Da Nessuna Parte*.

Yet this Italian Deborah (or these Deborahs) felt sufficiently motivated to do what few others had. Among all the millions of Cash fans, Deborah, Francisco, and Martin were uniquely committed; they were the only voices we have from Italy, Spain, and Argentina, respectively. Unlike some contributors, who responded because they were somehow connected to us, they had found their way to the survey, and alone among their nations, they had contributed to it. The apparently neutral format of the survey for them became a hot medium, a passport out of their domesticated selves into the singular intrepidness and self-fashioning that Cash modeled. They exhibit another way of being themselves.

4

CASH ON PAPER

Global Fandom Before and After the Internet

Before websites and pan-global art projects, Cash fans connected internationally through fanzines and newsletters. These publications performed a variety of functions, giving news about tours and releases, helping people share music or memorabilia, and offering fans opportunities for self-expression and dialogue. Their writers recounted experiences of meeting the artist and offered strategic advice about how such meetings might be achieved. Viewed now, the publications provide an archive of the global progress of Cash through the perspective of his fans. Although passion plays a defining role in the growth of Cash fandom, these publications show how it was also shaped by the growth of modern media, anticipating the possibilities offered by the internet.

Cash's presence around the world was not universal in the 1950s and 1960s but was dependent on the presence of American or Anglophone culture. Those who grew up in a country where there were English-language schools or where there were US military bases were far more likely to learn about Cash. Anecdotally, Silverman had a work colleague from Bangladesh who had gone to an English-language school in Pakistan, and this person was familiar with Cash. Another colleague came from the former French colony of Senegal and did not recall hearing Cash while growing up. A professor in

Havana had the same reaction. In Japan, on the other hand, Armed Forces Radio programmed content for American soldiers and their families; content was often overheard by local populations wherever American forces were stationed. Its influence peaked in the 1950s and 1960s, when the American armed presence overseas was at its height, and when Cash's star was ascending.

R. Stephen Craig suggests that such a "shadow audience" might have been a million a week, making Armed Forces Radio a formidable instrument of soft power, even if that was not its avowed mission, as Jack Gould (1966) notes: "If there is one abidingly strict rule governing the AFN, it is the provision that under no circumstances must the slightest taint of propaganda besmirch the network's program schedule . . . yet it is precisely that policy which has won the American Forces Network a significance that extends from Scandinavia to Italy and from Ireland to Austria." The popularity of country music grew in Japan with particular effect because of the demographics of the army, as Stephen I. Thompson indicates: "A disproportionate cadre of white southerners, many of them country music lovers, has traditionally been represented in the American military, and the Far East Network of the Armed Forces Radio Service has consistently attempted to satisfy this audience by programming an hour or two of country music each day" (1992, 32; see also Craig 1986; Gould 1966; Furmanovsky 2008). The occupation had a Southern accent. This in turn produced native performers converting to country music in order to get gigs at US bases, like Tomi Fujiyama, originally a singer of the traditional Japanese folk-pop genre of *enka*. If she converted to the genre of country music at first out of economic necessity, Tomioka became both a lifelong fan and performer, touring Japan and elsewhere, even appearing at the Grand Ole Opry on the same bill as Cash. Fujiyama's story is told in the documentary *Made in Japan* (dir. Josh Bishop, 2015).

In contrast to how fandom was being shaped externally by the volatility of geopolitics, fan clubs organized themselves in more predictable ways. Johnny Cash had several fan clubs, some based internationally and some based in the United States. At least two long-lasting publications emerged from fan clubs, both of which aspired to communicate across borders, one *The Johnny Cash International Fan Club*, which ran from 1971 to 2001, and the other *The Johnny Cash Fanzine*, which Peter Lewry ran out of England from 1994 to 2019. The Johnny Cash International Fan Club was not the first fan club, as there was the Johnny Cash Society run out of California and the Johnny Cash Appreciation Society in England. England also produced

Barry Rowden's *Strictly Cash*, "a monthly magazine about Johnny Cash," according to an ad run in *The Legend*, the Johnny Cash Society newsletter.[1] From Rowden to Lewry, English fans of Cash have trusted in print media as the most effective method of self-organization; in this way, they also served as gatekeepers for the international communication of news about Cash, also reflecting how their country was often his first port of call when touring internationally.

Just as technology enabled the increasing availability of Cash's music, the development of the photocopier as a readily available publishing technology allowed for a revolution in the transmission of his multinational fandom. Whatever their production values, newsletters functioned to provide information and services often not available otherwise. However, they also served to give an identity to groups of fans who had not realized they possessed such collectivity. Cash fans could commune and communicate in these pages; they could discuss how best to encounter his work or the man himself. Because national stations were often slow to feature popular music, fans recommended alternatives, such as Armed Forces radio or pirate stations. They discussed how to persuade other key influencers, such as record shops and tour promoters, to bring more Cash to town.

When Xerox released its first mass-produced copy machine in 1959, the first fan club newsletters and fanzines started soon after (O'Connell 2013). Such an invention gave license for people to more easily circulate their ideas, as Clive Thompson (2015) notes: "In essence, the photocopier was not merely a vehicle for copying. It became a mechanism for *sub-rosa* publishing—a way of seizing the means of production, circulating ideas that would previously have been difficult to get past censors and editors." As Henry Jenkins notes, "A history of participatory culture might well start with the photocopier, which quickly became 'the people's printing press,' paving the way for a broad range of subcultural communities to publish and circulate their perspectives on contemporary society" (2006, 555).

Once Cash reached a certain level of popularity in the 1960s, fan clubs began forming, and they started to make connections and create publications. The first issue of *The Legend* had a variety of international material that seems noteworthy. For one, there was a letter from Pat and David Deadman, the heads of the Johnny Cash Appreciation Society, which discussed how its membership had reached over five hundred but also commented more generally on how Cash was becoming more popular in the United Kingdom:

"Johnny's tour of the United Kingdom last year has proven to have been a bigger success than we realized at the time." Their excitement about being part of a wave on the rise is palpable: "Once upon a time when Johnny's name was mentioned over here most people said. . . . 'Who's he'? . . . Now the name of Johnny Cash is becoming well known."

The Deadmans gave credit for this rise to the pirate radio scene in England. Pirate radio stations, such as Radio Caroline, were highly organized and monetized responses to the BBC's restricted playlist, which barely played popular music (Chapman 1990). Their work was significant in that they embraced an entirely different model of popularity than the one the BBC understood as its mission. Pirate stations ran by the law of the market, and record sales and advertising were their metrics. The BBC's mission was to educate and inform the populace, not give them more of what they already said they liked.

The Deadmans found themselves affiliated with the pirates. They clearly found their transgressions exciting, describing themselves as grateful partners in crime: "A lot of credit for this must go to the 'Pirate' radio stations, which our government has now decided to ban; but during their short spell they played Johnny's records a great deal. In fact, we were lucky enough to obtain a special Johnny Cash Spot in one regular country programme, which was broadcast every day; for this supplied the 'Cash Material' and sometimes introduced the records." The program they are likely referring to is Don Allen's "Country and Western Jubilee," which played on Radio Caroline North, one of the primary pirate radio stations (Martinsen 2013; Pirate Radio Hall of Fame, n.d.). There is a strange combination of the outlawed and the officious in their tone; the Deadmans really saw themselves as a BBC in waiting rather than pirates. In the aftermath of the banning of pirate stations, they stress the righteousness of what they are doing, not least by indicating how the BBC had consequently changed policy and responded to the need for a greater diversity of popular music: "Since the pirates went off the air, the BBC have tried to boost country music a little more, and they did have a short interview with Johnny a few weeks ago, in which Johnny talked about Peter Le Farge, and the way he felt about the Indians of America" (*Legend* 1967). This last detail is intriguing because it indicates that Cash's activism was critical in securing the attention of the public broadcaster; they were interested in Cash because there was more to him than his being just another performer of popular music.

The Deadmans had a second article in the same issue, again (unsurprisingly) proclaiming a surge in Cash's popularity and reporting how subscriptions to their newsletter had grown since Cash's tour: "We now have members in Germany, Sweden, Holland, Denmark, Czechoslovakia, Australia, Karachi, and of course all over the British Isles" (*Legend* 1967). As often happens in fandom culture, proactive people like the Deadmans become doubly appreciative of not only their object of affection but also their own success. Another group of British Cash fans, affiliated with the Official Johnny Cash Society, were rewarded by Cash. First he invited them to his recording sessions in Britain. Then Cash invited the presidents, Diane and Barry Rowden (editor of *Strictly Cash*), to visit him in Nashville (*Strictly Cash* 1974).[2] In other words, fandom could generate a type of intimate affiliation, especially for fans who took it seriously.

By the mid-1970s, the American-based Johnny Cash International Fan Club had become a consistent and increasingly influential presence in the fan club infosphere. First headed by Virginia Strohler, an elementary school teacher in Indiana, and later by two North Carolinians, the newsletters were generally straightforward sources of information about Johnny Cash, presenting some material gathered firsthand by the editor-presidents, and the rest a bricolage of newspaper and magazine clips.

This organization was internationalist in conception, but a critical attraction for fans was that the editors could provide information from the United States and report directly from the Fan Fair in Nashville. They would often report meeting Cash there, but it was also important to present a compelling fan anxiety that this should not be taken for granted. People also placed advertisements both for materials they wanted to sell and for materials they wanted to get. Europeans were always well represented here, seeking and selling records and photographs, then videotapes and cassette recordings as these technologies came and went. This made a lot of sense, given how they were at a significant geographical remove from the main flow of Cash goods. Newsletters and advertising always sustain one another, but this acquired particular focus within the context of a group of fans who were generating a uniquely specialized market. Trading with like-minded people no longer felt like shopping. Rather, fans were operating within an exclusive economy of friends. Who else should a Johnny Cash fan deal with but a Johnny Cash fan?

The International Fan Club newsletters included a dedicated Trading Post for the exchange of goods from United States readers and those from a variety of countries. One ad from 1983 from Czechoslovakia wants to trade a local recording for a United States one—a significant example of détente, given that the Berlin Wall was still intact: "For Trade: Will trade copies of Johnny

Cash In Prague Live For USA country albums" (*Legend* 1983, 19). Another ad from Denmark wants to do the same: "FOR TRADE OR SALE: Rare Johnny Cash TV show recorded and produced in Denmark in 1971. Taped from the master tape to VHS video PAL system—also on audio tape. Will trade for records of video tape. Have lone [*sic*] list of other video shows" (*Legend* 1986, 60). The marketplace shows another manifestation of fandom: collectors become completionists. Cash's own internationalism created a vast market of possible exchanges, with recordings of performances in far-off places acquiring a particular allure. A woman in Tallahassee might covet a recording from Prague, and a kid there might covet the latest from Nashville.

The growth of Cash's international fan base has to be linked to the sheer labor of the man himself—his preparedness to go both on the road and overseas. Through his touring, he had a lot of personal encounters with fans, and a definite pattern emerges when the accounts of these encounters are surveyed together. They inevitably describe the history of their own fandom, then the process of making a connection with Cash (or Cash and Carter), the experience of the encounter itself, and how nice and/or genuine Cash was. These encounters are almost invariably described as thrilling. In writing about Elvis Presley fans' participation in their fan newsletters in the 2000s, Mark Duffett (2012) finds similar behavior, though more in the sense that fans are looking to promote Presley. The Cash narratives seem more dedicated to documenting fan behavior.

For example, the narrative of journalist Ole Romm from Sweden sustains a note of euphoria: "The day of November 3rd, 1983 was a very special day in my life. That day I had the great privilege to meet my favorite country music singer of all time, Johnny Cash, for the second time." Romm had previously written about Cash, and when he meets Johnny and June, he presented them with samples of that work:

> I had with me every issue of the two magazines which had published my biography on Johnny Cash (a 6-part story, with an LP discography in the sixth issue), twelve issues in all, quite an impressive pack! These magazines are the Finnish *Folk & Country Music Magazine* and the Swedish *Kountry Korral* (Swedish spelling!), both of which are published by two different non-profit organisations promoting country music in Scandinavia, and I'm proud to be a part of that, and to promote Johnny Cash here!

As with the Deadmans, Romm was happy to meet his idol, but he also was pleased with his own work as a kind of Cash missionary. There is a delighted humility in meeting Cash but also an impulse for self-congratulation. These fans took pride in their work, and they liked the feeling of being an adjunct to the artist's organization. A fan is a willing intern.

Carter and Cash were appropriately gracious, and Romm responded in kind: "Johnny and June were very grateful for the magazines, and said that they would be invaluable for the House of Cash Yearbook, and I really hope so." Romm then described how he and a colleague from the magazine made presentations to Cash, when they "gave John two reader's awards for winning out in the yearly reader's poll for best country-gospel singer of the year, two years in a row (1982 and 1983)." The next sentence serves to indicate Cash's decency and modesty—vital qualities for his fans: "John was very pleased to receive them, and he said that those awards 'means more to me than a gold record,' and knowing Johnny Cash is also knowing that he means it!" The move into calling Cash "John" is interesting. It signals a venture into intimacy and serves to give Romm himself an aura of someone entering into a kind of friendly confederacy.

The highlight for Romm, however, was Cash's call-out to him in the concert, and his writing moves into a final crescendo as Cash's stardust enhances a press conference:

> After that followed photo and autograph sessions and then the press conference was over, the greatest I've ever witnessed! And when John at the concert that evening dedicated a new gospel song (not yet on record!) to "his friends at *Kountry Korral*," you can understand that we felt very proud, and you can be sure I've filed that day under the title "special" in my mind! (*Legend* 1984, 5)

The strange thing about looking at these pieces of writing that stress the specialness of an experience is how they converge. This observation isn't meant to devalue these experiences; rather, it shows how fans are after the same thing in pursuit of the special. These fans wanted access to Cash, and when they got it, they wanted him to live up to their exalted expectations. That said, as was seen in Charlie Taggart's accounts of Cash, a fan will also make allowances for occasions when Johnny is not so sociable or accommodating.

Another contribution to the International Fan Club newsletter comes from an American woman who visited Jamaica while Cash was living there. She did not meet him, or even see him, but she stayed in a hotel across the street from his estate and asked locals about Cash to get a sense of how the natives felt about him. After a short description of the island, she talked benignly about the attitudes that natives have about Americans: "Although poverty is abundant here, natives still find smiles and kind words for their American visitors." A context is being prepared for an idyllic description of Cash's life.

In the course of writing about Johnny and June's reasons for buying their home, the woman found her way into assuming their dual personae, as if she were party to their collective consciousness: "They soon recognized the charm of Jamaica and found that when they wanted to escape from the pressures that fame brings, this was the place where they could come to relax." After realizing her hotel's proximity to their house, she began the experience of retracing the couple's steps: "Their place is also quite close to the illustrious Rose Hall Great House, which Johnny sang about in 'The Legend of Annie Palmer.' Remembering this song, I was very fascinated to explore the mansion and find out more about its history." The correspondent performed the feat of actualizing Cash's song, as if his words had become a real place through which her body was moving. This is the impulse for the unison of virtual and real places common in literary and cultural tourism, which has Dracula fans venturing to Transylvania or *Game of Thrones* (2011–19) fans visiting Ireland and Croatia. She could "almost hear Johnny's words echoing" in her ears:

> I felt as if I had already seen this place before because Johnny's song had been so real to me. At this point I wouldn't have been surprised to see Johnny slowly walking through the grounds. Actually a few years earlier he had given a concert in the back gardens surrounding the old home and many Jamaicans had thus had a chance to hear his unique style of music.

The correspondent's interviewing was set on a particular goal, to see if people thought well of Cash: "Everywhere I went on the island, I spoke with people from all walks of life and they seemed to agree in their feelings about Johnny. Whether it was a security guard, tour guide, cab driver or wealthy landowner, all considered him a warm, sincere and down to earth person." The fan narrative demands that their hero be kind, and since she did not have the chance to meet him herself, she interviewed those who live in Jamaica, trying to confirm her own good opinion. Arguably, it was better that she did not meet Cash, given that what she wanted to do was make something that was practically a myth.

Even though the choice of interview subjects indicates a commitment to acknowledging racial and class diversity, this barely matters. The fact is that all the people she named also have a vested interest in thinking well of Johnny Cash. This would be problematic if she were reporting for the *Times* of London, but in terms of writing for the Johnny Cash International Fan Club, you must make Cash capital where you can. Indeed, this report is a remarkable case of someone making substance out of an absence: "Since I find it far more pleasurable to be around people who are natural, it was refreshing to hear the security guard say that when he met Johnny, talking with him was as relaxed as our conversation during the past few minutes had been." One might wonder how a conversation between someone whose livelihood depends on a tourist economy and a tourist can ever be natural, and how one might define "natural," but the report relentlessly drove toward its conclusion: "There are not many big name stars who can truly claim to be so down to earth." Everybody said so.

In another interview with a cab driver, when "it wasn't long before we got on the subject of Johnny and June," she recalled that "this middle-aged black man" "seemed very eager to tell me how Johnny often rode down to the Rose Hall Intercontinental Hotel on his motorscooter." This led to her looking for Johnny Cash arriving on a scooter, but again to no avail: "Needless to say I spent a lot of time in that hotel lobby but unfortunately Johnny and June weren't in Jamaica during my stay there." She concluded: "There certainly is no doubt that Johnny and June are very highly thought of on this Caribbean island. Not only have they become involved in such charity projects as donating to a Jamaican orphanage but they have also shown a genuine interest in the people here. Best of all, they are always themselves which is a lot more than you can say for many people" (*Our Kinda Cash* 1978, 11–12). The entire text is careful in its avoidance of being directly racist, but it makes overconfident assumptions about what constitutes authenticity in a security guard and Johnny Cash. In saying that Johnny and June are "always themselves," it must also be understood that "themselves" is defined according to this fan's definition. As Charlie Taggart's love for Cash's contradictions has shown, not every fan needs Johnny to be so benign all the time.

These anecdotes do not encompass the entirety of foreign reports to the newsletter, but they are representative of many of them. They assume Johnny Cash's essential goodness, and they build narratives around that affirmation. This is not surprising. After all, the newsletter is for fans, and it seems intrusive to look at such writing with a conventional critical lens. These narratives show how these fans want to record the impact that Cash is having on the world, which indicates that they are not wasting their time in being his fans.

The international aspect to this is vital. American fans can express satisfaction at seeing how Cash's achievements surge across continental borders. Fans from elsewhere can reflect on the sense of achievement they experience when they encounter Cash, whether in person or just by hearing his music in an unexpected place. The most idiosyncratic recollection of this kind came from a writer from Norway:

> One day my family and I visited a Zoo with lots of animals and ONE SPECIAL THING. This was an old American Railroad Depot and a train called WESTERN EXPRESS. At the Depot, we could sit down and taste juice and popcorn and the BEST of all . . . they played ONLY JOHNNY CASH RECORDS . . . non stop!! My sons said, "We'll NEVER get Mommy out of this place." Needless to say, she DID enjoy the Zoo this time!!! (*Our Kinda Cash* 1976, 13)

Again we see fandom as a family affair—how Johnny Cash permeated the consciousness of fans and their relatives. It also shows how the peculiar pleasure of fandom can be activated most intensely in unanticipated situations. It engenders surprise by the inclusion of what we consider to be personal or particularly contextual material in unexpected places. The pleasure is intensified because it is so out of context.

The International Fan Club newsletter was the organ of a Cash network, even if it was published infrequently and was limited in scope. The newsletter also had a section for pen pals, suggesting a movement toward creating relationships that might go beyond the mutual expression of love for Johnny. They all began as Johnny Cash fans, then tried to distinguish themselves through their other interests. (Names and full addresses have been removed for privacy.) Here is one from Ireland: "Hello, all you Johnny Cash fans. My name is Patricia and I am 49 years old. I would love to hear from some new pen pals, female only, and from a similar age group. I love country music, of course, mainly Johnny Cash. I also enjoy reading, films, TV, walking, etc. Write soon!" The "female only" can be decoded in various ways; it may have been a strategy to close off romantic overtures from single men, but the double emphasis on Cash shows a desire for friendships that begin with him, making it clear that his work is offered as a sound basis for social intercourse (*Our Kinda Cash* 1996, 9). Here is another one, this time from Scotland: "Heather . . . would like to hear from pen-friends from the US, Canada and Britain. Interests are listening to country music, loves Johnny Cash, likes collecting cuddly toys, buying records, writing letters and watching TV" (*Our Kinda Cash* 1993b, 26).

A Frenchwoman similarly wanted to establish connections with people and did not even mention Cash, perhaps taking for granted a shared regard for him, given the context of the publication: "Odile-Marie . . . would like friends from any part of the US and would be interested in writing in English or French. Blond-haired, single 40 years of age and living in a small French city. Works in a public library so favorite hobby is reading along with listening to music, classical as well as country. Would like to find pen pals with same interests to exchange thoughts on ways of life, etc." (*Our Kinda Cash* 1993a, 16). For these correspondents, the newsletter was a way to find other people with similar interests in a closed and safe environment.

A love for Cash's music was the prime source of that sense of safety, and it relates to fans' needing to believe in Cash's fundamental decency. It also allowed them to believe that the people who loved him would share that decency. Making contact with people in an epistolary culture was genuinely hard work and represented a certain daring and trust, for all that safety. What relationships emerged from the correspondence is unknowable and private, which only adds to their poignancy.

Lists of fans' locations often appeared in the newsletter, communicating a sense of mission as well as community. In an article titled "How Our Club Began," the founders of the International Fan Club, Virginia and Charles Strohler, explained the expansion of their global reach: "After one of my letters was then printed in Country Song Round-up, we became International with many, many new members from Canada and before long we had members in West Germany, Sweden, England, Philippines, Japan, Norway, Holland, then, Bahamas, Australia, Netherlands and the end is not in sight." They added, "The membership as of December 1972 numbers approx. 1500 members. There are new members being added every week" (Strohler 1972, 2). Like many technological items from previous eras, the newsletter now seems antiquated compared to the web. As Duffett notes, "Undoubtedly the internet has radically increased the visibility and accessibility of fan communities, as it has allowed much wider access to fan networks, accelerated the speed at which information travels, provided new means through which people can communicate, blurred the line between public and private life, and augmented the means and metrics by which fame is propagated" (2012, 317). The internet has effectively captured the raison d'être of a fan newsletter, and fan communication has followed in adapting to the terms of discourse set by new media. As Nancy K. Baym notes, "No sooner did the first nodes of what become the internet make their first connection than fans began using it to build stable and persistent group infrastructures for their fandom" (2018, 79).

One of those sites is the Johnny Cash Infocenter, run by Elvira van Poelgeest out of Groningen, the Netherlands, and here the kind of work instigated by the newsletters has both expanded and sharpened in focus. Websites can provide links to external sources and archive all sorts of material, so no communication or detail goes astray. Elvira's site offers a comprehensive archival listing of all Cash public performances, for example. More importantly, fans can interact quickly, sometimes in real time. Pen pals have been replaced by posting on Facebook and web forums. Monitoring fan numbers has been translated into the enumeration of likes, hits, and posts. Nearly every Cash website proffers playlists and affects the ears as well as the eyes.

The need for speed inevitably becomes a problem for producers of this fan news, as the demand for new content is felt much more pressingly than if one is only producing a quarterly print publication. There are many Cash sites, but quite a few have not altered much over the past few years, and some are periodically disabled altogether, owing to issues with servers, among other things. Longtime Johnny Cash collector and fan facilitator Bill Miller in the past offered a weekly webcast from Cash Country, but as of this writing, his site is inactive, as is Elvira's Infocenter. In the meantime, they still operate through Facebook, which allows for the immediacy of discourse that people now instinctively demand. Another shift in fan media is already taking place. Websites are useful because they can store quite a bit of material, yet there is only so much fan labor that even the most dedicated fan can perform. Just keeping Facebook stocked with updates and information is work enough.

It also allows for the kind of mutual affirmation that fans feed on, and to a degree it equalizes the fan experience. On Facebook, people have the feeling of participating together, whereas in fandom's hierarchical terms, priority exists with the provision of a website's content.

As Paul Théberge notes, it is almost impossible to know how many fan clubs exist for any star. Websites and Facebook groups are easy to start, and once online, it is hard to know their real level of impact: "Indeed, the magnitude of official and unofficial fan-club activity itself poses a substantial problem to anyone attempting to study it. It is not even possible to get a clear picture of the number of fan clubs in operation, even for a single star or media text" (2006, 492). The sites that succeed in getting people's attention may not be the best designed, but they are probably the best at exhibiting their particular purpose.

5 WHAT ENGLISH FANS MAKE OF JOHNNY CASH

Class, Culture, and Belonging

The newsletters show that England was critical in the formation of international Cash fandom, not least because of his frequent touring there. From early 1963 onward, Cash played London and the industrial cities of the Midlands and North, such as Manchester, where he played ten times in his career.[1] Friedrich Engels based his 1845 study *The Condition of the Working Class in England* on what he observed in Manchester, and in the mid-twentieth century, it still represented a hub of working-class life in the country. Audiences clearly made Cash feel at home there. Even as cities like Manchester lost some of their economic power, Cash continued to play them, implying a loyalty between fan and performer that went beyond market forces. Thinking about Cash fandom with reference to class makes particular sense in England, where its stratifications are an inherent part of society.

Cash is more popular in Britain today than ever. The Sky Arts TV channel regularly runs evenings of Cash programming, blending documentaries (such as *Johnny Cash: Song by Song*, Ovation, 2012) with concert footage, and commissioning new programming about Cash, such as the *Urban Myths* (2017–) episode "Johnny Cash and the Ostrich" (2018), a one-off comedy drama based on a real event in Cash's English touring history. The BBC runs similar programming on Cash in the shape of themed evenings on its own dedicated arts channel, BBC Four. He also features prominently on BBC radio playlists, particularly the specialized Channel 6 Music, and is only rarely regarded within the prism of the genre of country and western. All of this suggests that Cash has become and remains a powerful current in the cultural mainstream, and that he has acquired a cultural respectability that is unusual for an American country singer in the United Kingdom. At issue is whether Cash represents the kind of mainstream cultural capital that is endorsed by institutions like the BBC, or whether he represents the kind of subcultural capital cherished by intimate fan communities—communities where a different Cash exists, one whom fans have to be in the know about, in the same way that football fans pride themselves on having the inside track on their team.

If Cash has become mainstream and respectable, that might also suggest that he has lost his edge. Yet when many English fans describe Cash's appeal, they tend to do so in ways that stress his edginess, relating that quality to class. Such ideas seem to ring true for another foundational (and decidedly edgy) field of English fandom: the world of the football (soccer; we use the term "football" throughout) supporter. Cash comes into focus for a group of football supporters as they discuss him on a web forum. Half Man Half Biscuit parses who is the real Johnny Cash fan, and Cash serves at the locus in other aspects of English popular culture, even getting into the dressing room of the English cricket team—another space definitively complicated by class. Across the scope of this study, fans have stressed the integrity and honesty of Cash; this might be linked to class in a different way. One of the things about Cash that inspires fans is that he never forgets where he came from; despite the improvement in his material circumstances, he was grounded in the memory of his poverty. According to this reading, Cash remained working class in attitude and perception throughout his life, irrespective of material wealth; this conception is a familiar trope in country music.[2] Cash might thus be seen as a kind of middle-class hero; he represents the ability to improve on the circumstances of one's birth while remaining mindful of them. But who talks about middle-class heroes? Cash is a working-class hero in another way: he allows his fans to feel like members of the working class, or at least connected to the values of that class. So in England, Cash fandom comes into play as class significant, a club that may be joined only by those with the right class credentials. Cash fandom shows how a country's obsessions and ideologies wrap themselves around a foreign icon. But it also shows how that icon can itself foster a reckoning of one's values.

Johnny and the Gentleman Thugs

The idea of Cash fandom as a working-class privilege is proclaimed in a song called "L'Enfer C'est les Autres" (Hell is other people), by Half Man Half Biscuit (http://halfmanhalfbiscuit.uk), a postpunk band from Birkenhead in the northwest of England (just beside Liverpool). They have famously made a barely remunerative career out of writing increasingly mordant satires on English life, summoning the deadpan shades of Byron and Philip Larkin. "L'Enfer C'est les Autres," a song that appears on the album *90 Bisodol* (Probe Plus, 2011), takes its title from Jean-Paul Sartre's existential drama, *No Exit* (1944), and in its spirit, it generates a scenario to illustrate the sense of nausea that other people bring. Principally this is done by lyricist Nigel Blackwell describing an encounter with an overbearing man who announces how he has just "discovered" Johnny Cash by buying his greatest hits album on discount at the supermarket.

The hellishness of the scenario might just be that the man is a bore, or that he is unbearable because he came to his fandom so cheaply, which parodies the question that reemerges in this study about whether some actions belong to fandom at all. It might just be a classic example of Anglo miserabilism, part of a long tradition that runs from Anglo-Saxon poetry to Morrissey. It could be that the singer of the song wants to keep a liking for Cash to himself and resents the intrusion; or perhaps the lyrics despair that Cash is too easy to like, thus daring to think that Cash might not be worth following when even a fool may do so. The song does not answer any of these questions. Rather, it infers that there is something undefinable about an ineligibility for Cash fandom.

If the song simply resents the lack of labor that goes into liking Cash, however, the speaker of "L'Enfer C'est les Autres" should be equally annoyed by the fan who owns nothing but just listens through Spotify or YouTube. The arriviste Cash fan is hated not just because he got his music too easily but also because of how the greatest hits compilation exemplifies a banal logic that the best things are necessarily the most popular. A greatest hits album shows the ruthless economizing of an artist's work, trimming away any extraneous material. Yet the gathering and keeping of that material is exactly what inspires the traditional fan, such as Charlie Taggart. For fans who might cherish the complexity of "their" Johnny Cash, a greatest hits album also means that this is being erased in the name of making the product appeal to everyone.

Yet the dislike of the Cash discoverer has another explanation based in class and sport. Half Man Half Biscuit is famous for its support of a local football club, the doggedly unsuccessful Tranmere Rovers. Most famously, this led to them passing on the opportunity to appear on *The Tube* (1982–87), a Channel 4 TV program that was hugely significant in enabling new bands to make a break during the 1980s. The program was broadcast live on a Friday evening from Newcastle in the northeast of England, and Tranmere Rovers were playing at home at the same time, so the band refused to contemplate missing the match for the recording (*Lancashire Post* 2010). The loss this represented in terms of mass exposure was nothing compared to the feelings of betrayal that would have attended them had they not gone to see their team. This act is also what has led to the canonization of the band as models of the peculiar madness that is fandom.

In "L'Enfer C'est les Autres," that understanding also extends to how music fandom emulates football fandom in England—a country that in many ways (often violently) defines the terms of how followers of the game conduct themselves. Football hooliganism may or may not have originated in England, but its prevalence there in the 1980s led to it being referred to repeatedly in the media as "the English disease." For the determinedly antisocial government of Margaret Thatcher's Conservative party in that decade, acting to suppress the violent impulses of football fans became an activity analogous to breaking the power of trade unions.[3] Any form of working-class collectivity, whether unionistic or sporting, was targeted as potentially seditious. As a result, football was remade; it was turned into a sport for a sedentary audience rather than a standing one. Whether at home or in stadiums, football fans were commanded to sit and consume rather than engage (Giulianotti 1999). Richard Giulianotti has identified this as leading to the age of the postfan, where "post-industrial society and the remarkable commodification of top professional football underpin the possible realignment of the game's class identity":

Since 1990, the structural nexus of football and the working classes has been strongly undermined. Football clubs and the police are less tolerant of expressive forms of support. Ground redevelopment has replaced the old terraces with more expensive, family-friendly stands. Those locked out must forfeit a hefty subscription fee to watch on television. Merchandising and share issues mean that clubs pursue wealthier, national fan groups rather than satisfy local supporters. On the park, the local one-club heroes have become peripatetic national or international "celebrities," drawn increasingly from affluent suburbs rather than poor housing estates. (1999, 147)

The new type of fan that emerged was no longer identified as a suspect part of a potentially violent collective but rather as an individual who used fandom as a lens to identify his or her own identity. A key text in understanding this is 1992's *Fever Pitch* by Nick Hornby, credited with defining a new form of football writing and taking football fandom out of its working-class enclave. To some football fans, however, Hornby is symptomatic of everything that has gone wrong with the game, but to others, he is a fairly typical football fan. In fact, what Hornby describes very well is how his fandom put him in a liminal place, totally dedicated to his team but not altogether part of the terrifying mass that installed itself in sections of the terraces. To add to the trepidation of how football fandom might be imbricated with Johnny Cash, it is worth adding that Hornby's narrator (another love-him-or-hate-him figure) in the novel *High Fidelity* (the 1995 follow-up to *Fever Pitch*) states that "my all-time favorite book is Johnny Cash's autobiography 'Cash' by Johnny Cash."

This brings us back to another dimension of Half Man Half Biscuit's encounter with the neophyte Cash fan. The key marker of difference between protagonist and antagonist is that the newfound Cash fan also says that he has just come back from a drinking weekend in Riga with some "rugby pals." It is here that class becomes an overt consideration in the song. Rugby in England signifies inherited power and its abuses; it stands for money, the military, and elite education. By comparison, the origin story of football is determinedly working class, a sport that emerged out of the workplace rather than the institutions of the establishment. As Oscar Wilde is alleged to have said, "Rugby is a game for barbarians played by gentlemen; football is a game for gentlemen played by barbarians."[4] Half Man Half Biscuit's lyrics want to deplore the claiming of Cash by a barbarous gentleman in a rugby shirt, insisting that he belongs to other people. The lyrics also hint at the fear that just as English football is separated from its working-class roots after Thatcherism, so too might Johnny Cash. The real presence of poverty in Cash's imaginary world runs the risk of being turned into merely an attitude of style.

Johnny the Hammer

Out of nowhere, on August 3, 2017, a fan of the English football club West Ham United, Far Cough, decided to post a discussion about Johnny Cash:

> The Man in Black
>> Anyone else like him?
>> One Piece at a Time is fucking hilarious also his back catalog of more serious stuff, can't sing like Pavarotti but more than makes up for it by pure emotion
>> Thoughts?
>> Anyone (West Ham Online; forum at http://westhamonline.net)

The poster inspired a week of comment—maybe not as much as what happens with discussion of team concerns on the site, but considerable compared to other discussions about cultural matters that occasionally take place there. The fans who post on the site evidently have eclectic tastes, and they reference these freely at times, but it was unusual to see a thread dedicated to a recording artist, particularly one with no particular context. To warrant a discussion, musicians ordinarily need to have either recently died, to have supported West Ham, or both. The controversy about the Cash T-shirt in Charlottesville had yet to happen, so the only apparent prompt for Far Cough was his own fandom and the instinct that he might venture it to his comrades. The Cash discourse was much more orderly and free from profanity than most of the sporting talk—an indication of the particular reverence that Cash might inspire. It also showed that the forum members were happy to have Cash as a topic because he was somebody who fitted their knowledge and self-perception. Cash was welcome to their club.

The contributors appear to be all men, and men based in a range of countries, hinted at by their user names: Sydney Iron, Worse Case Ontario, Chajon Bubble, Norwaytips, and Lily Hammer. Even as West Ham's identity is intimately connected to the docklands and the working class of the East End of London, where the club emerged out of the Thames Ironworks (hence the nicknames the Hammers or the Irons), they have also acquired a far-reaching fan diaspora, like many English teams (a West Ham fan club meets in Nashville). It is practically impossible to determine from the postings whether the various posters were transplanted Londoners or foreign nationals, yet wherever they came from, they all had something to say about Johnny Cash.

As the discussion rolled out, no contributor really had a bad word to say about Cash—unlike what they had to say about their football club. What the exchange replicates is the kind of themes-with-variations dialogue that might sustain a group of people in a bar over an evening's drinking—a feeling that many such forums generate. At first, this centers negatively on the figure of Jerry Lee Lewis, who is condemned all round for his sexual conduct. Grumpster posts about "the great balls of fire chap who married his cousin and rocked up into Britain with a 12-year-old (or close to) on his arm." Beginning with talking about the reprobate Jerry Lee clears the way for talking about the comparatively clean Cash. Cash is regarded as exemplifying a live-fast masculinity, and even his drug use gets approval. As Lertie Button posts in the final message of the discussion, "The movie Walk the Line was class. . . . Got to love a fella with a serious speed habit."

Others keep intervening with jokes. One played on terminology, as "rubber Johnny" is English slang for a condom ("Yogib: I thought that Johnny Cash was change for a Durex machine"). Another's remarks were based on Cockney rhyming slang, the mode of London working-class speech where a word is replaced by another rhyme word, so when poster Saul Bollox writes, "I've just been to the bog for a Johny Cash," he means he has just urinated. These comic interventions are checking mechanisms deployed to prevent the discourse from becoming too reverent or sentimental, as in Far Cough's (whose username is also a defensively comic pun) many posts. Consider the following remark by Chim Chim Cha Boo:

I absolutely love Johnny Cash.
    When I was a kid my paddy Pal's parents (who were pikey ****s) loved him so naturally I hated everything they liked. So I chucked him in the mental bin with Elvis Presley (who I still don't like).
    Live at Folsom Prison is one of the greatest live albums of all time and right through his career he came up with fantastic songs. Great lyrics too. Stuff like fighting his dad in "A Boy Named Sue" with "well I've fought bigger, harder men, I just can't quite remember when. He kicked like a mule and bit like a crocodile."
    The real genius of the man was the stuff he recorded in the ten months after his wife, June Carter Cash, died. Every word he sang is

full of pain and longing which is why "Hurt" works so well. You can hear how much he wants to die and be in heaven with June. Songs like "When the man comes around" almost dare you NOT to believe in God—even a cynical Godless bastard like me.[5]

Chim Chim Cha Boo alternated between intense statements of love and counterassertions of what he does not like: his Irish friend's parents, Elvis Presley, and ultimately himself. But again, Cash expresses contradictions, and fans feel empowered to experience them in turn. Saul Bollox's joke was posted straight after this, practically puncturing the potential for an awkward silence that was generated by Chim Chim Cha Boo's emotional openness. Another poster, Eerie Descent, took issue with a remark by Chim Chim Cha Boo, correcting what he sees as the other man's unfettered emotionalism: "I personally can never fully immerse like that when the words are not originally from the singers own mind."

To this piece of authenticity-based analysis, Chim Chim Cha Boo did not respond at all. As this study notes elsewhere, YouTube comments are fan parliaments, often rowdy ones, but this relatively closed circuit of English posters operates in a different way—as a clubhouse doubling as a symposium. There is a great deal of profanity in places, particularly directed at Jerry Lee Lewis, but there is also a remarkable atmosphere of agreement in the thread (as BrookingisGod said, "Nice thread!," with no further comment). These posters were pleased with their discussion and their ability to perpetuate it. Cash as a subject seems to elicit a desire in them to represent themselves in a positive light, whether this be positively funny or positively knowledge-able. Grumpster identifies himself as the positive epitome of the good son:

> Never really been overly mad on him, but he does have a couple of classics.
>
> Took my mum to see the Million Dollar Quarter recently which was good.
>
> True life impromptu jamming session that Elvis Presley, Jerry Lee Lewis, Carl Perkins, and Johnny Cash done back in the 50's.

Mostly, however, the fans offered isolated reflections on favorite songs and gradually build a discourse that proves both the effectiveness of their social network and Cash's capacity for activating that social network:

SYDNEY IRON: Legend IMO, love his stuff and even some of the later covers he did are great, "Hurt" not long before he died is by far the best version of that particular song, you almost get the feeling he knew the end was close.

MALLARD: Plays "One" better than U2

TED FENTON: I play Hurt on my guitar at least once a week . . . I love it sad as it is!!!!!!

THE STOAT: Clever mash up by Puddles Pity Party (you'll all be singing it later);-)

Different types of fandom are evidently in play here, starting with Sydney Iron's testimonial mode; Mallard brought in a comparative dimension and took us back to the question of who owns a song once it has been covered; Ted Fenton was an example of the performative fan; and the Stoat introduces a note of play, although it is not apparent whether anyone follows his link, which is not mentioned in any subsequent posting. More lines of minute difference and discrimination appear:

LILY HAMMER: I like most of what I've heard, especially the last few albums where he covered some then contemporary artists, but I'm more a Woody Guthrie man.

SWANS OF NEVER: The Mercy Seat is brilliant.

DUKE OF DEVO: How many times does "When the man comes around" get used on film soundtracks?

Surprised The Walking Dead haven't purloined it

KEEP DREAMING: The mans a legend. His voice are is pitch perfect in my head

YOUR MUM: THE best autobiography out there!

HUFFERS: 150/250 of my most played songs are his. The best in my opinion.

MR. BURNS: Have you been to his museum in Nashville Huff?

User Your Mum varied the discourse by stressing Cash's writerly capabilities, while Mr. Burns shifted attention to the experiential to find out who has (and presumably who has not) engaged in some Cash tourism. Curiously, everyone provided a different song or type of text to praise. There is an anxiousness here to contribute but also to show specialized knowledge. The posters were conforming even as they also wanted to express difference:

CHAJONBUBBLE: a real talent, kept pushing boundaries until the end.

Walk the Line is a film well worth seeing.

WEBBY 25: The Closing Medley at San Quentin is just brilliant.

Standard of musicians, no fancy equipment and the atmosphere of the prison setting—top stuff.

SURFACE AGENT X2 ZERO: I don't listen to albums all the way through as much as I used to.

One of the few that I do regularly do that with is American IV: The Man Comes Around.

15 songs, almost all about death, love lost or both and yet still somehow uplifting. It's an album that could probably only have been recorded by a man who had just lost his wife/life partner and knew his own death was imminent.

Wonderful stuff.

Surface Agent X2 Zero almost ruined the conversation by affording himself more room for discourse than the others, only to squander it by moving into a critical summary that is based on assumptions that are groundless: June Carter was not dead when the record was made, and she appeared in the video. It is fascinating to note that he and Chim Chim Cha Boo made the same error, though, as if they cannot resist the idea of Cash as Orpheus, someone who sings out of afflicted uxoriousness. Cash as the ideal husband models how you should love your wife, in contrast to the outcast Jerry Lee. In this company, Cash is not an outlaw figure but a mythopoetic figure of supreme integrity.

This is a remarkable chorus of approval, with a practically eulogistic quality as solitary verdicts are provided one after another. Argument only really enters the forum twice, when the discussion veers at the end into discussion of the Live 8/Live Aid phenomenon. More pointedly, however, Far Cough intervenes at one stage to correct Swiss, who has dared to write, "He's stuff is all the same really though isn't it?" Swiss might well be saying this merely to goad Far Cough. If so, it worked. Far Cough responds emphatically: "NO, Hurt and One Piece at a Time, couldn't be more different." Gamely, Swiss came back with a calculatedly offhand description of chick-a-boom: "Yeah Hurt is different but the rest are pretty similar with those twangy chords. Prefer Nine Inch Nails version." Far Cough had to have the last word:

Ragged Old Flag and A Boy Named Sue.

Different.

Having started the discussion, Far Cough also wanted to define it. In this, the competitive aspect of fandom appears, but what also appears is the way a discussion like this will necessarily generate a contest for hierarchy—a miniature class struggle. Swiss's insubordination might comically derail the entire order of tribute and deference that Far Cough has evoked. He needed to be put in his place.

In the middle of this, a particular post stood out: "It took me weeks to get over the fact he didn't write Boy Named Sue." The poster uses the name Ray Winstone, the English (West Ham–supporting) character actor who has made a career out of playing variously cultured thugs.[6] When the real Ray Winstone appeared on the BBC Radio 4 program *Desert Island Discs* (1942–) on January 2, 2015, a British institution where guests select eight songs and one book to bring to a hypothetical state of being castaway, he chose Cash's "When the Man Comes Around." Winstone first explains the choice because it offers a scriptural vision of judgement, "Do unto others as they would do unto you," which he then reinterprets in karmic terms: "What goes around, comes around." In Winstone's mouth, the words nevertheless carry a meaning that is as menacingly profane as it is sacred. Winstone has played a lot of East End gangsters and hooligans, and he lets us hear that strain of menace in Cash's theology.

These West Ham fans opt into the discourse around Cash almost as if they feel obliged to, such is the power of Cash's peculiar demonstration of what a man ought to be. What persists throughout these fans' every utterance is a related question about their relationship to one another. Are they a real collective, showing solidarity and political potential in their communications? Or are they related only by the fact that they are browsing in a supermarket called fandom, whether the supermarket has football or Johnny Cash on offer? The answer is that they are both together and apart, without feeling confident or content in either way. None of them refers to having just picked up his greatest hits album in the supermarket—a tacit admission that to do so is to break a code of working-class authenticity, that frail commodity so beloved by football fans. The dilemma is whether they are fans or postfans, as Richard Giulianotti terms it. Giulianotti argues that the "notion of the 'post-fan' is an important heuristic here; this new supporter category has white-collar employment, and shows a greater reflexivity and critical distance when engaging with popular culture" (1999, 146). This would appear to perfectly well describe the phenomenon of West Ham supporters' agreeing to hold a weeklong discussion via the internet on the merits of Johnny Cash, yet those same fans would be fearful that such a description might suggest that they have lost their vital edge. In loving Johnny Cash, have they gone soft?

Cash the Enabler

Another celebrity Cash fan, and one who has made something out of his football attachments, is English comedian Frank Skinner. A native of Birmingham in the English Midlands, where Charlie Taggart worked on the buses, Skinner became famous in the mid-1990s for his blokey (a key English word in the frail new masculinity; *OED* 2002) comic partnership with David Baddiel, which saw them host a TV show called *Fantasy Football League* (1994–2004) and compose a rally song for the English national squad when the country hosted the 1996 European Football Championships—an event cited by old-time supporters as being decisive in extinguishing whatever was left of English football as a predominantly working-class sport. In spring 2018, after a long career in television, a TV show written by Skinner was announced for the Sky Arts channel, with him playing the role of Johnny Cash. As he wrote in the *Guardian* in 2018, it was "a drama about the hellraising singer's infamous fight with an ostrich."

Skinner (2018) produced a thirty-minute film that emphasized the hallucinatory grotesqueness of the tale, but he was at pains to say this was not an entirely comfortable exercise for him. As a comedian, he felt obliged to find exaggeration in an already exaggerated reality, but as a self-identified Cash fan, one who had first seen him perform live at the age of fourteen, he felt somewhat guilty in doing so. He looked guilty as he acted, with a strangely rueful expression achieving permanence on his face. In what is a familiar narrative mode of the clown who is crying on the inside, Skinner writes to express a pronounced duality, thrilling to external fantasy while simultaneously mustering a darkness within himself. In discovering Cash, which he did unprompted by simply taking a fancy to the cover of the *At San Quentin* album (Columbia, 1969), he acquired an initiation into a world of violence and wounding that he found irresistible: "Songs about being in the run from the law, one about a train wreck in which the driver was 'scalded to death by the steam,' and another about a man called Sue brawling with his estranged father." Skinner provides a necessary reminder that there is a hard-core aspect to Cashworld as an imaginary universe, a place of poverty and brutality that fans actively recognize as working class. They do not aspire toward that world but rather enjoy Cash's ability to describe it. Skinner uses the reference to "A Boy Named Sue" to introduce a series of stories about troubled and troubling relationships within the male members of Skinner's family—relationships that center particularly on addiction. The newspaper article highlights that "Johnny Cash started me on the rocky road to alcoholism," but this is not what the story communicates as such. Skinner rather tells us that he first understood how to recognize his father's alcoholism when they went together to see a Cash concert, and he then describes his own induction into drinking (and his own alcoholism) by going to see a Cash tribute act with his older brother: "My elder brother, Terry, suggested we visited a nearby pub in Smethwick to see a Johnny Cash impersonator. I'd never been in a pub before so I was a bit scared, but I couldn't resist the opportunity to relive that glorious first gig, albeit with a stand-in for the great man." This effectively defines Skinner in terms of addiction: the need for Cash was irresistible, and this need then referred him into other things he could not resist, even if they were more banal. His first pint of beer is described in such a way that, in a weird moment of transubstantiation, it practically becomes the body of Johnny Cash: "My brother . . . got me a big, dark pint of beer." That the dark beer led to the Man in Black is the key idea in Skinner's poised and melancholic piece. He understands that Cash's outlaw persona was something that enabled him to pursue his self-destruction, but it also subsequently enabled him to understand this in analytical terms. Cash's unique ability was to be inside and outside of the experience of addiction—something only a real addict might intimately understand.

Skinner (2018) is peculiarly sensitive to the ways that success can crumble into disaffection and destitution. He sees it in himself and Cash. Even more poignantly, he sees it when he describes how the Cash tribute act performed a great gig, only to be called over afterward by Skinner's brother: "'Yeah,' said my brother, 'but he's seen the real Johnny Cash live on stage.' Copy-Cash looked crestfallen. 'Why did you bring him here then?' he said and walked away. I learned a valuable lesson that night: when you meet a big fish in a small pond, never acknowledge the existence of a larger body of water." The peculiar cruelty of this relates to any performer, of course, where one negative comment can destroy (as a comic, Skinner knows this very well), but for a tribute act, the illusion of authenticity is everything, for all that it is an illusion. Nothing is worse than being compared to the real thing. This recalls Charlie Taggart's insistence on the total absence of aura in a tribute performance. But it is even more painful here, because the tribute performer himself exhibits that understanding. After Skinner quits drinking, Cash becomes just as real a presence in his recovery as he had been in his addiction—indeed, Cash becomes part of Skinner's evangelization into recovery. Curiously, but perhaps expectedly in an English context, this also finds expression through Skinner's suffering through football fandom: "Sans booze, Cash's troubled outsider lyrics didn't move me as much as they had, but I still loved him. Over the space of a few long drives, mainly to and from West Bromwich Albion matches, I listened to him recite the entire New Testament on 16 CDs." This is an extraordinary fandom, reaching into a zone of Cash's activity that only the deeply committed (and afflicted) might do. However, it also makes sense. The love for Cash is Skinner's bedrock, and within that love, Skinner is able to identify and fashion a particular Cash for his particular needs: "I concentrate on Cash the decidedly unstable Old Testament prophet, a sort of Isaiah on analgesics."

Through Cash, Skinner is able to show us several comedies or life studies (tragedy has death covered), and they are mainly funny in profound and implicating ways. Skinner declares how anxious he is not to "mock" Cash's addiction, yet in a way that is what he does in life, emulating it in action and understanding. To mock is to copy, in the oldest sense of the word. The key comic understanding is that Cash enables a form of social compact to exist between himself and his fans, and that his pain is a matter of everyday recognition, something we are all used to enduring. Skinner (2018) cannot resist the lure of a pun to communicate this. The bitter joke is realized in what turns out to be that most strangely English of contexts: the supermarket. Skinner notes, "I still get a pain in my heart when a checkout person asks me if I'd like cash back."

It Started "De De De De De De De"

A final proof of how Cash becomes particularly class active comes with a game that is perhaps regarded as the most quintessentially English of all: cricket. It is famously the game of the English summer, and historically it is the sport that both rugby men and footballers would play in their off seasons, their cleats hung up. This belies cricket's reputation for being uniquely posh and socially exclusive. The truth of the matter is more complicated. Cricket was played both by coal miners and mill workers in the north of England's industrial heyday—though that should not obscure the fact that the game has always been administered by the establishment, people from good schools.

The game's history describes an ongoing tension between gentlemen (the posh) and players (the ordinary). Captains of the English cricket team have tended to be gentlemen, although there has been an occasional shift, not least when a working-class cricketer of such ability emerges that the case for promoting him to the captaincy seems unassailable. Andrew Flintoff was a fine example, nominated Man of the Series (or MVP) when England defeated Australia, their biggest rivals, to win the trophy known as the Ashes in 2005. Flintoff was also quick to achieve notoriety that same summer, when he was visibly drunk at a reception at the residence of the prime minister, Tony Blair, while the queen was present. As Flintoff became more famous, so did scrutiny of his drinking; at the same time were implications of Flintoff's being a wonderful player, but not a gentleman, and definitely not the right sort to lead the country. That said, Flintoff was elevated to the role of vice captain, and he became captain in 2006, when injury forced the incumbent, Michael Vaughan, to take a break from the game.

While the team won, Flintoff's antics were tolerated. The highlight of his tenure came in March 2006 with a victory against India in Mumbai. The team's fortunes turned dramatically on the fourth day of the game, when Flintoff introduced a motivational tactic that would have seen him scorned if it had failed. Even in victory, though, there were some who held their noses. Here is how the profoundly establishmentarian *Daily Telegraph* reported on the game, underneath an image of Flintoff holding a can of beer that carried the byline "Lager Rout" (a pun on the common term for a drunken undesirable, "lager lout"): "Having dominated the game for four days, they found themselves second favourites behind the draw at lunchtime yesterday, at least until their inspirational captain, Andrew Flintoff, called for a rousing rendition of Cash and June Carter's 1963 hit Ring of Fire, a song no doubt popular with the squad for reasons not entirely unrelated to India's spicy food and its after-effects." The transformation was astonishing, as Flintoff promptly removed Rahul Dravid with the third ball after the break (Pringle 2006). Flintoff himself promoted the story that Cash's song had been the spur: "Usually a lot of drivel gets played but 'Ring of Fire' is one song all the lads enjoy. We played it through Pakistan when we needed a lift and we played it in the lunch break here. It certainly gave us a spring in our step." The *Telegraph*'s rendering makes it sound as though Flintoff was leading the team in a jolly sing-along and ventures a contextualization in toilet humor. Ten years later, on *Desert Island Discs,* on July 10, 2015, Flintoff gave more color to what exactly had happened:

> The series was in the balance on the last day, so I went into the dress-ing room and, rather than giving a team-talk, I had a shower. I walked out naked with a towel over my shoulder and went to my iPod and found Johnny Cash. "Ring of Fire" was on. It started "de de de de de de de" and, naked, I started dancing and swinging my towel around my head. And then, one by one, the team started getting up and dancing. Bearing in mind we're going back out to field any minute. I was naked, swinging my towel around my head, swinging everything about, while one of the world's best ever players, Sachin Tendulkar, pokes his head around the dressing room, saying: "What is going on here?"
>
> I said "Sachin, don't worry about it," and we went out after "Ring of Fire" and bowled India out to win a Test match in Mumbai for the first time in 20 years.

Even as this story describes a famous victory, it is also full of Flintoff's own sense that he was not really captain material. (Indeed, his tenure was short lived, curtailed by chronic problems with injury). Flintoff notes, "I had to give all these team talks. I was bored of my own voice, to be honest" (NME 2016). "Ring of Fire" saved Flintoff from having to bear that responsibility. Cash's song freed him entirely from the connotations of duty, hierarchy, and deference that the singular job of English captain carries with it. It could not have been a less appropriate choice for that occasion in the dressing room; he could not have been further away from the apparent domain of Flintoff's authentic responsibilities as captain of England. Yet this is precisely why Cash serves to allow a playful sense of the carnivalesque to erupt, as evidenced by orgiastic dancing. Half-naked, Flintoff strips cricket of its connotations and complications of class, allowing it to become nothing more or less than a game. Cash allows the English, deliriously, to forget that they are English.

Shakespearean American?

Cash fandom allowed Flintoff to break out of a mold he could not really fit; one man from Cash-loving Manchester having love of Cash is his last possession, a last means of connection to society after he has fallen down the full extent of the class system. There are several online videos shot on its streets of a man called Homeless Paul, impressively performing close to the entirety of the core Cash canon, including a Cash medley as well as an imposing spoken-word version of "A Boy Named Sue." A bearded figure of both affability and pathos, Homeless Paul seems Falstaffian, channeling Shakespeare as he recites Cash. Sometimes fandom can seem to honor two artists as once. Homeless Paul is English in the same way that Cash is American, through birth and diction. When the Englishman lovingly quotes the American, an action further complicated through the videos' being posted by a range of people on different websites, it is a type of international, transnational incident, a demonstration that the broadcasting and dissemination of Cash fandom has found a home in Homeless Paul. The videos also provoke questions about the ethics of representation. It is not clear if the postings are intended to celebrate Homeless Paul and his love of Cash, or to regard him patronizingly as a drunk piece of local color (AshersAdventures, YouTube, May 10, 2016).[7] Yet Homeless Paul is comfortable on camera, meticulous about his presentation, even stopping a recitation of "A Boy Named Sue" because he blames the holder of the phone for making him miss a beat, though the motives of whomever was holding the phone remain inscrutable.

Another video featuring Homeless Paul is posted on YouTube, including his impressive recall of "Cocaine Blues"; the performance is forceful and compelling, shot on a barely lit street, reminding us that Paul might not yet know where he is sleeping that night ("Homeless Paul as Johnny Cash"). More revelatory is another video posted by City Jackdaw of Homeless Paul from around the same time, one that does not appear on YouTube but rather on a blog entitled "City Jackdaw: Notes in a Life" under the headline "If a Drunken Donald Sutherland Did Johnny Cash" (2016).

This video was originally posted to the Facebook page of an online Manchester newspaper, The Manc (2016), with the simple heading, "Drunk Guy Outside MMU." Homeless Paul is standing outside Manchester Metropolitan University, where he spots a group of students who are conducting video interviews for a class project. In character, he offers to perform for them. He adopts a pose, enquiring, "Rolling? Rolling? Rolling?" He is not in such good form vocally here as in the other videos, and he appears almost overanxious, moving through a succession of Cash songs in a headlong medley, starting with "Ring of Fire," then "I Walk the Line" and "The Man in Black," which he launches into when he spies a black-clad security man approaching (out of shot) to help another yellow-coated one—someone who is attempting to move Homeless Paul along. Suddenly we are watching not only Homeless Paul's fandom but its interruption. Underneath the posting of the video on The Manc is a note that the video has 1.3 million views.

The posting on The Manc inspires abundant commentary from people who had encountered Homeless Paul on nights out in pubs, either joining in with him in singing Cash or giving him some kind of a handout. Homeless Paul is a local celebrity of sorts; he clearly enjoys being called "Johnny Cash" by the security men and those who film him. The commentators also find an online sense of community in discussing his situation. He is also clearly enjoying the performativity that Cash manifests in him, which mitigates the unease that watching the videos might entail. Through Cash, he is still recognizable in his society. He prompted one commentator to remark, "I love this city." Homeless Paul is a positive proof of Manchester's resilience, a character who discovers a robustness in adversity that Cash models for him.

Homeless Paul emerged from nowhere and now lives on in these videos, but he remains otherwise unknown. Cash might be the only comfort that he has. Yet this seems grossly sentimental and patronizing. The videos show a man for whom Cash really means something; Cash is deeply imprinted on his memory, despite his evident afflictions. How he enacts Cash's songs reflects those circumstances, heartbreakingly but also with a degree of archfulness. The hard facts of Homeless Paul's existence are expressed by the hard truths of Cash's lyrics. Here is both England and fandom. Many boundaries are crossed in unifying them.

PART TWO

A YEAR IN THE LIFE

OF CASH FANS AROUND

THE WORLD

6 GATHERING OF THE SUPERFANS

*How Contemporary Cash
Fandoms Network, June 2017*

The second part of this study is structured substantially around what happened as a consequence of meeting Elvira van Poelgeest, the Cash superfan (although this is not necessarily a label that she and other fans would welcome) who began the online Johnny Cash Infocenter as a way to share previously unshared and unshareable forms of information and music.[1] Along the way, it became a bigger vehicle, establishing and fostering relationships among fans from around the world.

We traveled to the Netherlands to interview her in her hometown of Groningen. For a year, we visited and traveled with Johnny Cash fans and tracked some of their behaviors online. The year was filled with unexpected turns and experiences, but mostly it was filled with the passion and ingenuity of Cash fans, both those who were part of Elvira's network and others who had gone their own way.

As it turned out, the Johnny Cash Infocenter website was inactive, but only because Elvira had redirected her energies into other areas of dynamic fandom, creating other types of networks and connections. Communication continued through Facebook, and Elvira was spending more time working with her bands: the Memphis 4 (who mainly played Cash's music) and the

Black Suspenders, a country-rockabilly band that also came along to perform on the day of the interview. Elvira was every bit as consumed by Cash fandom as Charlie Taggart, but her fandom manifested in a radically different way: through performing, curating, organizing, and traveling.

Elvira's Facebook post about our imminent visit to the Netherlands drew the attention of another Irish Cash fan and tribute performer, Barry Winters, who offered to fly over to be interviewed. This encounter led to a collaboration between Barry and Elvira. Their activities over the next year provided a fascinating opportunity for live study, not least because of the way in which these fans invited us into their world and work as fans.

Meeting a fan like Elvira in the context of her home was also vital to our project. It gave us a local context to the international phenomenon and allowed us to compare her to a fan like Charlie, despite their contrasting commitments to performance and travel. It was remarkable to find out how far everyday people would go in their fandom, not only geographically but also in terms of committing their money and time. Perhaps the eagerness of these fans to participate in the project was also an indication of their desire to be noticed and validated through that acknowledgment—impulses recognizable in the work older fans had performed in Cash newsletters. Or perhaps these fans saw the project as part of their project to bring further attention to Cash and his fans.

Elvira and Barry did fandom through fieldwork. Yet we were doing our own fieldwork, seeing where and how fans live, and situating their fandom within their own origin stories while also considering the ways extrapersonal forces might influence what appears to be a very personal business. It also allowed for the understanding that even if fandom is a pleasure, it must be taken as seriously as any other form of work.

Groningen seemed to be as vital a site of Cash activity as anywhere else in Europe. Looking through just the first hundred contributions to the online Johnny Cash Project, there were three frames uploaded from different individuals based in Groningen, including Elvira. People said it was a vibrant and free-thinking university town, the sort of place where a complex figure such as Cash might enjoy an aptly complicated regard.

Country music is popular in the Netherlands anyway, but it had also become clear from a number of sources that the country was unusually receptive to Cash's work. Internet searches revealed a range of tribute bands hailing from all over: The Boys Named Sue from Amsterdam ("rock-oriented," according to Elvira), Eindhoven's Def Americans ("more authentic"); and Elvira's own groups, the Black Suspenders (seven or eight years in existence) and the Memphis 4 (sometimes 5). The Netherlands was also the source of the weirdest account of Cash fandom we had yet encountered in the project—a case that had been reported across international media of a man from Nijmegen whom medical researchers had claimed was cured of OCD after deep-brain stimulation therapy (Mantione, Figee, and Denys 2014, 8). The only side effect had been the patient's developing a love for (or obsession with) Johnny Cash. This was held to be benign, given the grievousness of the patient's prior suffering (Woolf 2014).

In our trip to the Netherlands in June 2017, we stayed in the west side of the city center, close to the university, and prepared questions. When we checked out the city, we stopped at Plato, an archly named record store that was almost idyllic. It was orderly and comprehensive, its stock reasonably priced, with a mix of new and used CDs and vinyl.[2] Silverman went hunting for Cash vinyl, perhaps to buy (even though he did not own a record player)—perhaps to use as artwork, but also to assess Cash's presence in the commercial world of Groningen. Here were many of Cash's studio albums from the 1950s through the American Recordings era, as well as a number of compilations and anthologies. This was not necessarily surprising, given the presence of Cash material in almost every record store we had ever been in, but there was an appreciable difference in quantity and choice in this particular store. The man behind the counter turned out to be a knowledgeable and generous music fan. As conversation turned to the Cash fandom project, he said he did not know much about the presence of Johnny Cash fans in his town. After he was informed that the Johnny Cash Infocenter was based in Groningen, as well as the high level of participation from denizens of the city in the Johnny Cash Project, he thought again. When it was put to him that there were a lot of Johnny Cash records in his store, he responded, "That's because they sell well"—an entirely reasonable business strategy, and an example of the mercantile pragmatism of the Dutch (Coates 2015).

Elvira soon picked us up in her car. She announced that she was going to pick up another guest, the aforementioned Finbarr Winters. This was unanticipated, and it became another thing to think about en route, not least it indicated that this project was a source of potential excitement for Cash fans because it might offer them a voice in a different forum from where they were usually heard. Elvira's instincts about his potential as a contributor proved correct. Finbarr was a skilled performer (which we would observe later), but he was also a well-versed Cash fan, and someone with a keen sense of what might make for a meaningful story.

Elvira told us she had come to Johnny Cash fandom through an initial passion for Elvis Presley, an artist whom her mother had played for her. She came to this fandom young, and it found its way into both her life at home and at school. Whenever she had a report that she could present on Elvis, she did. Once she got internet access in 1998, she started looking for Elvis Presley material online. In the meantime, she worked at McDonald's, working her way up to manager of first one, then two, restaurants. Then she decided to go back to school part time, earning a degree in business. In this period, she also began to redirect her fandom toward Johnny Cash.

She began to acquire the equipment and materials to become an even more active fan. She traded cassette tapes, then CDs, which she duplicated on a slow CD burner. She only exchanged material that was not available commercially, and she sought out trading partners through internet forums. She turned her attention to Cash in the 2000s, trying to undertake the same process of sharing music, but she did not find Cash fandom immediately receptive. Elvira identified this as a generational problem: these fans were older and adhered to a different fan economy. Many were used to selling or buying their material rather than exchanging it, but the lure of free trading eventually broke their resistance.

When asked whether she thought there were divergent political views within Dutch Cashdom, she said of course. In the Netherland's current political binary, there were more or less centrist values represented by the coalition government of Mark Rutte, or the anti-immigrant populism of Geert Wilders's Freedom Party. Elvira was for Rutte, but she would not speak for her bandmates.

Finbarr emerged, immediately telling everyone to call him Barry. When they arrived at Elvira's house, she showed them a room that had photos of Elvis and Cash, as well as an American sign related to the terror attacks of September 11, 2001: "United We Stand." The kitchen had more Americana, including posters of *North by Northwest* (1959) and Hank Williams. Most notably, there was a collection of basses and guitars, seven in all, plus a stand-up bass, which turned out to be Elvira's new passion. She said later she had been playing for two years, first taking six months of lessons to "avoid learning how to play wrong."

This dedication corresponded to her motivation to start the website, which was designed only for fans. Other Cash sites were working to promote Johnny Cash directly, to sell material, or both. Elvira's Johnny Cash Infocenter was self-explanatory; it existed to share information while offering more than that. She admitted to being on a personal quest to collect all of Cash's recordings, especially those that have not appeared commercially. As Lee Marshall notes, "The individuals who collect unauthorized recordings are in general the most dedicated fans an artist has" (2003, 60). Elvira claimed that she wanted to have everything to make her own judgments about the quality of recordings rather than relying on the verdict of others; often she preferred bootleg cuts to the released ones. Marshall argues such collecting "is mimetic of the understanding of processual creativity," which he sees as "a living organic entity rather than as a hypostasized product" (61). Barry was not identically motivated, but nevertheless he had modernized his collection by putting nine hundred songs onto a drive in his car playable through Bluetooth. He had fifteen versions of Cash's "I Walk the Line," which he revisited frequently, taking pleasure in identifying all the songs' nuances, performance by performance. As with Charlie Taggart, minute particularities of context became vibrant texts in their own right, revelatory events in Cash's history.

Discussion began about how fans might relate to one another, as well as Elvira's generally positive relations with other fan clubs. She insisted that the real difference was that she had no commercial element attached to her venture, whereas some fan club leaders wanted to be paid for their work. A fundamental problem in fandom is that no one really can be compensated adequately for their work, at least financially. Elvira was nevertheless mindful of the value of her work as a price she was prepared to bear so as to facilitate her version of free Cash trading. The site cost her about €100 (a little more than $100) a year for server space. She had also experienced some frustration in terms of trying to instill a pro bono culture in Cash fandom circles, like when she had done translation work for a Cash fan newsletter, which was unpaid (tolerable), then was asked to pay for the issue she had helped translate (intolerable). It was also entirely probable that a man would not have been treated in the same way, hinting at sexism. Clearly Elvira's generosity had been exploited, whether consciously or not.

Elvira had a pragmatic interest in connecting people so they could share information and music files—hence the title of the site. Her determination not to monetize her fandom or her collection of Cash materials seemed absolute, just as her bands were not playing Cash music for money (beyond their expenses). Performance was another mode of sharing and communicating, and it facilitated travel, another particular passion. As for the mercantile pragmatism of the Dutch, Elvira had much of this quality, but in a curious way. She was interested in trading Cash, but the only currency worth using was material related to Johnny. That said, she knew exactly what it cost in euros to run the Infocenter, and she knew that not everybody understood Cashworld as she did. In order to do her fan work, she found the resources necessary even as she revised the very definition of "necessary."

The Infocenter served best the interests of people like herself, who wanted a productive line of communication between Europe, the United States, and the rest of the world. She and the other site users needed each other: "What you really want is not available in stores. I hooked up with some diehard collectors. People are very open to share stuff."

Elvira's immediate circle of fans in Groningen were incredibly active and inventive. She detailed a busy performing schedule for her bands across festivals in the summer months; she described how Ivo, the singer from her Cash tribute act, the Memphis 4, had written and performed a play about Cash's life. Elvira also spoke of her involvement in a special prayer meeting that only used Cash's music, organized by a preacher named Piet in Papendrecht, near Rotterdam. The idea originated with another preacher named Fred, who had previously held Elvis and Dylan services.

The Cash service was enormously successful. It was held on three occasions, with regular attendees at Piet's services having to be turned away. It also received substantial media coverage in the Netherlands. Elvira was quick to assert that she was not religious herself, but her own mission of widening the Cash community took precedence. She viewed the work of others in this regard with a degree of ambivalence. She said that the Cash fan in Holland with the highest national profile was probably Matthijs van Nieuwkerk, whose magazine program on Dutch TV, *De Wereld Draait Door* (The world keeps turning; 2005–) featured a long-term segment entitled "DWDD Recordings" that would see invited Flemish and Dutch artists sing cover versions of songs that had a special meaning for them. The direct inspiration for the project had been Cash's American Recordings series, as was indicated by the playing of a sample from one of these albums before the live performance of every DWDD recording began. Elvira was clearly pleased by this phenomenon, if not by the way in which Cash-related events were organized by media or institutions: "They never ask the fans, but always the same experts from the newspapers."

She was determinedly uninterested in the story about the deep brain–manipulated Cash fan from Nijmegen; this was the sort of fandom story that the press would run, sensationalist and grotesque. Fandom was only interesting to conventional media if it was frivolous. She was serious, and so was Barry. Talking thoughtfully and moderately, he seemed very much the former communications specialist in the Irish police force from which he had recently retired.

Then an anecdote revealed another side to him. Another Irish fan, Brendan Woods from Tipperary, owned a Scania R620 truck and trailer that he had custom painted with a series of elaborate images of Cash.[3] Driving on a busy dual carriageway (highway) en route to a holiday with his wife, Barry suddenly saw Woods's truck heading in the other direction, so he did a U-turn so he could follow. The truck soon turned off, and Barry ended up following it up the laneway to the Woods' residence. Just as its private gate was closing, he ran in, yelling, "I'm sorry, I'm sorry. I'm just a Johnny Cash fan." After an explanation, Woods allowed him to take photographs of the truck and even sit in it. Barry later bought a limited-edition model of the truck, one of two hundred made. He also showed photographs of other Cash trucks in circulation, mostly of German origin. Barry no longer seemed quite so moderate.

Elvira had never met Cash and had no regrets about it, while Barry had enjoyed two fairly intimate encounters with him, based on a relationship he had forged with Cash's sometime piano player, Earl Poole Ball, to whom he offered a tour of Cork City while the latter was touring Ireland. In the first meeting, Barry had purchased a ticket to one of Cash's shows in Cork, and Ball had alerted Cash to his Irish friend's presence at the show. Wanting to be close to the stage, Barry took up a seat in the middle of the front row by himself, because for most people that was too close. He remembers the comedy of his sitting there alone in a new denim jacket with a white fur collar, feeling self-conscious.

Before the show, Cash came out and met him there; he met him again in a back room after the show as well. A photo of this encounter is the picture ID on Facebook for Strictly Cash, Barry's tribute band (you can see the denim jacket). Traveling in America another time, Barry planned a trip to a Cash show in which Ball was playing. He bought tickets and left a note at Ball's hotel to say he was in town. At the show, Cash was in a feisty mood, asking audience members where they were from and playing an appropriate song. For an audience member from Alabama, Cash started up "Oh Susannah." The band tried to catch up, only for him to pick another face and state once they had. Then he asked, "Where's my friend Finbarr?" When Barry raised his hand, the band played a full version of "Forty Shades of Green."

These stories prove a double truth: Cash was remarkably cognizant of his fans, and Barry was an exceptional fan worthy of exceptional attention. Barry is from Ballincollig, near the city of Cork, and his fan genesis is shaped by the degrees of access he had to Cash. His first memories of Cash come from watching broadcasts of *The Johnny Cash Show* (1969–71) on RTE (the Irish national public station), the only channel on TV at the time. Barry was thus part of a captive audience. As with the story of Charlie Taggart, a curatorial broadcast decision taken by RTE turned out to be a critical moment. Barry recalled how the camera zoomed in on Cash's hands at the end of the song "These Hands" (PeterRabbit59 2011). He added his pleasure at reuniting with that scene via YouTube years later, and how that foundational event in his fandom became reactualized: "I just watched the television show, and it just stuck. It was in my mind. Records were very expensive, so I saved my pocket money, which was scarce and went to the shop and bought 'The Man in Black' at Black's Shop in Portlaoise. So I got my 'The Man in Black' from the man in Black's; it came to me years later. I was interested in Johnny Cash and that led me to country music, American, of course." This last remark clarifies that Barry, like Charlie, is not a fan of country and Irish, and that to like Johnny Cash is to indicate that you are not part of Ireland's conventional herd.

Early interest in Cash also took on a scholarly aspect; again, with amazing serendipity, Uncle Bill's Heraldite Club section of the national *Evening Herald* newspaper advertised an essay-writing competition on the subject of Johnny Cash. Barry, who had just started secondary school, researched the essay by going to record shops and cribbing liner notes from whatever albums he found. He won the contest and received his prizes, the double album *Star Portrait* (1972) and a promotional copy of the single "Kate" (1972). The story even comes with a cliffhanger. When Barry opened the prize package, a Johnny Nash sticker fell out, to his horror; he recalls his older brother saying, "Ha ha." But the rest was pure Cash.

This is a great collector's story, even if Barry denied that was his thing: "I never wanted to be a collector, but I wanted to get as much Johnny Cash as I could." He describes the peculiar gratification of finding Cash records in unlikely places, like when he found the album *Hymns by Johnny Cash* (Columbia, 1959) for seventeen shillings and sixpence (about a dollar) by going through racks of albums in what was usually a household store dealing mainly in furniture and drapery.

When performing Cash, Barry took pleasure in identifying others in his audience who would recognize a song if he chose to play one from outside the familiar repertoire—someone in the room who might be slightly disengaged from the main body but nevertheless singing along, enjoying the opportunity to act out in public their knowledge that ordinarily remains a private activity. So Barry checked out the fandom levels of his audience, but he also wanted to show that there was more to Cash than "I Walk the Line." In this, Barry was also singing for someone like himself—people who do not like Cash but love him.

Barry did not say "Hello, I'm Johnny Cash" when he performed, and he disliked the designation "tribute artist," partly because he sees it as having become a brand identity rather than the genuine paying of tribute. Of the acts that emerged since *Walk the Line,* Barry remarks that they should be called "Joaquin Phoenix Tribute Acts, not Johnny Cash." There is genuine tribute, and there is imitation. Barry makes tribute, but he is not a tribute act: "A tribute act is more of an actor than a musician. You have to assume the role. It's putting on a visual show."

His band toured Ireland with some success in the early 2000s, until the collapse in 2008 of the briefly ascendant Celtic Tiger economy (the Irish economy had unexpectedly boomed when Ireland's currency became the euro) devastated the fabric of Irish social life. People stopped going to pubs, and Strictly Cash found themselves without a regular clientele. It meant the end of the band, but Barry persevered by going solo, giving free concerts in care homes: "After the financial crash, no one wanted to pay the band. I went on a year on my own. Now I'm back to playing Johnny Cash for myself."

Barry also had a Barnumesque talent for event conception, demonstrated in 2008's staging of a Strictly Cash show at Mountjoy, Ireland's largest and most notorious prison for adult men. Given his working life as a policeman, it was a transgressive thing to do—but not in terms of honoring Cash to the fullest extent possible. He noted that the prisoners were unaccustomed to coming together as an audience, except when they would congregate to watch the English soap opera *Coronation Street* (1960–) at 7:30 in the evening four times a week: "That's the only home life they have." The gig took place in that weekly slot of precious free time that was available to the prisoners, and Barry did not want to waste it. He was motivated in part by the desire to reenact Cash's most radical decision about performance, but he was also motivated to explore his own sensitivity to the deprivations of a prisoner's life. He continually stressed the humanity of Cash as a core part of his appeal, and he was also sensitive to the idea that he was entertaining people whom he and his work colleagues had worked hard to put behind bars, sometimes for violent and cruel crimes. The experience was necessarily difficult, but that was precisely the point. Barry wanted to celebrate the forthcoming anniversaries of the Cash prison performances at Folsom and San Quentin; he was anxious to continue the commemorative work of fandom, but also to reexperience how jailhouse performance enlivened Cash's own work. Cash had his own concerns and anxieties before Folsom—concerns and anxieties that Barry wanted to approximate.

Cash fandom also had social impact. When Barry played his Cash tribute, he said people would come up to him and talk about their favorite songs. All of Elvira's work colleagues knew she was a fan and a musician; some would ask about her activities and Cash. Barry and Elvira both noted that they would gear their responses to these enquiries according to how committed a fan the person asking might be. Fandom might unify, but it is also stratified. A frequent point of discrimination in this way is the film *Walk the Line*, released in 2005. Many fans came to Cash through this movie, and Elvira and Barry both expressed a dislike for it. However, both are careful to either hide their opinion or downplay their dislike to new fans so they do not alienate them.

Matters of preference and discrimination were important as ways of demonstrating the kind of fans they were. In measured ways, they were even critical of Cash's work. Barry cited Cash's attempt to write the theme for the Bond movie *Thunderball* (1965) as a bona fide error of judgment. Elvira leapt up to play it, drawing on her de facto completist library, and Barry modeled visceral distress. Then they played another unreleased song, using a nearly identical arrangement. Elvira acknowledged that she would still want a new Cash recording, even if it was terrible. She also made a far more radical claim: "My musical taste stops at 1975." In this, she was effectively ruling out about thirty years of Johnny Cash music. Barry was far more inclusive. Still, many songs from the American Recordings albums played in the background, so there was evidence that Elvira had not dismissed them entirely. Either way, she enjoyed a good epigrammatic declaration. When asked what she thought of samplings of Cash by hip-hop artists, she answered in a flash: "'Get Rhythm' is the only rap song I like."

When asked if Cash's music provided a soundtrack for the personal lives of Barry and Elvira, with Cash's music complementing events of significance for them, both declined to comment. If Cash fandom was a way of life, then it was not their only life. When Barry referred to his U-turn on the highway, he acknowledged that he had to explain his actions to his wife. For Elvira and Barry, Cash was every bit as much of a passion as he was for Charlie, but it motivated them into radically different behaviors. Charlie had always found a way of bringing Cash to work with him. Elvira worked hard at an educational publisher, then gave much of her time over to following and performing Cash. Fandom was not a mere pastime for either Barry or Elvira.

Barry and Elvira were also keen readers of Cash-related literature, having most, if not all, of the books written about Cash. They knew his life story and its related controversies backward and forward. Elvira claimed to be unsentimental about Cash's life, but that implied an understanding that Cash was seldom sentimental about it either. Yet while she asserted that she did not care for the American Recordings phase of Cash's career (even as Barry indicated his liking for it), this appeared to be a coolly aesthetic measuring. But when "Hurt" was sung by Theunis Lourens, the vocalist of the Black Suspenders, Elvira declared it "depressing," thus suggesting that a sentimental relationship to the later music did exist.

Elvira's frankness was not always appreciated by other fans and Cash forum mediators, who would block users for merely mentioning some unflattering part of Cash's life or catalog. Elvira disliked such piety; it ran contrary to her sense of how Cash fandom should be performed, as an all-engaging creative activity that would emulate Cash's own hard work. Fandom was a prompt to action and mobility; it was a way to deliberately unsettle herself. In the year that followed, she would organize a music tour of Tennessee, Arkansas, and Mississippi, then come to Ireland to perform with the Black Suspenders. Barry would be joining them there, having also traveled on a Cash pilgrimage to the United States, accompanied by his Austrian friends who ran a Cash museum and were organizing a European Cash festival. Cash fandom was a window for all of them. It took them to his native place, but also to each other.

Non-American Cash fans always had much to say about Cash, but even more to say about the local circumstances that had connected to him. Their fandom was a matter of self-assertion rather than merely evidence of the dominance of American culture. Despite not fully engaging the idea of Cash's Americanness, Barry later wrote an email in response, an indication of his desire to contribute as comprehensively as possible:

> As a very young lad, our gang would go to the cinema most Sunday afternoons where we'd watch among other things, the old Westerns, Audie Murphy etc. . . ., and re-enact the story on the way home, that evening, and during the following week. Happy carefree days. A few years later, we discovered Johnny Cash singing about the cowboys, prairies and such.
>
> Perhaps he subconsciously brought back those happy carefree days. I don't know, that is something for the psychologists. Why Johnny Cash? There were lots of other country singers around, but they didn't have the same exposure. Here he was, in our living rooms every Saturday evening.
>
> You may not have realized it . . . Michael might, but America at that time, and for years before, was the Promised Land for us. President Kennedy's visit, and subsequent tragedy, created an affinity. Also, our first TV station came on air in the early 60s, which brought never before seen images of skyscrapers, big cars and everything else that we could hardly imagine, as the American TV shows were shown.

American influence on popular culture was evidently pervasive, but it does not explain why Barry (and not everybody else) became fascinated with Johnny Cash; the answer to that was fundamentally unknowable. Yet if America was everything that Ireland could not imagine, it was also clear enough that the positive influence of America was also a negative expression of being Irish. Barry stressed the poverty of his family's local circumstances. In finding Cash, he found someone who talked about prevailing over such circumstances.

Elvira and her band did not talk about Dutch or American identity but rather about Groningen and Friesland, the province to the northeast (pers.

comm., June 9, 2017). The interest in American music and Americana was matched by a complementary pleasure in detailing the quirks of being Friesian. So as well as expressing a transnational ability to move beyond national boundaries, these fans were also defined by their translocality. Cash fans affiliated through Cash, but they could relate their own particular places, plots, and contexts.

Friesland produced an album called *Fryske Cash* (Marista, 2011), featuring twenty-one different performers singing lyrics in Friesian to Cash tunes and rhythm. "A Boy Named Sue" bawdily became "In Man Named Tyt" (A man named tit). Cash satisfied the transnational impulse here, letting Friesians transgress against the idea of both the cultural homogeneities of nation and globalization. However, he also let them express their regionality and locality, as the performers came from a variety of villages and towns within Friesland. So the translocal answer to "What do you think about the Americanness of Johnny Cash?" was "I come from Friesland. Where are you from?"

The members of Elvira's band, the Black Suspenders, were not dedicated Cash fans, although guitarist Albert and drummer Kees found room for him in their complex and knowledgeable love of rockabilly. In a discussion about how one might come a long way round to Cash via a more long-abiding interest in punk, metal, or blues, Albert animatedly talked about crossover elements between the modes, while Kees stressed the circuitry that could relate Cash to a multiplicity of rock narratives, with multiple references to his other love: heavy metal.

The Black Suspenders had a show the next day, so they rehearsed a set of rockabilly and music by Cash, with Barry guesting. The singer, Theunis, had been notably shy when introductions had been made. Now in performance, he was hollering and crooning in a Southern accent. This was a total transformation. An environmental officer in his day job, and only twenty-one, Theunis was more of a country fan than the rockabillyists Kees and Albert, and by his own admission, he was mainly channeling Hank Williams. Clothing accentuated his performance: tapered boots, a boot-lace tie and trim cowboy shirt, black pants, hair slicked back. He had only been interested in the music for four years, and it was intriguing to hear that his bodily and intellectual voyaging had begun (as increasingly trips into Cashdom do) with a first viewing of the video for "Hurt." He had worked through his fandom fast. Elvira had begun with Elvis and arrived at Cash; he had been a departure point for Theunis.

Irish singer Barry Winters jams with the Black Suspenders in Elvira van Poelgeest's living room in Groningen.

At the end of the rehearsal, he alone had started into singing "Hurt," and Barry immediately joined in, moving toward Theunis, drawn irresistibly by the sound of a Cash song. An Irishman in his everyday clothes, a Dutchman in costume—they genuinely seemed to want to play Cash forever. One had been a fan for four years, the other for over fifty, and they had just met for the first time. Unsurprisingly, their vocals did not quite harmonize, and gradually Theunis granted the floor to Barry.

After the music was done, Elvira left the room and came back with two boxes of Black Suspenders T-shirts, stickers, and business cards. She then revealed a box of sample Cash shirts she hoped to sell on her website, including designs that featured Cash's classic hairline, and shirts that read "I shot a man in Reno," "What would Cash do?," and "Will you miss me when I go?" So the pragmatism had a mercantile aspect after all, even though she had not yet sold anything, and the idea was only to finance the Infocenter and her other work: "It's expensive, you know?"

Elvira had to consider the financing of her activities because they were so sheerly energetic; Charlie's fandom took the form of a determinedly contained enjoyment, Barry's was expansive and compulsively performative, but Elvira went beyond both in terms of her determination both to meet fans and enable them to meet. She did not offer an origin story like the Irishmen, but instead used action to express her fandom. In this she also connected to the organized business of Cash fandom, which had taken heed of her work, not least because they saw opportunities for their own enterprises. In the space of the next year, triangulating Holland, Ireland, and the American South, she and Barry would be in motion, bringing their fandom with them and growing it as they went.

CHAPTER 7

YOUTUBE, CASH TALK, AND TRASH TALK

Fandom in the Comments,
June 2017–June 2018

Fans can be busy in remarkably different ways. There are so many comments on the September 6, 2009, YouTube video of Johnny Cash's "The Man Comes Around" that keeping track of them is virtually impossible—there are over 19,000 on one video alone (Johnny Cash Channel 2009). But it is not only the number of comments that makes it hard to keep track of; it is also the types of discussions, which can range from high-level discussions of the song to philosophical examinations of the existence of gods to people insulting each other about their perceived sexuality. Then there is the matter of fandom. YouTube commenters on a video of "Hurt" are clearly not fans in the way that Charlie, Elvira, and Barry are, yet many comments on that video are identifiable as expressions of fandom, even if the fans are not themselves identified as international. More than that, they are having to affirm their fandom in troll-infested environments, far from the relatively safe enclosures of the domains inhabited by the Dutch and Irish superfans discussed so far.

The abundance of Cash material generated on YouTube necessitates its separate analysis into two parts: one of the commentary found beneath Cash videos and the other of the performative fandom represented in cover versions of "Ring of Fire." YouTube is a commons for a variety of fan behaviors, suggesting that fandom comes in many digital forms and that people come to Cash in many ways. For many younger Cash fans, YouTube may be how they first encountered his work, and it demands to be read as a location in its own right; it might represent a kind of home for Deborah from Nowhere. YouTube servers are all around the world, and posters' IP addresses are known only to YouTube, so in a sense, nowhere is not an accurate description of the geography of a posted video, but rather the sense of its geographic ambiguity when we cannot determine it.

Additional and strange tensions are also at play in YouTube videos. The complexity and technological advances required to create YouTube content are concealed by the range of fan behaviors associated with it. Posting a ready-made Cash video requires little effort, although it risks infringing copyright law; however, posting a video in which a Cash song is covered might be the most frequent labor-intensive fan activity there is, given that the posters often do the performing and/or the filming themselves. Finally, Cash's presence as a visual text, sophisticatedly constructed, often contrasts sharply with the level of discourse below it in the comments. Yet if anything matches the weirdness and idiosyncratic nature of Cash's fifty-plus years in show business (and his fifteen-year posthumous career), it is the multiplicious and variegated nature of fans' YouTube responses to his work, be they pontifications, insights, mutterings, insults, and empathetic responses.

Do You Speak Johnny Cash?

In terms of Johnny Cash, what YouTube does directly is to present him as a phenomenon of the English language. In this way, these videos contextualize Johnny Cash as not only American but English; part of his accessibility is not only his nationality but his lingua franca. English is the language most taught in the world and has official status in at least seventy countries (Crystal 2012, 4–5). Yet American content dominates English-speaking popular culture for a variety of reasons, including the means of production and distribution. The English that most people tune into is frequently some kind of American.[1]

Johnny Cash speaks and sings perfectly enunciated English, despite (or because of) his Southern accent. But in a sense his work's themes are the more relatable language. His concepts—life, death, regret, faith, humor, and anger—are universal, whether they are songs he wrote, like "I Walk the Line," or whether they are written by others, like "Hurt." His clarity, added to the key terms in many Cash lyrics, form a basic vocabulary for any student of English as a foreign language. Indeed, a YouTube video posted by a teacher of English, Randhawa, as a second language in Gwangju, South Korea, demonstrates as much, with a class of children singing "Ring of Fire" in giddy chorus (December 12, 2011).[2]

Fans themselves would not likely identify the transferability of Cash's language and sound grammar as reasons for why they became fans. YouTube commentators often do admit that they appreciate a song because of its appearance on a movie soundtrack, but it is unlikely they would say they do so because the movie is distributed through a culture economy that relies on English-language listeners and watchers, if not speakers. They almost invariably describe their movement through YouTube in emotional terms, in this way reflecting the affective core of all that Cash produced. As Andrew Tolson notes, "Although there is some guidance on the home page with its featured videos, and although there is the preselection of links, crucially it is the computer user, not the institution, that makes the connections. . . . In post-television users construct their own viewing experiences, from user-generated videos" (2010, 285).[3] Such viewers recognize the feelings that Cash generates and how he makes those feelings seem real. As Paul Booth notes, "Fans use digital technology not only to create, to change, to appropriate, to poach, or to write, but also to share, to experience together, to become alive with community" (2010, 39). In YouTube, that aliveness takes complex forms, both sublime and grotesque.

Most YouTube postings of Cash's own videos begin as tribute, with posters simply wanting to display another exemplary Cash text. Yet such postings often lead to arguments as soon as an opinion is ventured about the meaning of the song or the quality of the performance. However, they also evolve into discussions about subjects and between people, with Cash only tangentially involved. Often comments center on how someone has responded as participants indulge in summary judgment.

The practically lawless zones of the YouTube commons show not so much a model of international cooperation as a chaotic postnational space that can turn hilarious, distressing, or solemn in an instant. In the middle of all that, posters sometimes return to the comforts of national identification to remind themselves (and others) that they have another life outside the screen. So in the chaos of comments beneath "The Man Comes Around," user Arshad Rashid Reed just posts "Hardcore Johnny cash fan from INDIAIN," and Matt Loutzenhiser replies, "Arshad rashid reed Awesome man, cool to see how far music can still reach people" (Johnny Cash Channel 2009). Internationalism is reassuring and civility is restored—until the next comment.

Empire of Dirt

Every fan group or individual has a Cash entry point, whether it is the rockabilly phase of the 1950s, "Ring of Fire," or the prison concerts of the 1960s. Newer fans mostly have come in by finding on YouTube Mark Romanek's video for "Hurt." In this, YouTube provides the role that older fans may attribute to a parent (especially a father) or some other tutelary figure, who might have given them a record or taken them to a show. "Hurt" appears in many ways on YouTube, so it is practically impossible to measure its impact overall. However, just an analysis of one posting is instructive. YouTube user DFtranslateBR put up Romanek's video on April 5, 2012, with a short supporting text in Portuguese (the BR in the username appears to stand for Brazil); as of August 28, 2018, it had received 121,983,272 views (DFtranslateBR 2012), although the video has since been taken down. According to Social Blade (https://socialblade.com), this makes it the 17,967th most watched video on YouTube, and the video had been watched 5,405,927 times in the previous thirty days. Social Blade estimates that this matriculates in potential revenues for advertising as between €14,800 and €236,000 (about $15,000 to $250,000), although it is not clear whether anyone has actually benefited monetarily from the posting.

The video has also been posted by another Brazilian, Roberto Leopoldino, getting 9.3 million views, and also by an Italian, Turicampo, who attracted fifty-three million views. Another poster, Beachbuggy, got 81,787,114 views (as of September 5, 2018). There are 15,843,231 views for v94j's lyrics video (simply presenting the text on a black background) and another 6,351,024 views of kyle72895's conceptually similar video (they use different fonts). All of this and more amount to close to three hundred million views of the "Hurt" video, making it overwhelmingly the most watched Cash song on YouTube, with perhaps "Ring of Fire" a distant second.[4] As of July 5, 2018, DFtranslateBR's video has generated 52,735 comments; much of the discourse focuses on the relationship of Cash's version to the original by the Nine Inch Nails, or on the poignant biographical context in which the video was shot.

This poignancy results in remarkable and candid testimony from some fans, obliterating barriers between private and public experience. In mid-June 2019, Alba Andreu comments on the video posted by DFtranslateBR:

> This song reminds me of my father who passed away 2 days ago. My father mistreated my mom for 20 years, also my big brother who has a disability. My father wasn't a great man, he lied and he abused of his beloved ones but, at the end, he is my father. What disturbs me is the idea that my father died with the sense of no being loved. Dad, even all the pain you have caused and all the hate I have on you, I love you till the end of my life. I will always be your "cuchipú" and your "tiny star." I will regret the rest of my life don't tell you that I love you.

There is no direct reference to Cash here, yet the song triggers a stream of confession and mourning. It is unclear whether this was a premeditated posting in connection with "Hurt," or whether it was something spontaneous, a reaction to a random viewing. Either way, the post inspired responses such as the following:

> **MOMOMATHEW O:** Alba Andreu just reading this comment brought tears to my eyes. I'm so sorry.

> **THE PUNISHER:** Alba Andreu I'm sorry for your lost I was sad when I read it I hope u will be fine . . . I Don know why I said that to you but I did ☹☹

The Punisher and Momomathew O are clearly pseudonyms, and this dialogue is performative (as all dialogue is), but one nevertheless feels real sympathy and community in these moments. We should note here that we do not really know anyone's nationality; we can only infer it by their use of English or perhaps by a name. Yet it would also be wrong to assume that they are all American, English, or Spanish. This discourse takes place across borders, even if these borders are not declared. Yet posters take turns to express their caring.

One commentator, Nathan P. Russell, or rather "Nathan P. Russell" (we note here that even traditional-sounding names might be pseudonyms), offers advice: "Forgiveness is the key. To purify oneself is also very important. To hate a parent who mistreated you and others in the family is natural, but not useful." He then offers his diagnosis: "You seem to have much love inside and the ability for forgiving. Childhood makes deep impressions into your physical and mental constitution—if you can look with an open and forgiving mind on yourself, the negative emotions can be transformed into wisdom and strength and you'll become a whole and loving person." After his own confession of grief, he suggests a few resources for dealing with grief, including a meditation video. Peanut Head chimes in: "Sounds familiar let em burn!" There are a few more sympathetic responses. Then Nazbol Miner responds:

Abusing dad?
Cant feel sad for his death now. He deserved it.
Stop loving an evil creature, or you're retarded as well.

Rainbow TheOne responds:

Nazbol Miner What are you for an a*shole? Her father died and you cant even understand her emotions? Leave.

After a few more responses, Lucy writes,

Im sorry for your loss:(I worry about this everday. My dad was abusive towards my mom and I for 20 years as well and now that we were able to get away from him I worry that he will die thinking he is unloved when in reality despite everything he is my father and I love him so much. I hope you are able to heal slowly with time.

Confession, life coaching, compassion, rebukes, community policing, group therapy, and awkward silence at the funeral parlor—these may well be exactly what draws people to YouTube videos of "Hurt," as it allows people to put their emotions on display, whether for themselves or for Cash. Whether or not this is fandom, it is full of the raw material from which fandom is made.

It is also fascinating to notice how quickly these strangers (from an unspecifiable range of countries) move into talking as if they know one another (in contrast to how the West Ham fans converse online about Cash through their preexisting community). If this has a certain solemnity here, not least because of the traumatic material under discussion, it can quickly mutate into other expressions of abusive familiarity in another context. We also see here the notion of self-policing that rules online communities. As Nancy K. Baym notes, "Fan communities have strong ideas about what constitutes appropriate fan behavior and are not shy about policing one another for adherence online or off" (2018, 85).

A later post from Andy Appleton is more generic in its use of the language of homage, one of millions of online RIP gestures for Cash: "We love you Johnny Cash. We love you and we thank you. I love you so much. Your voice was one of a kind. Thank you for covering NIN song. It's truly amazing."

Both Andra Albeu and Andy Appleton have expressed a desire to become visible, even globally visible. Such a desire is often irresistible, and a demand implicit throughout YouTube. No content is bad content; in this way, YouTube needs to be read as a carnival of utterances moving between borders of experience, identity, and culture. Alba Andreu's posting spawned a relatively dignified and respectful discourse, but Appleton's did not; things quickly move into gross-out comedic language, occasionally violent and gratuitous. Here is a sample from the eighty-three replies:

SOLON: G@Y

KNIGHTS: Andy Appleton kiss him already

ANDY APPLETON: D I don't love him that way

TIGGLYXTEDDY 1: I'm reading all of this shit while listening to a depressing song

ANDY APPLETON: Ignore us. If you like this music, then like it

DARK WESTERN 1: Andy Appleton Fuck him.

He made this music for us.

The needle tears a hole, the old familiar sting

It was never about you, nor him.

This was situational, suit to fit anyone with similar mindset.

He's helping listenners relate via situational experience we all will face one day.

So beautiful, so amazing.

Don't make it about you, selfish assholes.

PIPER JUST PIPER1: Paul Go in son, I'll do the deed if that's how he is, be careful, south of the river, DUBLIN.

These exchanges are familiar in the sense that they show avowedly straight young men calling each other gay, an abiding pastime of avowedly straight young men, but linguistically they are also bizarre and babelistic, bending English into barely comprehensible hate shapes. It is not always apparent which person is saying what to whom—but more to the point, who cares? Language is being used here in such a way that no one in usual circumstances would read it as an overall proceeding. English has become diffused and difficult while retaining a brute power. One trolling participant appears to be from Dublin, but it may not matter; trolling might be regarded as a postnational mode of address in that it seeks to undermine the words and views of others for the sake of mockery itself. Yet this all starts from the same song—one that inspires others into a form of communion.

Fandom—whether it is indeed fandom—is tested stringently on You-Tube. It is not a safe zone, as in the relatively closed loops of fan clubs, gigs, and more circumscribed forums that are policed for inappropriate or irrelevant commentary. If YouTube comments pages are congresses where the contributors have elected themselves, then they are such spaces in the most radical sense: largely uncontrollable, as liable to lapse into anarchy as consensus. They are also the most inscrutable international spaces that might be encountered, because it is not always possible to determine users' origins, unless they declare it. Users' level of English usage does not necessarily indicate if they are using it as a first or second (or third) language. Mistakes in spelling and grammar are just part of the scene and general disorientation.

The results can be depressing, as evidenced in both the stupidity and the wisdom commenters exhibit as they respond to "Hurt." This in turn manifests as what an "Empire of Dirt" might look like: a place where people are as likely to behave impeccably as they are appallingly. With all of the bile being chucked around, Arturo Núñez intervenes in the thread to contribute (in the fullest sense of that word) the following: "Querido amigo hace tiempo partiste pero te tengo en el corazón gracias" (Dear friend, I have kept you in my heart for a long time, thanks). It is almost as if Arturo has not understood a word of what has been going on around him in the thread, but maybe that is precisely the point. The ghastly Anglo babble finds its modulated Latin reproach. In this case, the reassertion of a language border also serves as an ethical constraint.

What Are They Doing Here?

Similar things happen elsewhere but take on a different character depending on the song's text. Looking at the comments of any YouTube video, especially if the video is popular, long-standing or both, there will be many disagreements. People disagree on the quality of the recording, the reputation of the artist, or the merits of various fan interpretations. They may disagree about something tangential to the video's content; the reaction among the seventy-five million views of the celebrity-heavy video for "God's Gonna Cut You Down" is notably negative, as ordinary fans take exception to having their space invaded by the famous, who are portrayed as covetous of some of Cash's authenticity (YouTube, Johnny Cash, November 1, 2009). As a Greek poster, Kallio3.14159265358979, notes, "What the hell is kanye west doing in a johnny cash video?" (Those closest to Cash in real life, such as Kris Kristofferson and Rubin, get less of a hard time.)

There are some "so what" responses to this, although the potentially racist aspects of it are not explored, and there is no adverse comment on the presence of Terrence Howard, Chris Rock, and Q-Tip in the video. Generally an accord is expressed that West is unwelcome, related by some posters to his May 2018 tweets of support for Donald Trump.[5] Yet a counter-reading emerges that insists that this video critiques the entire culture that has spawned West, Trump, and everyone else. The reaperdom of the lyric extends to the vainglorious participants in the video: "This song is about those celebrities that sold their soul to the devil for fortune and fame. Pay attention to the symbolism in the video. God is going to cut those down who sold their soul." This reading hints that the celebrity fans are participating in a pageant of their own damnation, perhaps seeking atonement. Yet this is not necessarily what the commentators want to see in the protagonists; nor does anyone reference the actual friendships that Cash had with many of them.

Engagement with "Hurt," "God's Going to Cut You Down," and "The Man Comes Around" also shows that the later Cash is a relevant and quite different Cash, which transforms his place in the world. Johnny Cash has become engaged with a renewed public through these songs, but this engagement also invites other creative people to attend to the Cash oeuvre, whether they are filmmakers, documentarists, or even advertisers, and their work brings yet more people to Cash's music.

The Corrections

Many responses to videos are tied to the song's meaning, its association with another text (like a movie or television show), and political or cultural circumstances, along with too many other factors to catalog, like those coming from the personal circumstances of commentators themselves.

"The Man Comes Around" generates a variety of disagreements. One long thread is about the song's content, which is based on the Book of Revelation from the New Testament. Simon says he likes the music and does not care about the religious component. This leads to an argument between Christians and atheists, with Simon, mostly in vain, trying to separate his atheism from the song. The argument is mostly respectful and shows how fandom is a means through which people can relitigate eternal questions. There is a remarkable tension in the comment space around this song, which in itself is a matter of theology and philosophy.

A Czech poster, Alžběta Ponková, affirms, "Cash come to Christ and he wan't to write songs about him and bible why you guys are here arguing? When someone become christian in heart he want to tell everyone about Christ," and another poster (Excatholics) proclaims, "Jesus is Lord!," only to be corrected by Jafer Jebari, "Excatholics Jesus is not Lord, he is a prophet. He was never crucified, God sent him on to him. Please brotheran understand that." This poster inevitably runs into a profiling query from The Miserable Man "jafer jebori muslim?," which gets the retort "The Miserable Man Securalized Muslim." Then comes another correction, from J Shay: "Jafer jebori Jesus was God. He died on the cross and rose again, 3 days later, just as the Bible prophesied 700 years earlier. And He's coming again! The Bible cannot be disproved." This in turn is corrected by C**tservatives Are Filthy Scumsucking Maggots, who notes, "J Shay Nor can it be proved. Give me a break"—a sequence that eventually ends with three different posters simply writing, "Amen." If it is not necessarily possible to identify the full international dimensions of this discourse, it is nevertheless evident that a wide number of ethnicities and faith positions are being expressed, all promoted by Cash's writing and performance (with due acknowledgment given to Rubin's extraordinary production).

Slavoj Žižek identifies "The Man Comes Around" as "an exemplary articulation of the anxieties contained in Southern Baptist Christianity" (2006, 186) but extends his reading of the lyric into a post-Marxist exploration of what he sees as the prevailing culture of fatalism and impasse, which extends to everyone living in an apocalyptic twenty-first century, one defined by arbitrariness, torture, and terror.[6] The YouTube philosophers are less stringent than both Žižek and the theologians; they range between the Epicureans, who only want to speak of musical pleasure (like Aussie Loads, who acclaims Cash as "the true country singer, timeless perfection," or Web Magician, who notes in Russian, "One of my favorite songs. A real classic!" and in English, "Very good music") and the panic merchants like Bjshd Ejdh: "I listen to this song and I think in my head that the world is falling apart around and civilization is breaking." But there is also an existentialist debunker, Bassistdave109, who just wants everyone to know who and what he is: "Just doing a dance in my living room. Don't mind me." Nothing more, nothing less.

New Cashworld

The YouTube commons are public but populated by mostly anonymous people, and so it is hard to know who is from where except through subject clues, like saying you are "at university" rather than "in college." The ethnic diversity of many developed countries also means that it is hard to use names as a reliable indicator of nationality, whatever some might believe. In how many places might Jefar Jaberi or Aussie Loads reside? An imagined community, as Benedict Anderson notes, is both real and virtual: "It is imagined because the members of even the smallest nation will never know most of their fellow-members, meet them, or even hear of them, yet in the minds of each lives the image of their communion" ([1983] 2006, 6). In the YouTube comments, self-identification through geography is infrequent, with it manifesting instead through assertions of preferences and beliefs, although the significance of location can evidently be an important factor in the generation of the latter.

These postings generate their own virtual geography of twenty-first-century Cashworld, with intensifications of population and movement. Every contribution represents a potential alteration of the landscape, bringing in new people and driving others away—not forgetting that there is a massive silent majority that does not comment but only spectates. In this new geography, posted videos and songs are cities, and commentators are dual citizens, at once a member of their own community and the commentariat below. This new role is simultaneously temporary and lasting—that is, until the video is taken down or the comment deleted.

In terms of locations within the transnational Cash nation, the posting of "Hurt" is a sprawling megacity on the rise, the growth of which can be measured in hundreds of millions; its citizens are more or less connected to Cash and Cash fandom. One of the most watched postings of "Hurt" is by Mono Pilot; with over thirty-five million views, it presents a still photograph of Hugh Jackman as Wolverine and relates to the soundtrack of the film *Logan*. In its comments section, there is barely a mention of Johnny Cash, with people mostly posting RIP messages to Logan, Professor Charles Xavier, or others in the Marvel universe.

It is evidently hard to think of these citizens of Cashworld as living in the same country as Elvira, Barry, or Charlie; their residencies seems so long term as to be permanent. Matt Hills (2013), building on John Fiske's concept of textual productivity, notes that before the internet, it used to be easy to tell who was really a fan: "Textual productivity—the creation of fan fiction, fan art, folk songs and fan videos—appeared to demarcate fan communities and identities since non-fan audiences would be far less likely to engage in these practices of textual production." Hills and others feel the categories are too strict in terms of understanding what fandom is in the modern era. Hills (2013) notes: "I would argue that online postings, reviews or commentaries themselves become textual in the sense of being digitally reproduced and reproducible . . . these fan productions are no longer embodied or spoken in a precise spatiotemporal moment, they are instead mediated to indeterminate or unknown others (a forum/Twitter followers who may re-tweet/YouTube viewers etc.)." The permanent residents of Cash fandom relate to the posters in YouTube in the way that people who have fully paid their mortgage might be compared to members of the new international precariat, for whom dwelling is a matter of impermanence, dependent on shifts of employment circumstances enforced by twenty-first-century capitalism, the only game in town. As Rebecca Pearson notes, no one is really sure what online fan community is: "Clearly the issue of community in all its ramifications (definition, the nature of fan networks, the relationship of fans to corporate structures that mimic fan networks and practices) constitutes a key and unresolved tension in fandom as well as in the digital economy as a whole" (2010, 93).

Whether fans on YouTube are vacationing from another reality or apparently rootless, the same technology that has created such ephemerality is the same one that produces all those videos. Yet Cash speaks to all of them, with equal authority, and above all with clarity. Whatever your circumstances, you will find a Johnny Cash that you can understand. The tension between what it means to be a fan in general and an international fan in particular is endlessly explorable, and it acquires even more depth when people decide to cover Cash, as the next chapter demonstrates.

8

A CLOSE WATCH ON
THIS SONG OF HIS

*International Fans Cover and Post
"Ring of Fire," June 2017–June 2018*

In 2015, Kristian Ordulj sang "Ring of Fire" on *The Voice Croatia* (YouTube, January 24, 2015), his English almost perfect, his pitch excellent. He wore a modified Western outfit, entirely black. While Ordulj sang, one of the judges made a "yee-haw" sound, and another put his feet up on a chair. They seemed delighted by both the choice of music and the singer.

Cash's work appears often on *The Voice*. In an initial search, we found *The Voice* performances of Cash songs in the following countries: Australia, Croatia, Germany, Portugal, Ireland, the United Kingdom, Norway, Quebec, and the United States. If the YouTube comments show how Cash prompts community debate, then performances on *The Voice* show how Cash inspires imitators and even embodiers. The contestants on the show are not necessarily Cash fans, but they surely understand the way his music communicates across cultures. If you want to generate an illusion of authenticity, Cash is who you channel.

Through his imitators, Cash knows how to win such contests, perhaps in ways that would have surprised the man himself. Cash was/is a traditionally handsome American man; his voice has a singular quality, one not obviously easy to imitate. Non-Anglophone performers take on an even more unenviable task in trying to emulate it, yet they find it irresistible. But if his voice is hard to copy, his music is relatively easy to learn on guitar, which explains why so many of his fans are drawn to performing him.

Surveying performances on YouTube provides another compelling alternative to recording charts as a mechanism for understanding popularity, not least because of how such charts are notoriously manipulable. However, the performances also reframe the idea of the popular in terms of activity rather than revenue. In many countries Cash has an unimpressive chart history as a singles artist, yet he inspires countless covers. A YouTube search of "Ring of Fire cover" returns 1.75 million results, and international covers represent a large portion of them. There are performances in kitchens, front porches, recording studios, street corners, bars, and stages; there are covers on network television and with CGI vision; there are covers that are professionally produced and some that are essentially trailers to advertise the performers for future gigs. There are dozens, maybe hundreds, of covers of all kinds on YouTube, from people filming themselves to performances by bands like Blondie. What better way to pay tribute to a great artist than by covering a song of his? Or what better way to pay tribute to yourself and your good taste than by covering a legend?

The covers often do not do much of what might be thought of traditionally as cultural contributions, as they often are not particularly accomplished, so they do not make a compelling case for their own existence, at least musically. Yet the covers from a wide range of countries and nationalities invite us into a type of dual citizenship of music experience or double vision; we see Johnny Cash from another country, and we see another country from Johnny Cash.

"Ring of Fire" is remarkable in Cash's canon for the performativity it inspires and the relatability it simultaneously demonstrates, its presentation of a conundrum of fear and desire that goes right back to the earliest expressions in lyric, and the ancient Greek poet Sappho's conception of desire as bittersweet.[1] In the newest language of the twenty-first century, it can be represented conceptually in just two emojis: 💍🔥. On YouTube, that conceptual core inspires an explosion of creative twists—indeed, too many to list. Whether these artists are fans seems dependent on whether their desire is to honor Cash or themselves, or inevitably some combination of the two. In exploring this question, we present a taxonomy of transnational performers and performances of Johnny Cash's, mostly of "Ring of Fire," according to mode and type, with a few other notable examples.

The Early International Cash

International covers of Cash began early and sometimes under his supervision, as with the Japanese singer Takahiro Saito's performance on *The Johnny Cash Show* in 1971, posted by PeterRabbit59 in 2010 on YouTube. Cash heralds Saito as an exemplar of country music's transcontinental sweep:

> Country music today is the sound on radio, on television, all over the world today, whether it be in Japan, or Germany, or North America, country music is what more and more people are demanding, and with each passing day it is being accepted in an even greater variety of musical styles . . . and from Tokyo, Japan, comes a young man who learned to sing country songs from listening to records, even before he learned to speak English, because of his love for country music, he completely handmade the guitar he's playing. Backed by the Tennessee 3, make welcome my friend from Tokyo, Takahiro Saito.[2]

Saito begins to sing "I Walk the Line" with Cash providing beaming encouragement in the background. He starts in English using a conventional baritone, but the highlight of the piece is when Saito switches midsong to Japanese. In that instant, he also switches to a deeper tone that is more directly an impersonation of Cash. The TV audience recognizes the double transition and whoops in approval. Saito walks the line between paying homage by performing a mild imitation in English, then actual impersonation in Japanese. Saito becomes Cash in his own language, whereas in English he was trying to be like him. There is the fandom of resemblance and the more radical fandom of becoming, which Saito performs in the more intimate zone of his mother tongue.

Takahiro Saito's performance foreshadows one of the dominant roles in twenty-first-century fandom: the cover or tribute artist. In this era, fans, or those in fans' clothing, often try to distinguish themselves by performing the work of artists they admire (or think others admire) online, but also nationally and across local communities. Both Ireland and the Netherlands have many current groups committed to playing Cash music, as fans and for his fans.

Monika Mueller explores some of the creative license that international interpreters have taken with Cash songs and wonders which Cash it is who inspires such varied tribute: "It might well have been this distorted image of the Man in Black in its mythic, transnational appeal, rather than the singer

Johnny Cash, that inspired the creatively twisted German versions of Johnny Cash" (she cites Bernadette La Hengst's electro "A Boy Named Sue," a Croatian version of "Five Feet High and Rising," and Ramesh B. Weeratunga's Bollywood "Ring of Fire" as examples). She posits, "In spite of the elusive nature of the 'authenticity' of folk rock music . . . [Cash] . . . managed to convey an 'authenticity' or 'realness' of intent that easily transcended genre boundaries. This 'realness' also made for their worldwide appeal which in its turn resulted in fascinating transnational adaptations of their songs" (2013, 115)

Cash's "realness" thus invites a wide range of "creatively twisted" responses, and YouTube is home to them all. In a way, Johnny Cash gives permission to his imitators of "Ring of Fire"; after all, he covers many songs himself, including "Rowboat" on the underrated album *Unchained* (American Recordings, 1996). In covering the song, Cash finds a way that recalls Beck's original, yet he makes it very much a Cash song, not only by deepening the musical accompaniment but also simply by singing in a way that is recognizable to his audience. Indeed, the first step in covering a song is to separate yourself from the original in some way; covers that only imitate usually work the least well because they remind us of the original—which, if it is performed by Johnny Cash, is not likely to be surpassed.

Not every cover is meant to do this work, and because Cash is a master cover artist, the bar for covering his work successfully seems high. Cash's professional bona fides automatically give him authority to interpret someone else's work, reinforced by the acceptance of performing other people's music in his genre and the eras through which he moved. Frank Sinatra hardly wrote any of his music, and country music songwriters have a good amount of authority in the Nashville musical landscape. What Cash does in the American Recordings series is often different from Sinatra's performance work; producer Rick Rubin imagines Cash as a genre-fluid interpreter of music from a variety of sources to discover both the genius of the song and Cash's performance.

The Cash Actor

YouTube shows an international cast of Cash tribute acts who perform within local and national networks as part of their cultural economies. Such performers are not necessarily fans; rather, they are entrepreneurs responding to the postmortem swell in Cash's popularity. They are attempting to feed (and feed from) Cash fandom rather than simply express it. One example is the Australian touring show Johnny Cash Live (Daniel Thompson and Stuie French), whose video not only shows the performers in question but also critically includes footage of the audience arriving in anticipation at the theater and postshow testimony attesting to the good time they have had. This is not only a performance but also an advertising video, and a reminder of the particular economy that the Cash actor works within a video posted through his username, DanThompson875 on January 8, 2018. Fan performers more recognizably work out of the idea of homage, trying to fill the perpetual gap opened by the death of the original artist. These tribute acts all contribute to what might be called an industry of Cash emulations and projections, playing festivals and tours worldwide; as in other production processes, it could be argued that some are more organically or carefully produced than others.

Tribute acts do not get that much attention on YouTube—something sometimes cruelly revealed by their total number of views. Charlie Taggart's logic is useful here: if you want to watch a video of a Johnny Cash song on YouTube, why not just watch Johnny Cash? Yet despite the low number of views they attract, they tell us something about how Cash has a peculiar power to inspire performance. Some act as Cash, some sound like Cash, some summon a Cash aura in a range of ways while doing their own thing; some are making a living of sorts out of being Cash, and others are just making a night of it by playing him.

Some Cash tribute acts are literally acts, in that they basically offer a theatrical experience of sorts, in which the value of the performance is based on the quality of the illusion being presented. The audience members are key to such a performance, in that they are required to enter into a fictional compact with the performer, to allow themselves to think that they are watching the real Johnny Cash. Sometimes such performers not only wear black but also a wig. Cash actors capitalizing on the success of the Mangold biopic *Walk the Line* will have a June Carter replicant in tow; others favor the economy of playing the role of Man in Black, unaccompanied. They will probably start their concert with "Hello, I'm Johnny Cash"—something Barry Winters refuses to do.

The Cash as Cash Player

Most tributes fit into the category we call Cash as Cash player. The singers will not necessarily dress as Cash, but they will probably be styled according to his powerful example. There will be black, maybe pomade or Brylcreem. They will move into the role of the Cash actor in that they will emulate Cash's voice, but they will not necessarily attempt theatrical re-embodiment. The emphasis is on Cash's music, and on attempting to replicate its sound above all else. Going to hear Johnny Horsepower from Denmark perform "Ring of Fire" is trying to get as close as possible to listening to Cash's record, at least according to Streetcruiserdk's September 13, 2013, YouTube post. On YouTube, however, they face the problem that the best Cash actor is Johnny Cash himself; they cannot compete for attention with the very man they emulate.

The Out-of-My-Fandom Player

Out-of-my-fandom players are the tribute acts that proclaim Cash fandom as a pretext for performance. They will resemble the performance of the Cash actor and the Cash for Cash performer, but with the crucial intervention of "my fandom" as a mediatory lens. This takes many forms and would apply to Barry Winters, whose performances are prefaced with his drawing a line between himself and the kind of tribute act that proclaims, "I'm Johnny Cash."

Cash is an inspiration for doing and a reason to bring other people who love Cash together. By contrast, but within this same type, the Danish metal band Volbeat's singer Michael Poulsen performs a fragment of "Ring of Fire" at nearly every live show, which has been recorded by fans many times, such as the June 19, 2016, YouTube post by Leanie and Loque. When Volbeat fans like them post these moments, they are in effect expressing their fandom through how Poulsen expresses his own. He presents the Cash fragment as a vital text in his musical autobiography, a song that enables him to do his own music, which he then moves into by playing the song "Sad Man's Tongue," the chorus of which describes how its outcast protagonist is repeatedly told to take his Johnny Cash records and go. For these players, Cash is a muse.

The (Perceived) Outsider

When a YouTube performance of a Cash song is foregrounded by the non-Americanness or nonwhiteness of the performer, as when a Korean tourist sings at Willie Moffatt's in Memphis, the performance is presented by the person who posts it as a narrative in which "Johnny Cash's talent refused to pass on when he died, and it jumped into the body of a passing Korean tourist." Even the introductory text posted in 2007 by Kumbah for the video describes the tourist as "unsuspecting." Unsurprisingly, and despite this patronizing ordeal, the Korean singer turns out to be a highly proficient interpreter. As one of the commenters reports: "Holy shit, he's good." When a posting of a video leads with reference to a nationality, the viewer is always being asked to comment on the same thing: the degree to which the performer succeeds in spite of his nationality, as in "Folsom Prison Blues Johnny Cash by Johnny Black an Italian Tribute," as posted by MusicaCountry on November 13, 2014, or an excellent performance titled "A Tribute to Johnny Cash—German JC Cover Band," posted by Xl Medical on August 28, 2012.

In a video posted on May 5, 2015, Michael entitled "Czech Cash Tribute Band," the title provides us with the key elements to discuss. The band's members are playing Johnny Cash, and they are Czech. Next is "Karim Kandil (Egypt) Folsom Prison Blues," posted by OJLPWC (March 4, 2011), and then "Johnny Cash—Thailand" (posted by The KaC Himself on YouTube on February 9, 2011). As this one plays, an American-accented voice says, "This is unheard of, in front of all these people. They are doing a great job. I am proud of him, I am proud of him." According to the post's introductory note, the singer does not speak any English. His teacher did well.

The Twisters

Twisting occurs when bands or performers manage to enhance viewers' sense of their own singular sound and feel, even as they remain substantially attentive to the Cash song that they are covering. Sometimes this is a matter of a subtle shift in genre, as with the Brazilian Cajuns' version of "Folsom Prison Blues," posted to YouTube by Way on November 16, 2013, which performs the unusual feat of entirely regenerating the energy of the original while giving it added amplitude—the benefit of adding an extra guitar and a washboard.

Similarly, "Ring of Fire" by the Hungarian band A Nyughatatlan (which translates as "the restless") make a striking impact, partly because they feature a female musician on rhythm guitar, thereby interrupting the maleness of much Cash tribute (YouTube, May 18, 2016). In this self-posted video, they are reminiscent of Elvira's bands, foregrounding their commitment in their

YouTube channel to Johnny Cash and rockabilly, although A Nyughatatlan also records original material in Hungarian.

The French Betty G and the D-towners (September 18, 2017) command attention just for Betty's vocals, which seem to add the words, "I fell for you like a bag of child." Posted by Eureka on January 21, 2014, the various ukulele versions of "Ring of Fire" on YouTube have to contend with one another for the role of the twister; after you listen to the first one, the novelty wears off. Sometimes, it remains open to question whether a twist has really happened at all, or whether it was a twist worth making. As in all categories, twisters can be inadvertent.

If you only listen to Juliana Strangelove's October 14, 2017 rendition, available on YouTube, it is genuinely impossible to determine whether the song is being sung by a man or a woman. A contralto from Russia, Strangelove's voice discovers and embodies the peculiar gender ambiguity already latent within the lyric (that Sapphic energy), combining depth and grace, sweetness and menace. Like all the artists mentioned, Strangelove (real name Julia Demyanskaya) is not a tribute act in the strict sense of the word, even though she appeared in the Moscow Johnny Cash Festival. She sings a broad repertoire from disparate genres, yet she provides a genuine contribution to Cash fandom in alerting listeners to new potentialities in his most familiar song. There is also the query inevitably realized by her name, with reference to Dr. Strangelove; is she learning to love the bomb, is the bomb her voice, bearing its way to the United States and Johnny Cash? Maybe not, but using the term "Strangelove" seems a peculiarly apt way of not only encapsulating the song's meaning but also of describing the interpretative history of these multiple Ring of Fires. The performance is motivated by some kind of love but is also potentially a way of introducing strangeness to the original Cash text, for better or worse.

The Auteur

Auteurs post videos entirely as pretexts for their own creativity. A Turkish poster called Ironcl posted many videos (now deleted) using Cash songs as pretexts. One is a comic acting out of "A Boy Named Sue," which is in its own way entertaining but baffling, giving the same kind of pleasure as any amateur video might. With other songs, however, such as "Best Friend," "Can't Help Where I'm Bound," and "I Hung My Head," the footage is of a kind of

Cash geography, sometimes just showing a dashboard cam of a freeway, or providing spectral mountain and desert scenes. Ironcl shows serious artistic ambitions and has fifteen thousand followers—not an insubstantial amount. He does not only respond to Cash songs, but does so with such frequency to suggest that he has a fanlike knowledge of his work.

The Fox

Romeo Capellato has 613,559 views of his 2012 video of "Ring of Fire," which uses Cash's backing track and uses visuals from Mangold's *Walk the Line;* whereas others show themselves, Capellato works by stealth. Giving people every reason to think of Cash's original via the backing track, and to think of Joaquin Phoenix via the visuals, he cunningly inserts his own vocal performance. It is a masterful use of the aura of others to inject himself into people's attention.

The Cynics

Some of the versions of Cash songs on YouTube show remarkable acuity and invention, while others express a baser instinct. It is hard to know what to apply to the video constructions of Marcus Nimbler, a German YouTuber who posted his own video response to both Cash's version of "Ring of Fire" as well as the cover version by Social Distortion. Nimbler dubs his own vocals over the original backing tracks and splices together videos from found footage. For the Social Distortion cover, he uses spectacular shots from action movies, then moves into soft-core footage of young women in lingerie and swimsuits. The video of Cash's version only has women in lingerie and swimsuits; his video for "Folsom Prison Blues" has women in swimsuits with guns. Nimbler is not much of a singer, and the word "egregious" seems a good one to use for descriptions of material like this, but it is very YouTube: self-promotion and sex. Unsurprisingly, Nimbler's videos pop up in other zones of the internet as well, such is his bottom-line appeal. His work still has to be understood in terms of tribute, however strange, as many songs get Nimblerized, but only "Ring of Fire" appears to have got it twice. Like the vanished auteur Ironcl, Nimbler also uses songs for his own video constructions, but they are much more Russ Meyer–like in their insistence on providing image streams of soft-core titillation for a male gaze, irrespective of the song. All Nimbler's videos look the same.

The Citers

Tribute takes many forms, of course, and one of the most interesting is citation. A rightly famous example is when Cash is sampled in De La Soul's "3 feet High and Rising" (Tommy Boy, 1989), a quotation that both proves the diverse legitimacy of Cash as well as the band's own ingenuity and nerve. The many lives of "Ring of Fire" in Jamaican ska and reggae served as a precedent for this, with the most overt example being Lee Perry and the Upsetters' full-on cover version (Upsetter/Trojan, 1972). Both before and after, however, phrases from the song, in particular its brass riff, have found their way into other recordings. The reggae forum Chatty Mouth: Reggae, Rants and Reasoning turned up the following: Augustus Pablo's "Put It on Dub" (Jamaican Recordings, 2006); the Ethiopians' "Hail Brother Rasta, Hail!" (Bb Inc., n.d.); Prince Jammy's (dub version) "Dub Is My Occupation" (Blood and Fire, 1999); Tommy McCook's "(Music Is My) Occupation" (Rocksteady, 1968); the Skatalites' (ska version) "(Music Is My) Occupation" (Trojan, 1967); Tristan Palmer's "Ghetto King" (Greensleeves, 1981); Ken Parker's "True True True" (Treasure Isle 1970); and Max Romeo's "Public Enemy Number One" (Upsetter, 1972). The extraordinary capacity of YouTube allows someone to almost instantaneously follow this circuitry of citation, all while being reminded of the insistent power of Cash's hook. Cash's love for Jamaica as a second home is a matter of record, of course, but these reversions of the song occur before he lived there and are thus indicative of a preexisting sympathy, and certainly some kind of fandom.

The Tourist

If buskers sing a Johnny Cash song only because they reckon it will elicit more money from passers-by, because people like to hear "Hurt," then that is hardly a communication of fandom. Yet YouTube videos of buskers are posted by the passers-by, not the buskers, and such postings often come from people on vacation, enjoying the moment when a performance of a song they like enhances their experience.

If not on vacation, posters may have enjoyed the moment when a busker's performance transfigured the experience of their everyday environment; in that moment, it can be said that they enjoy their native city as if they were a tourist. A Czech tribute band was performing "Jackson" in just such a street context; the poster, Michael (2015), is also an inhabitant of Prague, but he plays the role of tourist by taking the video even though he is walking around his hometown.

The Hopeful

Musically proficient to at least a fair degree, and equipped with a webcam, hopefuls sit in their bedroom or some other zone. They hope that we will subscribe, yet they remain marooned and housebound. Yet such videos may be the conduit to another life.

The commenters on Yoann Guay's August 19, 2016, posting of "Ring of Fire" on YouTube exhort him to enter *La Voix du Québec;* another says it is a shame about *La Voix du France.* It is unclear whether he ever entered either, or whether he is French or French Canadian (his name suggests that he might be Breton). What redeems him from the realm of the cynic is that he only sings Johnny Cash, steadfastly and seriously, while sitting bolt upright at home (2016).

A Polish YouTube website, Best CoverLive (2017), invites people to make recordings in their studio, with a view to attracting attention from producers or other performers: "Best Cover Live is a music project whose goal is to record, gather and then promote on YouTube channel BestCoverLive live clips of various performers, amateurs and professionals, from talented to outstanding." Thus a retired horseman, Wojciech Mickunas, sings "Ring of Fire" in a fine, deep voice, as well as songs by Patsy Cline. We await his fate.

The Missionary

Teresa the Traveler, in a YouTube post dated June 16, 2010, is playing "I Walk the Line," but the extraordinary circumstances of her performance demand inclusion, as she brings Johnny Cash to the uninitiated. On her peripatetic vlog, she visits the Western Desert in Egypt and visits the Farafra Oasis, the Kharga Oasis, and the Dakhla Oasis as well as the White Desert, Black Desert, and the Great Sand Sea—a lot of ground gets covered in four minutes.

At 3:12 in a 2010 video titled "Singing Johnny Cash Songs to Camel Herders in the Western Desert," as the herders make her tea, in an otherwise unexplained moment, Teresa dons an acoustic guitar and sings Cash while the herders look around, or indeed away. It does seem significant that a Cash song is what Teresa decides to play, as if he might be the American artist most likely to connect to a nomad. It is hard to know what they make of him, but her faith in the communicability of Cash is unbowed. It makes a striking contrast with another Cash-related curiosity on the never-ending stream prompted by the YouTube algorithms, a travel vlog by Erika Derrickson (February 6, 2015) that documents "Photographing My First Indian Christian Wedding w Johnny Cash." She appears in selfie mode, walking around the communal space where the wedding is taking place. This is framed by two comments, the first of which occurs as the opening riff in "I Walk the Line" can be heard: "So that's kind of weird music, especially for an Indian wedding." The second occurs at the end of the clip, when she turns to a generic observational comedy schtick to say the same thing: "[Shruggingly] 'I walk the line' Wait . . . what? Why? What music is this? It doesn't make any sense whatsoever . . . [a resignedly dismissive wave of the hand] . . . All right! [as in all right, do whatever you like!]."

Confusion is the result only for those unversed in fandom: both American and international Cash fans would find nothing weird about playing his music at their weddings, baptisms, and burials. What else would they play? The striking difference is that Derrickson cannot figure out how "I Walk the Line" would work in India, while Teresa is determined to make it work in Egypt, showing again how such performances of Cash by fans amount to a kind of speech as well as expressions of faith.

The Hipster

Hipsters play Johnny Cash in a cute little square in Paris like they play everything: with a certain disinterestedness and an excess of style. In the January 16, 2012, YouTube post by the label Mange Disques, there is vintage clothing everywhere as well as mannered movements, and probably somebody is recording this on shellac. What is interesting is the sheer persistence of his version of cool, yet the anxiety emerges that Cash has just become another lifestyle statement, like a beard or a pair of Ray-Bans—another item that white people like, as the blog of that name describes:

> White people love these Ray-Bans because they were very popular in the 1960s and the 1980s. This gives them a historical precedent and allows white people to classify them as "timeless." That way when they purchase these sunglasses they can talk about how they were inspired

by the fashion and music of these bygone eras. When a white person says this, you should just nod and mention how they look like young Johnny Cash, a dead Beach Boy, Audrey Hepburn, or an extra from a John Hughes movie. This will make them happy and likely to give you their old, expensive sunglasses that you can sell for a significant profit. ("Ray-Ban Wayfarers" 2009)

Yet whatever disdain might be visited on hipsters, Cash's appeal to them cannot be dismissed. In many twenty-first-century eyes, Cash is the definition of cool, a phenomenon of style above anything else.

The Butchers

Not everything can be cool, and no song is cover proof. ElFamo123's posting of "Trix 'O' Treat playing Ring of Fire by Johnny Cash at Bangkok Betty, Thailand" proves it—or maybe it is just the sound. In contrast, Alice Wolswijk, a YouTuber based in Malta with a modest following, sometimes posts images of Christmas services, Catholic street processions, and people singing hymns. She also posted two videos for "Ring of Fire." The first consists of her father performing karaoke in a restaurant while a solitary couple dance (June 28, 2011), while the other is shot in what appears to be the family home, with friends and/or contemporaries Johan and Mila singing while perched on kitchen stools (February 6, 2010). There is a bottle of J&B Scotch on a table, glasses, snacks in bowls. It is daylight. The singers converse in English, but most of Wolwijk's videos use Dutch for textual accompaniment, an indication of the family's roots elsewhere. It is a quiet party, the singing remarkably quiet and modest. Wolswijk films the scene from an armchair, sitting beside people who appear to be elderly relatives, with a couple of younger people also seated. As the song reaches its conclusion, Johan insists that the room join in with a reiteration of the final chorus, which they do. Everyone murmurs "Ring of Fire" toward a total silence.

One surprise occurs when one of the two commentators beneath the video identifies herself as having been at the party; her name is Undine LaVerve, and she turns out to be Malta's leading burlesque artist. Almost inevitably, another YouTube search reveals a tuxedoed Henk Wolswijk, Alice's father, singing "Ring of Fire" with a vamped-up Undine LaVerve at a wine bar in Balzan, Malta (2015). The song is an unlikely family hymn, but it is also an addiction.

The Namers

For some, it is enough to summon Cash's aura by name. La M.O.D.A. (La Marvillosa Orquestra di Alcohol) from Burgos in Spain sing "Los Hijos de Johnny Cash" on the streets of Mexico City sporting beards and white undershirts (Comunidad 18, May 15, 2017), or Britain's (highly professional but still starstruck) Alabama 3 (June 23, 2015) murmur, "Hello, I'm Johnny Cash." On YouTube, everyone is Johnny Cash.

The Live Ones

Silverman and an American friend were walking together in Oslo when they encountered an older man and a young child, presumably his grandchild, singling "Ring of Fire" as a duet. The rendition was highly competent, the contrast between old and young remarkable, and it worked. And the performance was live, unsanctioned, there for the moment for the Cash fan (or not) to discover. What you find on YouTube can also be found on the street.

9

THE OUTSIDER

A Veteran Punk Brings Cash to
the French, August 2017

When the opening of "Ring of Fire" is played, it commands attention. It is a musical phrase as internationally recognizable as anything else Johnny Cash put into words. It burrows its way into collective consciousness, and it still finds fans easily; it is a hard song to get away from. We found dozens of covers of the song on YouTube, but fans of Cash in a particular country do not easily appear in a database if fandom networks are not established. French Cash fans are not always easy to find despite their undoubted existence. Cash has a place among the many American artists that French people revere, but he is not as thoroughly a part of the cultural landscape there as in other countries. Marco Rockmilhaud saw this and decided to do something about it. He created the only website in French dedicated to the championing of Johnny Cash, and he put together a place of respectfully rough homage to Cash. Marco did this on his own terms, yet also in a way that was coherent and consistent with the maverick intellectual traditions of French culture.

Finding him took some detective work. It was impossible to find a picture of anyone by that name online. Marco's avatar image on Facebook was of a zombie Johnny giving the bird, and the surname was clearly a pseudonym. Finally, through Facebook messaging, a meeting was set with Hinds at a café in the ancient Roman town of Sommières in the Gard province, celebrated for its bridge dating to the first century BCE. Still, nothing seemed straightforward; it had been impossible from the phone call to gauge Marco's age, leading to yet more entertaining but futile speculation.

The dominant iconography of Marco's blog and web posts took the form of the rock gothic favored by bikers in general and Harley riders in particular. If Marco were a biker, then interviewing him would be an exciting path to follow, not least because it appeared to offer a different context for viewing Cash fandom compared to the rockabillyists of the Netherlands or the country fans of Ireland. The truth turned out to be complicated; it confirmed that the distance between an online presence and a real one might not be so large, but that beyond a web presence lies a much more complicated story that suggests appealing to potential fans is often a raison d'être for superfans.

It turned out that Marco had a motorbike, but he was not riding it. There are also a lot of beat-up Citroën saloon cars in France, and this is what rolled up at La Guinguette. A figure appeared from the car and seemed to hesitate, retreating to his car, then reappeared. Wearing combat shorts and a T-shirt advertising a bullfight (another great obsession in the region), this was Marco.

It was hard to estimate his age, but he clearly had done a lot of living, with a weathered face and a cautiously friendly demeanor. He had been sent questions in advance of the meeting, which would form the substance of our discussion, even if the questions were never precisely repeated. It quickly emerged that Marco's English was very good, and conversation moved into discussing Marco's website and the particularities of his singular Cash story.

Marco's Facebook page gives his birthplace as Freetown in Sierra Leone, but in discussion, it turned out that he had lived his early life in Nigeria because his father worked there. (It never emerged what he was doing there precisely, but the oil business seems likely.) Marco was doubly displaced, therefore; he was a French boy living in an African country that used English, not French, as its official language. Until his late teens, this was what Marco called home. He rarely, if ever, visited Europe, although his father would go to London once a year on business. On these trips, his father would stock up on all sorts of cultural matériel to bring home to the family, but in particular he bought records. From these records, he would teach his son to play guitar, and their favorite artist to play and learn together was Johnny Cash.

Cash came to Marco through the atypical circumstances of his childhood and his father's good taste. It is intriguing to think that if Marco's father went

Marco Rockmilhaud, founder of Fan Club Johnny Cash France.

to Paris, he would probably have brought back records by Johnny Hallyday (the French Elvis) or other Francophone artists, and his son might have lived a more narrowly circumscribed life. Marco spoke about his father with manifest affection, although he was clearly uninterested in speculating about why his father had been drawn to Cash. The why was not what concerned him; rather, it was the what. Yet the how is what gives us pause for this study, thinking about the way a fandom threaded its way between continents but also between a father and his son—a link that was now being reinvented by Marco's online work.

This was not the first time that a fandom story about Cash had also been a story of a father and son. The substance of this story was that loving Cash's music had been a shared passion in a life text that was nevertheless lived out in a zone of estrangement between Europe and Africa, although there is nothing to say that it felt strange for Marco. He is African by birth, and proud of it, but he is a proud son of the south of France too. He particularly enjoyed exploring this multiple identifiability during the 2018 World Cup, during which he faithfully updated scores and results through Facebook, giving particular attention to the achievements of the African teams, claiming he had to do it because the national broadcaster of France was only showing matches involving their own national selection.

In this context, who better to love than Johnny Cash, walking lines and inhabiting outsiderness wherever he went? Such an existential explanation is of course tempting, not least because it seems so much a part of the French philosophical tradition. This is the culture that produced Albert Camus's *The Stranger* (1942), an account of the senseless racial killing of an Arab by an alienated young man, a book that spawned a whole culture of existential querying and posturing. Cash's man in Folsom opens up a comparable space through shooting someone just to watch him die. The killings are not identical, but they are remarkable in their impact on the culture of the 1950s and 1960s, altering a sense of what it was possible to express in literature or song, and inspiring international followers.[1]

If France spawned the cultural cliché of the young man in the black turtleneck, then the United States offered the Man in Black.[2] Both were modeling ways of fashioning your alienation. In Marco's intercontinental youth, America was possibly less culturally dominant than if he were a European who had spent his entire life in Europe. This is not to say that the United States was not an active cultural presence in Africa during the 1960s and 1970s; rather, its influence was much more prevalent in the recently unoccupied country of France.

In 1970s France, he would have been immersed in a pop culture dominated by the United States, much as it was anywhere in Europe but even more so. For all the perceived cultural nationalism of France and the French, this is also the country that gave the world Hollywood chewing gum, and that has the second most profitable McDonald's operation in the world, even as it also has the world's most celebrated protests against the same franchise (Wile 2004). France is notorious for its lionizing of the comedian Jerry Lewis in spite of the widespread indifference to him expressed elsewhere, awarding him the prestigious Légion d'honneur in 2006, not to mention the abiding tolerance that France appears to have for everything that emanates from Sting, who is not American but did provide a song for a magnificent performance by Cash in "I Hung My Head" (Rioux 2007).

Johnny Cash does not have much of a profile in France, and he certainly does not have champions in popular media, unlike in the Netherlands. Nor was he awarded a Légion d'honneur, unlike Bob Dylan. AC/DC has more tribute acts there than Cash. This is precisely what Marco affirmed; Cash had *aucun profil*, no profile, in France, and with the evolution of an apt technology, Marco decided to do something about it. His website, Fan Club Johnny Cash France, established in 2011, with 2,500 members and over 75,000 views, was the result, although it has since moved to another address (https:// fan-club-johnny-cash-france.blog4ever.com/). The original site was packed with playlists and visual stimuli, almost overpowering in its confident but chaotic mission, which was to communicate to French people what they have been missing. The introductory text on the biography page on the site was a remarkably powerful and poetic statement, even in machine translation:

> It was one of those lovely nursery rhymes about everlasting loves, and horizons just as never ending, those stories that are a little sad, but very worthy, of men crushed down in the gutter, and who end up back on their feet, always. To let us in on this, he just leaned on his microphone, a nasty guitar in his arms, and the thrill was born. If Johnny Cash was in the movies, he would be called John Wayne. And if he played jazz piano in the back of a bar, he'd be Clint Eastwood, just the same. If a writer, he would have written *Journey to the End of the Night* or *The Grapes of Wrath*. Don't believe the figures: despite ninety million records sold, a career spanning half a century, and multiple successes, he actually incarnates the reverse of the American dream and chants the Saga of the Humble, of the man with nothing who nevertheless builds a civilization. Come closer: you will be told a beautiful story of love, of violence, of booze, and of people who are not the least, of money, of perdition and redemption. The Story of the Man in Black. (trans. Michael Hinds)

The original authorship of the French text is not clear, as it shows up both on Marco's site and the music blog Le Grenier Du Macumba Night, but either way, it works to lift his mission out of the simple provision of an information service to a form of teaching and acculturation. Yet for all that the site declared a lofty mission, it was also rough and ready, featuring ads for a Chevrolet and a Harley on its drop-down menu among the listings for playlists, gigs, and galleries. The vehicles are no longer advertised on the new site, but what Marco always presents nevertheless is a philosophy of the yard sale, determinedly down to earth. This mirrors his construction of

Cash as an existential hero with real experiential chops. Yet this too can be seen as a form of thorough acculturation, an invitation to think about Cash amid the jostle of other forms of commerce.

The site is a bricolage, a composition where collocated objects compete for attention, and these objects are assembled according to Marco's desires. This feels like a much more theoretical and French reading, yet its explanation lies in something more international and fundamental. Michel Butor expands on the idea of creative bricolage, originally engaging with it jokingly in its sense as the equivalent term in French: for the English, "do it yourself," and for Americans, "home improvement":

> I would say that the notion of bricolage has two levels. First, there is the bricoleur, the one who knows how to make something. Most men are bricoleurs. To tinker about [bricoler], they use the tools which are furnished them by department store chains. This is the vulgar aspect of bricolage. The other level is the invention of material. This is what I would like to call the gathering of significant objects, the recovery of what has been eliminated, thrown out. This is very important for me. It is recycling. (1994, 26)

Marco is the practical bricoleur; his site is an arrangement of capital, and he does not pretend otherwise. He has things he wants to advertise, like his business, Les Bulles d'Or (Golden bubbles), through which beer taps and pumps can be hired; and things he (or a friend) wants to sell, like that Chevrolet. There is no interest in fine polishing or branding; the dominant image as you scroll down the page is the zombified, bird-offering Cash. Yet Marco is also the generator of the creative recycling that Butor describes, the person who will not categorize things as dead or useless.

Intriguingly, Butor consigns the idea of American to the role of a ruthlessly carnivorous modernity. But Marco's work performs a vital role: it hangs onto American materials and American objects that he insists should remain in circulation. He is not selling Citroëns. He also moves across the class divide, between types of bricolage that Butor implies. Marco does the vulgar work of building something, but he does something with more dignity as well. He throws nothing out because he believes that everything is worth keeping.

By 2018, most of Marco's day-to-day activity had moved to Facebook; like Elvira and others, Marco is a restlessly intelligent mover through facets of web technology, and he quickly moves to whatever suits him best. Although the site has moved, he does a lot of his business by other means. What excited him more than anything is discussing the playlists that populate his site, which serve to communicate the diversity of Cash's achievement in apt context. So here is a playlist dedicated to Cash's own music; here is another devoted to country, and another to rockabilly. The site is a kind of laboratory wherein Cash might be discovered and then rediscovered through his relationship to other artists. The tenet that holds the entire mission together is that Cash is essential to everything.

Marco uses the web to do a lot of things, but his overriding aim is simply to get people listening. He does this as a celebration of Cash, of course, but also as a rebuke to the conventional thinking of French media (another theme familiar from the Netherlands). If France knew how to do its job properly with regard to playing Cash, then he would not have to maintain the site. This is the same attitude he takes when communicating the details of World Cup matches on Facebook.

Marco conforms in many ways to the figure of the unconventional French-man, a *citoyen* defined by always being in revolt. Yet at the same time Marco takes great pleasure in being the communicator of things that others forget to say, especially expressions of friendship and courtesy. If you friend Marco on Facebook, every Friday you will be treated to a joyous message of "Bien-venue au Weekend," with a differently phrased message every time. In this, Marco is out-Facebooking Facebook, which currently only reminds you of birthdays and (unnervingly) anniversaries of friendings. Marco performs this rite out of a thorough commitment to civility—perhaps the very thing that people most deplore the loss of within the rise of social media. Ever mercurial, in October 2019, Marco announced that he was retiring from Facebook, although he may have been joking.

In France, *patrimonie* is a key term, and a complex one. It communicates the idea of a masculine inheritance through cultural capital, just as the spirit of the nation is rendered in feminine terms, either as La Belle France or through the figure of Marianne, the goddess of liberty and the embodiment of revolution, seen in paintings and stamps. A *patrimonie* section in a local newspaper signifies the endless work of societies and local associations as well as the protection of the environment. It also signifies cultural inher-itance in a broader sense, as well as the concept of intellectual property. Marco is doing the work of *patrimonie* on many levels. He advocates passing on culture in the interest of preserving civility. His father gave Cash to him; now he was giving Cash to France, because this would substantially enrich France's culture. Marco might look like a punkish outsider, but not in this aspect. He was trying his best to be a good father figure, overcoming the problems of his past. In this way, he (in some measure) resembled Johnny Cash—but in a very French way.

Part of the pleasure of international fandom must be that your native culture is either entirely or relatively ignorant of what you love. As a French person, therefore, you do not go far into Cash fandom because it is something that you already share with the rest of France. There is an erotic quality to being attracted to something from another culture—and even more so from another language. Adorno (1959) describes this as linguistic exogamy; he links it to the pleasure of marrying outside of your own society. Marco liked the idea of Cash being something that only exists outside of France were it not for him, but to a degree this was wishful thinking. There are Cash tribute acts in France, and you can find Cash CDs in French record shops too. Our project survey received an interesting contribution from a French academic, Jonathan Fruoco (2017), one of many non-American academics with an interest in Cash, who comments in response to the question about Cash's postmortem representation: "I wrote a paper on that subject in which I tried to show that Cash somehow orchestrated his own death so that his musical legend would live on. I think our way of representing him since his death very much depends on this orchestration. Cash was a myth-maker." Fruoco also notes, "I know a lot of Cash fans. I love talking about his music with them, but I think my relationship with Johnny Cash is in a way also very personal." He also provides nuanced responses to other questions, but he situates these views in an emotional rather than an intellectual context. At the end of one answer, he even provides a brief Americanism, "It sure does," thereby indulging in a form of linguistic exogamy: "Because one cannot help but love Johnny Cash. He is a mythological figure whose music touches everyone differently, but it sure does touch everyone." Fruoco clearly gets fandom; indeed, another major research interest of his is *Doctor Who* (1963–89, 1996, 2005–).

Marco said he did not perform Cash's music, but without saying why. About an hour later, he provided an explanation for this in terms of the punk-rock philosophy of "do it yourself," rather than duplicating the work of others. Marco volunteered that he had been a bassist in a number of punk bands between the late 1970s and mid-1980s, most notably with the band Oberkampf (named after the Paris metro station), a band he described as the French Sex Pistols. Marco had even seen the original Pistols perform in London in 1977—another heroic achievement. In the video for Oberkampf's version of "La Marseillaise," the band is shown performing outside the street entrance to the station, when suddenly the bassist is attacked by a dog. Marco said he was the victim in question.

The idea of performance for Marco relates to the ideas of bricolage. Oberkampf takes the national anthem and flays it, but by doing so, the band remakes it. Marco draws a line between that kind of radical appropriation and what he sees Cash tribute acts as doing. These acts are repeating; they are not doing their own thing. Marco has no interest in playing bass in a Cash band (although he does help promote the work of a funk rock band called Folsom). Marco said he knew a good deal of tribute performers, but mostly AC/DC tributes on the French circuit; the only one of these he liked was the all-female version, the Ballbreakers. The most prominent online Cash tribute from France (or more precisely Marseilles) that Marco would admit to knowing was J. R. Black. In terms of the discussion of *patrimonie*, Black does something remarkable in his well-produced video of "Folsom Prison Blues," which is tellingly subtitled "Le Prison de Folsom," posted by TheMojoRanch on YouTube on March 23, 2012. The video begins with a cute little girl asking her mother, "Maman, quand est-ce que Papa va rentrer a la maison?" (Mommy, when is Daddy coming home?), to which a disembodied voice responds, "Jamais" (Never). The French Johnny Cash does something very French (although "very French" is an overused phrase). He does not even attempt to sound like Cash but instead translates his songs into French while adopting a determinedly cool look. He has great Cash hair, and the band is tight.

Yet in a sense this is a literary transcription. The whole exercise feels like an alienation effect from an experimental drama. Takahiro Saito sounded more like Cash when he sang in Japanese, but J. R. Black never sounds like him. This is Johnny Cash in a Francophone-only world in which nobody has ever heard Cash's original voice. Black does not care if anyone hears him; it is not his job. Marco was not really judgmental about such things. He was just disinterested. He waved them away as the kind of things that people do. Yet Black's video surely would have appeared empty to Marco because it is devoid of the thing—Cash's voice—that hooked him in the first place, and that has kept him going ever since. Contrary to the evocative Facebook remarks about Freetown, Marco said that he was born in Lagos, and that was where he and the voice first met. He was unsure about the first song he heard, but he knew that "Cocaine Blues" was the first Cash song that he learned to play.

Marco did not seem to care much about ostentatious displays of specialist knowledge. He did not discriminate between the various stages and manifestations of Cash's career. He simply said that there was always something compelling or interesting about Cash. He expressed surprise at the qualified responses to Mangold's *Walk the Line* that other fans like Barry and Elvira have expressed, saying simply, "It's fine; it's a good movie." He saw Cash live in Germany in 1992, and he said that it was great; he did not elaborate. Marco was a hard man to bother, although he was dismissive of some parts of Cash lore reported to him. He clearly liked to play the role of an outlier in Cashworld. He was not integrated with Elvira's network and was only vaguely aware of Barry's activities.

Yet he is also an organizer, like these others. Until 2012, Marco had spent over a decade coordinating the Sud Country-Rock festival in nearby Junas and had ambitions to put on a Cash festival there. When it was reported to him that an event of that kind was happening in Austria in 2018, it was easy enough to infer that he was not overly pleased. Marco was happy to lead the discourse on Johnny Cash in France, but he was happy to leave Cash fans elsewhere to themselves. In a sense, even as he was somewhat deracinated, he was not bothered much about travel or about *les autres*. Marco was incredulous when Charlie Taggart's daily observances were described to him, saying that he was happy enough to go for weeks without listening to Cash. He knew where he would be if he needed him.

This was the fundamental point about Cash for Marco. Cash was a homeplace for him, but it was a relaxed home. His life had been absolutely remarkable anyway, with his stint in Oberkampf and subsequent touring with Johnny Thunders in Sweden, once the Heartbreakers had relocated there in the early 1980s. Marco recalled the day he gave that particular gig up with mordant comedy: "He wanted me to go to Japan, but I knew I had to say no. I had the feeling that if I went there, I would not be coming back." The same logic saw Marco leave Paris and band life behind entirely, and by the late 1980s he had relocated to the south, close to his family's original roots in Marseilles.

An escapee from the rigors of the capital, Marco began working regular jobs. He embarked on a quiet life, working in Montpellier in the record-store section of FNAC, the French media retail chain, only to suffer a massive heart attack one day as he emerged from the shop. In his telling, the characteristically intense heat of the city in midsummer hit him as he emerged from the chill of the store's air-conditioning, and the shock to his system was too much. Next thing he knew, he was on a helicopter back to Paris to have a heart transplant, which saved his life. (He had never been told whose heart he received, but he had surmised it was that of a young girl, owing to its relatively small size.) Needless to say, this was dizzying stuff to hear. It helped put his entire demeanor in context. Marco had a posttraumatic serenity to him, the consciousness of someone who really has been saved. This also felt like the life text of a fan who was converging with Cash.

Marco preferred that there are not many Cash fans in France, not least because it provides the occasion for his own work: "I prefer to be the one who introduces them to Johnny Cash." It might be more accurate to say that there are not many Johnny Cash fans in France like Marco.

Thinking again of Charlie's Taggart's fandom, it seems like a solitary activity; then you realize just how plugged in that man is to his local community. Although Marco ran a website that had enough of a sense of mission to create a wide audience, he was resolutely and contentedly his own man. The emphasis of his site is on sound experience, and it therefore stresses being alive in the presence of the music. Funnily enough, this makes him just like Charlie. The cassette player in the shop and the tinny sound of the website through a laptop sound remarkably similar.

In a final exchange, after nearly three hours of talk, the subject of Cash's politics (and the politics of his fans) came up. Marco was curiously adamant. Not only Cash but his fans were "toujours à la gauche, à la gauche, à la gauche" (always to the left, to the left, to the left). Of course, within any discussion, conceptions of what left and right or liberal and conservative might not tally, but it was put it to Marco that you could be a libertarian, even a racist, and still like Johnny Cash. Marco did not loudly agree or disagree but just shook his head. It was not a thought worth having, even if indeed it might be possible. Marco was not a typical anything, whether Hell's Angel or punk. Marco made you think in more quizzical ways about such categorizations. He was not wrong in identifying the rebellious streak in so much of Cash fandom, and that mapped onto the veneration of revolt in French culture. It was not surprising to see in autumn 2018 how energized Marco had become with the rise of the antiestablishment protest movement, *les gilet jaunes* (yellow vests), and his Facebook activity became dually focused on Cash and contemporary politics.

The same held true elsewhere. In Ireland, a group called the Johnny Cash Appreciation Society met in Dublin in the late 1990s at the Hut bar in Phibsboro, a working-class section of the north side of the city. This was not a fan club in a conventional sense but an improvised community of punk and indie musicians who would convene to play renditions of Cash and other country musicians who spoke to alternative sensibilities. Contrarily, they would also perform countrified versions of songs from the alt-punk canon. This kind of crossover is practically standard in the twenty-first century, but in its time and place, this was radical work (Duggan 2006).

As part of a music scene, these people were already part of a network, albeit one made up of loose affiliations. Many of the members of the JCAS were also involved in leftist politics or union organization, and continue to be; adopting Cash turned that network into a more socially active and collectively creative community. Cash is thus a unifying presence in that one way or another, people were happy to acknowledge their regard for him, but he also acts as an organizing presence—somebody around whom people are ready to coalesce.

Yet if Cash enables people to rally, it is not necessarily preordained that it will be around a specific ideology; his gestures of resistance might be interpreted as just gestures, his oppositional integrity vulnerable to co-option by anyone who wants some of that precious quality. Exactly a week after the interview with Marco, the Charlottesville controversy erupted. He did not respond to an email asking what he made of the story. By any conventional measure of a fan, the man in question would qualify—the kind of fan who buys T-shirts and music, yet he was far from the left. Marco could not imagine such a fan existing, and yet the uncomfortable truth was that they did.

10 THE PERFORMER

A Fan Plays Cash Country, October 2017

Since Barry Winters met with us in Groningen, he updated us regularly about his activities, which frequently included engaging with other Cash fans. He was particularly enthusiastic about trips he made to the US air base in Landsberg where Cash was stationed; these led to a friendship with Walter Ringhofer from Austria, who had created a Cash museum at his house in the country town of Riedlingsdorf, not far from the Hungarian border.

In October 2017, Barry traveled to Tennessee and Virginia to visit Cash-related sites in the company of Walter and his wife, Brigitte. They could read and understand English but were not confident speakers, so they invited along Franz, a friend who acted as translator. This seemed like traditional music tourism. As Chris Gibson and John Connell note, "Music tourism constitutes a cluster of possible tourists, activities, locations, attractions, workers and events which utilize musical resources for tourist purposes" (2005, 16).[1] The activities the group had lined up—including visits to Cash's childhood home in Arkansas, Sun Studio, Graceland, and the Johnny Cash Museum—were certainly touristic. Yet both Walter and Barry had additional agendas beyond tourism. Barry hoped to perform at the Storytellers Museum near Nashville, perhaps with Johnny Cash's brother, Tommy Cash, as well as at the Carter Family Fold in Hiltons, Virginia, the Carter family homeplace and site to Johnny Cash's last performance. Walter wanted to promote his Johnny Cash festival at his museum the following year. He was also intent on photographing as much as possible of what was his first experience of the United States and his first trip beyond Europe. They demonstrated the ways superfans can bend tourist experiences beyond traditional tourism.

The trip began by following a familiar itinerary of Cash places: flying into Nashville, then moving to Memphis and Dyess, Cash's birthplace. Silverman, whom Barry had invited along, would join them once they returned to Nashville (Gibson and Connell 2005, 57). In Dyess, they had gone to the Johnny Cash Heritage Festival celebrating Cash, seen his childhood home, and, as Barry said, "We picked cotton. There is no cotton in Europe." Cotton is strange and exotic to European eyes, in contrast to how it appears to those who have had to farm it in America. For Barry, it was only another means of connecting to Johnny Cash's feeling of being in the world. While the group enjoyed this initial part of the trip, Barry was alive to the economic realities of music fandom—and how Nashville wrings profit from tourists. It cost $50 to go to Ryman Auditorium, the original site of the Grand Ole Opry, now located as an appendage to a mall: "Welcome to America." But as Barry noted, "You pay for everything, but you get value for your money." Barry pointed out the commercial nature of the Johnny Cash Museum relative to the purity of Walter's museum as a fan mission: "It's not commercial. It's a shrine. He's not in it for the money," he said.

After Silverman joined them, the trip began to feel like as much a quest as a tourist trip. Barry had sent materials to the operators of the Storytellers Museum, and they confirmed that when he was in the United States, he would be able to play there—an experience money could not buy (unlike the fan tourism experience), and a privilege that he could only get through acceptance by the members of the Cash family who were also performing there: Mark Alan Cash and Tommy Cash, Johnny's nephew and brother, respectively.

The Storytellers Museum is located just outside of Nashville in Bon Aqua. The plan for the day there was as follows. Mark Alan Cash would play in the morning; the group would next visit Bon Aqua, Johnny Cash's old farm; and then they would return to Storytellers and Barry would get to play—with Tommy Cash, they hoped. The Storytellers was as much a performance space as a museum, with a room featuring a stage and memorabilia, a gift shop in the outer room, and a manicured space outside. The posted hours suggested that the museum would be closed in the afternoon, but the museum seemed to be staying open to accommodate both Barry and tourists who had showed up at the museum that day. If it was an extraordinary privilege for Barry, his presence also represented an opportunity for the museum owners, the Oxley family, as they sought to establish themselves as part of the international Cash market. According to one report, Brian Oxley and his wife paid $895,000 for the farm and purchased a general store, which they converted into this theater (Thanki 2016). Brian's brother, Chris, said he hoped to install the museum and farm as part of the Cash narrative on the music trail from Memphis to Nashville.

In the morning, people gathered for the concert by Mark Alan Cash, who said of his uncle, "He was a humble guy; he hated attention. He didn't like to be put up on a pedestal." Although Johnny Cash's job was literally to put himself on a pedestal in front of as large an audience as possible, his nephew was operating within the vital country music trope of supposing stars to be humble in the face of adoration, as well as according with a fan demand that Cash be practically perfect.

After the set, Rachel Dawson, a worker at the museum and singer in her own right, was outside, writing a sign for Tommy Cash and Barry; unfortunately, it read "Barry White" and not "Barry Winters." At the same time, aside from acting as a kind of official photographer and distributing flyers for the European Festival, Walter presented a signed copy of his book about a forgotten guitar of Johnny Cash's to Mark Alan Cash. It was hard to know whether someone would travel so far to see Johnny Cash material when there was so much to see in Nashville, yet Cash fans did come from all around the world. Europeans would trek to Walter's museum if they had trekked to Tennessee. In a fandom trade-off, he was doing almost exactly what the Storytellers was doing: seeking a promotional opportunity for his version of the Cash experience.

Tommy would perform in the afternoon, so everyone headed to the farm a few miles away to take a tour under Rachel's direction. There was an empty barn—another performance space. There was a "car barn" that housed Johnny Cash's automobiles, including a Cadillac and a Mercedes, as well as a "One Piece at a Time" car, made according to the precise prescription of that song, which played on a loop while they were there.

In the house, individual furniture pieces were labeled, and Barry sat in one of Cash's chairs. Brian Oxley claimed that the bookshelves were stocked uniquely with Cash's library. Although he implied that the books indicated

Barry Winters sits waiting for his concert at Storytellers in Bon Aqua, Tennessee.

Winters meets Tommy Cash, one of Johnny Cash's siblings, before performing.

Cash's influences or preferences, he later admitted that some of his own books had infiltrated Cash's. In another little building, some of Cash's photographs were displayed. There was not much to the house in terms of traditional tourist expectations, as it was without the type of professionalizing that usually accompanies such sites. So the site had to stress insistently that is was actually a Johnny Cash place—somewhere he had lived. Photos helped with this, capturing the fact that Cash had been in this same spot. Beyond that, the site would only gather meaning as a tourist site as more tourists visited it, giving it credibility. If the house just felt like a house, that might be what a fan looking to evade the framings of tourism would enjoy, as it absolutely proved Cash's realness.

When the group arrived back at Storytellers, Tommy Cash was there, and he and Barry talked, confirming that they would play together. Asked about his status internationally, Tommy said his strongest fans were in "Ireland, Scandinavia, West Germany, Germany." When asked why, he said, "Just the special memories." He recounted that he was told, "You will not draw in Holland" (poor advice), although he noted that Germany was "still mad at me" for trying to reduce a three-week tour to two. He said his brother had fans all over the world. "I know he knew he loved people all over the world," Tommy Cash said. "He died too young." He conferred with Barry on the set list. When Barry asked if he could sing "I Still Miss Someone," Tommy Cash said, "I've sung it a thousand times; it's your turn."

Approximately thirty people were in the audience at showtime. Mark Alan Cash made the introductions: "I met this gentleman today, and what a fine, fine gentleman he is," he said. "There are some people with him, who are some great people, from Austria. I've been to their country, year before last for a country music festival over there. Put your hands together for Mr. Barry Winters."

Wearing black, Barry took a borrowed guitar to the stage.

"It's good to be here. It's such a privilege to be here. I come from Ireland," he said.

Bassist David Langley said, "It's a long walk."

Barry responded, "It will be an even longer walk back."

The exchange displayed Barry's comfort and preparedness. Many fans would not be able even to contemplate what he was getting to do here, but he was thoroughly at home, maybe more so than ever.

Barry got down to business. "I think we're all here for the same reason. I'd like to play 'I Still Miss Someone,'" he said. There was clapping in the middle of the verse as Barry played. The set was clearly well practiced, citing the origin narrative he had described in Groningen: "The very first record, the very first Johnny Cash record I ever bought with some pocket money when I was seven years old, I bought a record called 'The Man in Black,'" and "We all know that Johnny Cash spoke up for those who couldn't speak up for themselves and that was all about that song. I still have that record."

In introducing the songs and explaining his motivations for choosing them, Barry ensured that his performance was understood as an expression of fandom. But it also enhanced his difference; he was an Irishman in Tennessee covering Johnny Cash and highlighting Cash's connection to Barry's country of origin. He showed himself to be a connoisseur, picking rarities from Cash's songbook: "There are so many great songs, songs that people haven't heard. One such song is on the back of that single. It's called 'A Little Bit of Yesterday.' And I think it's a song that's even more relevant than when he sang it back then."

At the end of the song, Tommy Cash, sitting stage front, asked Barry, "Did John write that song?"

"He sure did," Barry said.

"I never heard it before," Tommy said.

"It's a beautiful song," Barry said.

Later, Barry talked about why he played "A Little Bit of Yesterday" in particular. "There are a few songs that haven't come to the fore, and I think they are excellent, and that's one of them," Barry said. "Well, I had it on the back of my record. Other people who didn't have the record wouldn't know about it. Tommy had never heard of it." All of this amounted to a substantial sense of vindication: "Records and knowledge. A fan would collect both. Became a fan then, or became a tribute then, people have done that. They have seen the movie, never known Johnny Cash, saw the movie, and, 'Yep, I can do that.'"

Barry said later that he had sent recordings of his work to Storytellers beforehand, and so his capacity for strategizing came more clearly into focus: "I sold myself as much as I could. I didn't sell myself short. I didn't sell myself low. I had one crack at it." Barry was exhilarated: "A stranger! I could have come in drunk. I could have come in rags. Or jeans. They didn't know I was going to wear my stage gear, bring it across to America. It is risky, yes. I could have given the place a bad name." He also acknowledged implicitly how the museum might have had business-oriented motives for inviting him to play: "I suppose Chris [Oxley] would have had a big say in it." Barry assumed his persona: "'We have this guy who has been pestering me, but he's got [a] good website. He's played in different places.' He's not chancing his arm." Back onstage, Barry said publicly what he had said in conversation in Groningen: "People often ask me at a show, why don't you come out and say, like some tribute artists, 'Hello, I'm Johnny Cash'? For me, there will be only one Johnny Cash."

Barry was not trying to be Johnny Cash; nor was he exactly imitating him. What he was doing was taking Cash's work and performing it so as to remind the audience of Johnny Cash, but through the lens of his own extraordinary fandom. Barry had a rare moment of comic metacommentary attached to his performance of "Five Feet High and Rising," summoning the onstage game playing of Cash that he had cited admiringly before. "I didn't actually mean to sing that song. The chords are the same. Am I going to get through with it?" Then he played "Don't Take Your Guns to Town," the song he meant to sing.

In natural showman mode, Barry played up his Irish connection: "There is a song I like to sing; it's a little bit of home I can take along with me . . . a song Johnny Cash wrote when flying into Ireland and saw how green the fields and forests were. Some of the people were pretty green as well. And June was being interviewed by a famous TV host as well in Ireland many years ago, and he wasn't too sure about what Johnny had written." He recounted the dialogue:

"What songs did he write?"
"Well, you know he wrote 'Forty Shades of Green.'"
"Aw, he didn't write that. I was singing that thirty years ago."
And she said, "that's when he wrote it."

That Cash wrote a song that was more Irish than the Irish is a familiar joke in Ireland, but it would not have been so familiar to an American audience. His anecdote served to show something of the special relationship Cash had with the Irish—which again made Barry seem special. Every transition was practiced, propelling the concert through thematic phases: "He sang prison songs; of course, he sang other songs as well."

"I often get asked: 'What is my favorite Johnny Cash song?' Barry said. "There is no answer there. I suppose whatever song I'm singing . . . they're all my favorite." He continued:

A song that meant a lot to me, though, was a hit in Ireland, got to the top of the charts in Ireland in '72; it was called "A Thing Called Love." It means a lot to me because we had the Beatles, who were still relevant.

The Rolling Stones, Glam Rock had begun, the Eagles were there of course, and people would say to me, what kind of music do you listen to? "I listen to Johnny Cash." And they would look at me and say, "But that's country music." I'd say, "Yep."

Then "A Thing Called Love" hit the charts, and everybody was singing it. And I met an old school pal and I hadn't seen him for thirty years and he said to me, "Do you still listen to Johnny Cash?"

"Yep."

"You know something, you've been right all along."

This was not only a celebration of Johnny Cash but also of Cash fandom itself, demonstrating that a life dedicated to Cash is not wasted. At one point in the set, Tommy Cash exclaimed, "I never want to follow him again. That's how good he is."

After playing a Kris Kristofferson song, Tommy Cash came to the stage. He said, "Since my brother passed away, there have been a lot of people singing Johnny Cash songs, doing impersonations, dressing like him, looking like him. This man is original; he's great. What are we singing?" Tommy Cash turned to the band.

"I would love to sing 'Silver Haired Daddy of Mine,'" Barry said. He had a reason for this particular choice: it was what Tommy sang with Johnny in the concert recorded in 1969, *Johnny Cash at Madison Square Garden* (Legacy Records/Columbia, 2002). This was a revealingly intimate and appropriate choice, one that again allowed Barry to fill the space left vacant by Johnny, this time as Tommy's brother. To affirm this, Barry asked if they could sing another from that set: "Do What You Do Do Well," a song not even listed by name on the album, appearing only in a medley performed at the end.

Tommy again complimented Barry: "You sound really good. We all agree you need to come back."

Barry responded politely. "I enjoyed it. Thanks for having me."

The next day, Barry said he was overwhelmed by the experience: "Yesterday was a very emotional day for me. Chris set it up because I had been exchanging messages with him. He said, 'Yeah we'll give you a guitar,' that he would do that for me, and that Tommy would do that for me." Tommy had even less incentive to let him play than Chris Oxley. "He doesn't even have to talk to me," Barry said. "But he shook my hand a number of times, tapping my shoulder."

But in addition to the ecstasy of the performance itself, Barry also stressed that he knew how lucky he had been: "I sang with Tommy the two songs I wanted plus whatever songs I sang. But I would have been happy if we had gotten out of the car, and I stood on the stage and sung to an empty hall one song. It was like winning the lotto."

Barry had understandably strong feelings about the farm and Storytellers, where nobody had asked anyone for money, unlike the Johnny Cash Museum.

In fact, when Silverman bought a T-shirt, Rachel voluntarily handed over an extra. Barry articulated the emotional economy of fandom directly to the economics of music tourism:

> The feeling yesterday, I had no emotion going into the museum because we were going back for "Cash for Cash." You pay for the trinkets inside. It's money. Going into the museum yesterday, I thought about the museum in Nashville, the commercial venture—Bon Aqua. Whether it's commercial, it's not lining someone's pocket. It's going to build up the place. That's a huge thing to me. It's like coming home. I felt comfortable in there, and the same feeling I got the first time I went to Walter's museum, back four or five years ago.

In Ireland, Barry had encountered mainly economic obstacles in the way of his fandom activity; now he had reached out to international Cash fandom and found that he could find an audience without worrying about people having the price of a ticket or a trip to the pub. This experience was more than he could have dreamed, but exactly what he had planned. He was in the extraordinary situation of having brought a fantasy into reality.

After Barry, Tommy Cash sang a few songs of his own. One was a song about modern technology, "The Way That We're Livin' Scares the Hell Out of Me," which proclaimed, "Internets and cell phones take the places of family." Yet these technologies had led Barry to Elvira and Walter, and had enabled him to persuade the Storytellers in advance that he was a competent performer. His fantasy was aided by twenty-first-century means.

The next day, they drove to Gate City, fairly close to Hiltons, Virginia, where the Carter Family Fold was. They took pictures of the fold (it would be dark for the concert the next day). Next they went to the Mt. Vernon United Methodist Church cemetery, which contained the Carter family plot. It included graves for A.P. and Sara Carter, musicians first in line of the Carter family, and June Carter Cash's aunt and uncle. June's cousin Joe Carter was also buried here, with his recently erected gravestone in the shape of a guitar. While Barry, Brigitte, and Walter took photos, Franz declared he was more of an Elvis fan, although he had been working hard distributing books and invitations on Walter's behalf and was willing to do Walter's talking for him. Franz was incredulous about all the photos Walter had taken—at that point more than seven thousand. (He was also a little dismissive about the health choices of Walter and Brigitte, who was an inveterate smoker.) His presence also added to a sense of the trip's theatricality: Barry was center stage, Walter and Brigitte were busy documenting and snapping just out of sight but saying little, and Franz was a slightly detached observer—not emotionally part of the Cash fervor but necessary to its functioning.

After the cemetery, they all moved on to Bristol for the Birthplace of Country Music museum, which commemorated the recording of folk and country artists by Ralph Peer of the Victor Talking Machine Company in 1927. The main reason for the group to visit centered on the recordings made there by A.P., Sara, and Maybelle Carter (the latter married to A.P.'s brother, Ezra), the mother of June Carter (Cash) and founder of the Carter Sisters.

They all went into a little theater where John Carter Cash narrated the history of the Bristol Sessions in a well-produced short film that referenced issues of race and gender, exemplifying modern museum presentation. The museum also featured fascinating interactivity: songs featured on the Bristol Sessions could be recorded or remixed. There was a show that explained the musicianship behind the recordings, and an aptly near 360-degree exhibit about the famous Carter Family song, "Will the Circle Be Unbroken?," which Cash and Carter routinely performed.

All of this was only tourism, however sophisticated; the question of whether Barry again would get to perform loomed larger. Entering the performance space at the Fold, they were asked where they were from. Barry was hoping to get on stage, but was trying to measure his expectations: "It's not as big a deal! Because I'm not expected." He may have said that, but it felt as if not playing would be a real disappointment.

The band on stage, the Jeff Little Trio, played traditional music with remarkable musicianship and some gently predictable humor. People were dancing with tap shoes, sometimes in couples, sometimes by themselves, one with a dog.

At the intermission, Barry went down to the stage and talked with Rita Forrester, the Carter family member who ran the Fold. She invited him to play. So he soon took the stage, again in his black performing clothes. Just as in the previous gig, he had thought of introductory words precisely designed for the occasion and had selected songs with special significance for both Cash and the Carters. This intimate knowledge folded him into the Fold:

This is a privilege being here today. I come from Ireland, and I want to sing a song that Johnny Cash sang, maybe sitting here in this chair in his last concert here. He explained that June . . . wanted this song sung at her funeral. Johnny arranged that; it must have been heartbreaking for him to sing it again on his last visit here. This is a tribute to June's memory.

He then played "Angel Band," an old folk song that Cash had played in July 2003 at the Carter Family Fold, and that Emmylou Harris had played at June's funeral a few months before. Barry sampled different parts of Cash's repertoire here than he had at Storytellers—another indication of how much care he had put into thinking about what he would like to perform at a particular site, if given the chance. There was nothing routine about his act. He clearly had wagered more heavily than he admitted that the Fold would let him perform.

A little teary, Rita Forrester talked about Johnny Cash: "He was very good to us. He didn't know what he was getting into." She added, "We miss him. . . . He carried the music of the Carter Family all around the world. We thank Barry, we appreciate it."

When Barry came back to his seat, he was clearly aglow.

After the rest of the performance, Rita arranged for someone else to show Barry and the group the museum and cabin. As in Bristol, there was a polished exhibition about the Carter Family and their history in the area. The cabin offered yet another chance to get close to Cash: the caretaker allowed Barry to sit in Cash's chair. He gave it two tries, once with his jacket on and the second wearing just his stage gear, again appearing doubly as fan tourist and fan performer—and seeing how far he could go in the second guise. Meanwhile, Walter continued taking photos, having already given his Cash festival materials to Rita.

A reminder that Barry had a life outside of his fandom came when they all arrived back at the place they were staying and the local police arrived. Barry liked to trade patches with local police on his travels and had brought some from his home station. The owner of the guesthouse knew local policemen in town and arranged a meeting. They exchanged pleasantries, then moved into conversation comparing conditions and procedures transatlantically. Barry was doing what many Irish policemen do when they travel to the United States, but he never made reference to his day job when performing and had been mostly reticent about it in Groningen. Even so, he was not embarrassed about it. Indeed, arguably it made sense for an enforcer of the law to be fascinated with Cash, who styled himself as living on the law's margins. In his own role as mediator, Walter took a picture of himself with the police. He posted it to Facebook, intimating that he had been joyfully arrested.

Months afterward, Barry ventured that the trip to Cash's America represented "closure." That certainly did not mean the end of his interest in Cash, but it did mean that he had been able to get physically closer to Cash's presence than ever before. "I've always wanted to see where he grew up," Barry said, "to stand where he stood, to walk on the grass where he walked."

11 THE COLLECTOR

Photographing and Displaying Fandom Home and Abroad, June 2018

Franz had said that Walter wanted to share his photos with us—a generous but daunting offer. Walter had been mostly silent throughout the trip, so his offer gave us a chance at least to see how he literally viewed his travels. The flash drives arrived in the post in late spring 2018. Sharing photos also showed us one way that digitalization had changed fandom: because his only limit was the generous storage offered by a digital SD card, Walter produced a relentless image stream rather than a select group of precious snapshots. His work was within the context of tourist photography nonetheless. Mike Robinson and David Picard note that tourist photography "is littered with performances involving those taking the photographs, those 'in' the photographs, those outside of the frame and all those who will later work with the photograph itself as a catalyst for storytelling. . . . The taking of photographs involves a framing of the world; a procedure of focus, both literally and metaphorically" (2009, 13).

That focus was collecting; he had an actual museum to give some context for the amount of photos. Museum curators have to sort through many objects as they put together their exhibits, making choice after choice. But first you need the materials, and Walter had been collecting Johnny Cash

Walter Ringhofer takes a photo of the grave of Carter family member Joe Carter in the Mt. Vernon cemetery in Hiltons, Virginia.

materials for decades. Now, with this trip to the United States, he would be collecting experiences. As Susan Sontag writes, "To collect photographs is to collect the world" (1977, 3). Walter's photos represented the footage of a once-in-a-lifetime trip, its abundance indicating uncertainty about what is significant, or maybe indicating a sense that everything experienced is significant or must be significant. Walter later termed the experience of creating his images as "indescribable": "The America trip was a dream. It was the first time Brigitte and me ever flew. We had Barry Finbarr Winters with us at the same time. He organized the whole program for America. It is indescribable, and I still dream of it. Barry Finbarr Winters showed us places where you would never go as a tourist, so every day was great" (Facebook message to M.H., October 11, 2018, translated from German).

Overall, the photos show one more aspect of how technology has changed fandom forever, with cheap storage meaning no image needs to be discarded. But Walter has the opposite problem as well. As a collector of Cash artifacts, he has only a limited space to display them. There is also the viewer: Walter must curate the photos to have any chance of an audience being interested in them—a process he is still undertaking through his Facebook site. Taken as a whole, Walter's life as a collector and tourist illustrate the paradox of digital abundance: it is easy to collect materials but harder to see them all.

In pursuit of documenting this dream, Walter took close to eight thousand photos and videos on the trip to Arkansas, Tennessee, and Virginia—and Brigitte took two thousand. Was eight thousand photos a lot when they might never return? When Silverman carried cameras and equipment for a *Sports Illustrated* photographer in 1986, she took eight hundred photos for a three-hour football game on old-school film reels. Now in the digital era, photos are cheap.

As a photo journal of a first trip to America, the first rush of images suggests the excitement of a first trip to the United States for a European, for whom all experiences seem both exotic and essential. It begins with getting on the airplane, with pictures of Franz and Brigitte, who is the unwitting star of many of the photos. There are photos of the plane wing and the flight. There are photos of general subjects at the Nashville airport, where a few Johnny Cash references emerge, including ads for the Johnny Cash Museum. Barry appears as another Cash subject. More shots of the airport follow, then the rental car, including its license plate. Then shots of the hotel, followed by shots of the pool, the skyline, the bridge to downtown, and the beers at dinner. But mode-of-transport photos (those set in a plane or car) are just one category of these photos. There are hotel photos; photos of eating; photos of exhibits; photos of performances; photos of people experiencing these exhibits and performances; photos of the landscape; and photos of the people in the landscape; some photos combine genres transcategorically.

Even though there are many photos of almost all aspects of the trip, Walter's emphasis and even pace changes as the roll progresses. Once Walter goes to the Johnny Cash Museum in Nashville, the capturing becomes singularly intense and pervasive. Walter captures every space of the museum—individual display cases, gold records, costumes, the chronology of Cash's life—everything except trying to capture the actual videos (which he does in the video section). One might think Walter was taking careful notes for his own museum, thinking how the American and domestic versions might translate. He was noticeably less energized and prolific in photographing Graceland, back in the role of not fan but tourist.[1]

Walter's camera really comes alive in Hendersonville, where Cash lived for thirty years. We see the remains of Cash's house on Old Hickory Lake (it burned down a few years ago), photos of the grounds, and photos of Barry, Walter, and Brigitte. There are a few shots of another house on the street; then it is on to the funeral home and cemetery. Here there are many shots of the group in various permutations around the graves of Johnny and June, as well as their parents, who are buried nearby. Finally the images show a restaurant, the Opry Mills shopping center, and the Grand Ole Opry. Some of these photos suggest an engagement with American culture; there are multiple photos of a jeep in the middle of a mall and photos of a military truck that serves as an advertisement for a barbecue place.

In a sense, the photos are an unprocessed tourism archive of a man and woman who traveled through the American mid-South in 2017 to experience its country music culture and heritage, with a focus on Cash. The reading of the photo stream is also necessarily framed by varieties of prior knowledge: the man and woman are from eastern Austria, and they understand but do not speak English. They are middle aged, and they were able to afford this trip. The trip was designed by Barry, but they trust that he knows what he is doing. They have a museum to promote; he has a stage to occupy. Finally, one of us (Silverman) was present on the trip. It is quickly apparent that this is something more complicated than tourism; this was material heading in different directions all at once.

These are not art images; nobody was channeling Ansel Adams here. Walter and the camera seem indistinguishable from one another in such moments; it is hard to imagine that he ever put it down, such was his appetite for capture. Now seen only via the lens, Barry appears from time to time in a playful persona, not consumed by the desire to be on stage but relaxing into the joyful rigors of road tripping. A shot in the Cash museum features Barry staring out through the bars of a prison door, with him assuming the glowering stare of an inmate. Compared to that actorliness, Walter grins in a rare photo of himself with a certain embarrassed eagerness. He looks like he would much rather be taking photographs.

A few days into the trip, starkly different photos appear, suggesting that the initial tourist glamour may have worn off, and that Walter's eye is admitting another aspect of American reality: there is a shot of people sleeping under a bridge, then those people with a policeman, then one staring at the camera. The photos show Walter to be the kind of tourist open to nonmediated experiences, but they also reiterate his desire to think that he is doing more than tourism, exactly what he credited Barry with showing him.

When Silverman joins the group, he starts to appear in photos, so in reviewing, he is a type of double witness. In Walter's pictures, Silverman is usually toward the margins of a shot. Walter saw him as a part of the group but also its observer—an ironic reversal of how Walter had appeared when Silverman was looking at Barry performing. Walter did not actually take many photos of his fellow fans; his pictures mainly communicate his love of things, which confirms that he is above all a collector.

Language is also an integral part of this experience, though it is almost invisible in the photos (not so much the videos, of course). In Walter's appearances on Austrian TV to publicize the festival, he speaks German animatedly but especially with reference to his collection and the various stories it generates. He speaks at the end of tribute shows to comprehensively thank all involved. On the American trip, however, Walter is silenced; these pictures rarely show anyone in conversation, only adding to the sense of distance from their experiences. To Silverman, on the trip, he was a genial participant at the mercy of a translator. But that was only Walter as a tourist in the United States, not Walter as a collector. Still, Walter's silence fits in with his collecting, as his objects do the talking for him. His images and objects amount to a kind of speech, and an international language.

The photo stream often emphasizes different stories and subjects than what Silverman witnessed. At the Storytellers Museum, Barry appears, but his anxious wait to see if he might perform is not apparent. The venue's Cashanalia takes prominence instead: quirky artwork, a piano, records, clothing, Cash's old cars, a display of photographs Cash took, and every stick of furniture in the house itself—things that did not seem relevant when Storytellers was being viewed through Barry's lens of performance.

One way or another, such a weight of material also begins to allow for the dimensions of his consciousness and drive to emerge. In a startling self-portrait, Walter stands contemplating himself in the mirror of a public bathroom, camera held in front of him. This is overt self-projection—but so is all of the photo trove, just in subtler forms.

One curious effect of looking at the members of Barry and Walter's pilgrim group is that when they are photographed among other people, whether on the street or at a museum or another venue, they look just like everyone else: day trippers or shoppers wandering from place to place. Yet when they are in a Cash venue and presenting a copy of Walter's CD or book—that is, when they are most clearly recognizing themselves on a particular fan mission—they are illuminated and energized.

The USB key also had thousands of photos and videos taken by Brigitte's camera. In her folder, it is not always clear who held the camera. At Sun Studio, she appears in a series of pictures taken by someone else. Yet Walter had also surrendered his camera at times, thus featuring in the odd shot. If anything, however, Brigitte took even fewer pictures of people yet more pictures of artifacts than her husband. All of this was a reminder that the work of Cash collecting was done by both Walter and Brigitte. He later confirmed that the museum was a thoroughly family enterprise: "Yes, Brigitte is just like me, a real Johnny Cash fan. . . . Brigitte helps and organizes a lot in the museum and my son is also fully involved in organizing the festivals."

Some photos in the stream appeared to need additional context, reminding us how an everyday scene from American life might look strange and intriguing to a European Cash fan. For example, there is a photo of a field with blooming cotton plants, where Walter had picked up a boll that he ended up showing off on Austrian TV. Barry had also talked about the power of encountering cotton for a European, and with Walter it became enshrined, a relic of material life in the rural South that also connected the fans to Cash's formative experiences there.

Both Walter and Brigitte's photo streams have a documentary feel, but the videos allow the inveterate performers in the group to show more of their stuff. For example, there are shots of Barry and Brigitte clowning around on the piano at Sun Studio. It feels somewhat more intrusive to look at these videos than at the photos; the capturing of the latter allows for some safe distancing, but video reminds you that this is (or was) a living subject. Video also allowed for them to shoot performances; in this case, the most important part of the technology was its ability to record sound. There are long and notably high-quality clips that Walter shot at the Heritage Festival, including video of Rosanne Cash playing songs from her album *River and Thread* (Capitol, 2014), which is partially about her childhood. There are videos of Sun Studio, both of the tour guide clearly saying *not* to shoot video and of the performance/recording area downstairs. There are videos of the performances of Mark Alan Cash and Rachel Dawson at Storytellers, and Walter films Brigitte in the courtyard there. There was very little shot during Barry's performances by Brigitte or Walter; for once they just enjoyed the show.

Then there is a video of Barry in the inn where they were staying, two minutes long, showing him making a paper airplane for the owners' son. Here we see another side of Barry, tender and patient, a link outside strict tourism. The video recalls the photos of the homeless in the way that it notices what is human and compelling between people who do not know each other. But it also shows Barry entirely out of character—the character of Barry the superfan from Ireland. The video also affirms that Barry and Walter are friends, that their mission to the United States is a shared mission, and that each advocates the other's cause, ensuring they got as much as they possibly could from the experience. Walter and Barry could not converse too naturally, given their language gap, but they communicated radically through their shared passion for Cash and their desire to do something with that passion.

These photos and videos convey what visitors to Cash country see when they travel there: what they want to remember, and what they are worried they might forget. If Barry is now established as a thorough performer, Walter is an equally thorough collector, and in the sense that his namesake Walter Benjamin famously describes, he is an historical materialist who collates materials in a way that generates a resistance to narrative conventions of epic history. Collectors of things from a given moment or period inevitably show the constructedness of history. Collectors are practical people who stake a claim through materiality that something is significant, even as another might deny that significance. Walter Benjamin writes, "Historicism presents an eternal image of the past, historical materialism a specific and unique engagement with it. . . . The task of historical materialism is to set to work an engagement with history original to every new present" ([1937] 1985, 352). An epic historian will thus readily proclaim the eternal significance of Napoleon and point to his glorious tomb at Les Invalides as positive proof of that. Walter, a materialist historian, accumulates Johnny Cash material as if Cash were Napoleon, and as if Cash's experience and sphere of existence were in themselves as significant and complex as those of Napoleon. The historical materialist collector "takes a Rabelaisian joy in quantity" (373). To provide his proof, he needs an abundance of material, and now with this trip to the United States, Walter could add experiences to his treasure trove of materials waiting for him at his museum back in Austria.

Museums are not meant to be private, however; they serve to display the vision of the collector and the collection. Any good museum does both, clueing the visitor into what is valued about the subject through the materials and actions of its curator. Walter's museum may be just a collection of things, but these things speak directly to certain viewers, makes them think about their relationship to Cash and the American context in which he emerged. Cash might be a relatively minor character in an epic history of America, but it is precisely that minority role that gives him significance. It particularly excites fans like Walter and Barry in their explicit attempts to show that Cash is not as minor as all that. They also do this by pushing Cash into the attention of the present, as Walter notes: "In 1976 I got a music cassette from Johnny Cash and since then I am collecting. I have collected forty years and there were already some boxes full. Someday I thought that I would make a museum so that the public can participate, and that is what we have done. I first set up one room, and over time it is now 150 square meters of museum space."

To Barry, Walter's work was profoundly complementary to his own activities. He described Walter's museum as "a kind of home to me," but like any concept of home, this turned out to be complicated, a combination of the modest and the richly spiritual: "I just had to stop at the door. I got emotional. To see all this stuff and to think there is a man I never knew was doing all this and here I was, and every time I've gone there since, I sit down—he has a short-armed chair—and just sit down. And it's like kind of a serene feeling that Johnny went to a church. Serene, quiet, peaceful; I feel that in there."

Barry and Walter come from two countries historically immersed in Catholicism and the power of shrines, and in their mutual comprehension of the value of a Cash site, they achieve communion. It hardly matters that Cash was not the same faith they are. To create the shrine, one has to complete the journey. Seeing the American landscape in the decades after Cash walked, drove, and performed there is a way of trying to understand him.

Every museum has its centerpiece, a *Book of Kells* or *Mona Lisa*. Walter prized what he terms Johnny Cash's Forgotten Guitar, which Elvira said had come into Walter's possession when he was purchasing Cash material from a woman. During that visit, she indicated that she also had a guitar, which she pulled out from under a bed and gave to him. It was Walter's self-published book about the guitar that he had been distributing on the trip along with his festival flyers. He posts about the guitar regularly on Facebook. In the guitar, he had struck fandom gold, and instead of hoarding it, he wanted to proclaim his good fortune.

But the guitar was just one piece in a place that radiated Walter's love for Cash. Barry's description had not quite communicated the scale of what Walter had made. Video and photographs indicate it to be both spacious but well filled, comprising the entire ground floor of a detached house set in prosperous-looking farmland. A TV crew from ORF, the Austrian public service broadcaster, arrived to film there in the week before the Johnny Cash festival in September 2018, and they revealed an unpretentious but entirely professional setup, with a smoked glass door that read MUSEUM in a Western font (ORF 2018).

There were things that one might expect to see, like vintage jukeboxes playing Cash 45s, and as Barry had said, there were posters—but more than a few. Mannequins sport a range of Cash costumes, and one of June Carter's too. Display cases show Cash recordings in a variety of media, including the recording that started Walter off, the *Best of Johnny Cash* cassette that he had been given by a friend. Real curiosities included an album of Cash singing with the B. C. Goodpasture Christian School (Goodpasture Christian School 1979), indicating the depth of this collection, which in turn suggests the passion of the collector.

This space is an intriguing combination of phenomena. It echoes the internet shrines that were built for many stars in the early years of the internet, and most of Walter's material was acquired through online transactions, yet at the same time the museum is something of a throwback to the physical shrines that have always been built in service to those who worship a holy figure. The fan sites that mostly serve Johnny Cash are the official ones run by Bill Miller and the Cash family, or FanPop.com, where forum questions go unanswered (and where Barry, posting as StrictlyCash, posted his website address, saying he was "glad to be among friends").

What was unfamiliar was the setting, a farmhouse in rural Austria. This space bore Walter's authorship because he was the presence coordinating the objects; his quest to make a museum in a fairly remote corner of Europe signaled a desire to create and share a world so that fellow travelers can have the opportunity to live vicariously in Cashworld. With his photo taking in Tennessee, Walter was continuing a process he had begun in Austria, moving between the physical and digital; you did not have to go to Austria to see the museum. There is footage from Walter's museum on his Facebook pages (one for the guitar and one for the museum) as well as many YouTube videos of performances there. As he took photos during the trip, they joined the photo stream. It is as real online as it is in rural Austria.

Walter says that he has two thousand Johnny Cash items, but not all of them are on display. In this, Walter's museum was like others in the world;

most have many more artifacts than they can possibly exhibit. Walter must curate his collection, must decide what is worth showing to the public. What is not on show still exerts an influence; the artifacts ask Walter to think about whether he might revise his opinion of them. The photos too continue to have life. As Robinson and Picard note, "Tourists, by definition, return home. While all life is a temporally bound condition, tourism is a particularly short one; a festive time that seems to allow people to recreate sense and signification associated with their lives" (2009, 19–20). Walter set to work curating the photos on his Facebook feed as soon as he got back, yet the sheer mass of that pictures folder remains a potent, intimate, and incomplete text. On Facebook, he has chosen the highlights of his trip. He has repeat posted one photo in several contexts: the photo of him holding hands, two handed, with Brigitte in front of the graves of Johnny Cash and June Carter Cash. The photo is notable for its parallel reflection between the graves and the couple—or at least that is how Walter and Brigitte see it, and it is another example of the fandom marriage that began with the two of them. It is a good photo, and intimate, but it is not as impressive as the exasperating, exhausting carnival that the flash drive contained, where the riotous impulses of a true collector could be felt.

12 THE NETWORKER

Making Fan Connections and Encountering
Race and Nostalgia in Cashworld, May 2018

Silverman revisited Cash Country with Elvira van Poelgeest and her friends from the Netherlands. Barry's group had precise goals that directed the shape of the whole trip, but this was a looser and larger confederation of people, and they were engaging more widely with the musical cultures of the American South, including soul and blues. The plan was to meet them in Clarksdale, Mississippi, spend a few days in Memphis, then travel on together to Nashville.

The American South offers so much in terms of music tourism that it is tempting to simply isolate a trail according to either a single genre or a performer. Because the Dutch travelers were not all dedicated Cash fans, the trip cut a broader swath through Southern culture and music, providing a broader context for Cash and his work. Put crudely, there was more to Johnny Cash than Johnny Cash.

As a consequence, the Dutch engaged necessarily difficult parts of the African American experience in Memphis, the South, and the United States. Writing about race in association with Cash and his career is as challenging as it is necessary. Cash himself had been targeted by hate groups, including the KKK, when a picture of his wife, Vivian Liberto, had made her appear African

American (she was Italian), and when Cash notably partnered with black artists on his television show. But because Cash ended up primarily working in a genre, country music, that is often associated with whiteness, race is not always a topic that comes up in Cashworld, with the notable exception of his work with Native American issues and perhaps his prison albums. As Geoff Mann notes, "In the construction of an idealized past-ness, country music not only 'talks white,' but it is 'whites' who hear it, and whose whiteness is produced and reproduced by what they hear. The songs of a racialized and mythic 'used to' sound a present in which whiteness makes sense retroactively, calling white people to their whiteness" (2008, 76). European country fandom is similarly white, and its popularity rises in the parts of countries like Ireland and the Netherlands that are least urbanized and consequently most monocultural (Blakemore 2017).

As Mann notes, country music often looks backward to how things used to be, and tourism related to country music, such as tours of Ryman Auditorium and the Country Music Hall of Fame, does too. As Stephen A. King writes, "Although cultural tourism 'preserves' traditional art forms, it also tends to 'freeze' these traditions in time" (2004). The nostalgia in country music culture is exactly what European fan tourists expect. Yet Elvira's group broke out of the cycle of countrified nostalgia, a consequence of their determination to see more than Nashville and just Cash sites. For Elvira and Barry, visiting the American past is only part of the process of contextualizing, reorienting, and rewriting their ideas of Cash.

To some extent, engaging with race was just part of the completionist project that seeing a broad sense of Southern culture would seem to necessarily engage. Barry's trip was more tightly focused on Cash, whereas Elvira had an extensive network of Cash fans and associates that she drew on as the trip progressed. Among the Dutch travelers were different levels of interest regarding Johnny Cash, and Elvira planned accordingly. Sometimes the broad outlines of the trip performed both the work of seeing the South and Johnny Cash, as the trips to Dyess, Arkansas, to see Johnny Cash's childhood home and Sun Studio in Memphis, where Cash first recorded, demonstrated. Still, because of her network, the Cashiness of the trip was never in doubt, and in pursuing experiences, Elvira demonstrated the possibilities associated with Cash fandom, a much more open system than fellow Sun artist Elvis Presley. On arriving to join Elvira's group in Clarksdale, two men and two women approached Silverman and asked if he was local. He said no. "Nobody is local," one of the women said, giving him a sense of the tourist background of the place. Yet someone must be local; while tourists might overrun the town, they cannot actually run it. Yet Clarksdale does feel strangely vacated, and one of its commemorative sites is where Muddy Waters successfully took a train to leave for Chicago. What differentiates it from country music sites is that the nostalgia built into them takes on a positively conservative charge, whereas in Clarksdale memory activates a once-vibrant culture that evolved a unique music—and a uniquely horrific history that gave rise to it.

Elvira was waiting at Ground Zero, the blues bar partially owned by Morgan Freeman. She introduced all of the Dutch tourists, of whom only Theunis was familiar, the vocalist in the Black Suspenders. The others were not talkative. One was blond, one was tall, and the other looked conspicuously younger than the rest. Elvira told Silverman they were content; so far they all had found something to like along the way.

They made it an early evening and met up for breakfast at the Bluesberry Café (pun intended) in downtown Clarksdale. There they listened to the Kimbrough Tradition, a band that had apparently played in three different places that Elvira's group had visited. She reported that the band was much better than they had been on Friday night at Ground Zero and on Saturday night at Red's. Silverman asked Elvira if they had seen any other patrons in the café at other blues venues. "The guy in the striped shirt," Elvira said. She took another look. "Everyone in here."

In other words, the brunch was very much part of the tourist blues scene, which built on Clarksdale's legacy as a home to an amazing array of blues artists, as Clay Motley notes: "It is stunning to consider the list of musicians who were born or lived in Clarksdale: W. C. Handy, Son House, Gus Cannon, John Lee Hooker, Muddy Waters, 'Pinetop' Perkins, Robert Nighthawk, 'Big Boy' Crudup, Sam Cooke, Ike Turner, and Mack Rice—to name a very few." Motley also notes the downside: "On a slow night—and there are many slow nights between festivals—the blues in Clarksdale can feel manufactured primarily to satisfy tourists. That can happen when Saturday night music is played seven nights a week. In these moments, Clarksdale can resemble what I call 'The Colonial Williamsburg of the Blues'" (2018, 92; see also Gussow 2017, 255–303). This is something of an overstatement; there were semiderelict spaces between some of the venues, but no more than in other cities in the South. Tourism brought more restaurants and record stores than a typical small Southern city, but there were also a city's typical staples: stores, churches, and banks. Unlike Colonial Williamsburg, people still lived there.

Sharp contrast came with the drive north up the Mississippi to Memphis and Sun Studio, a first engagement with Cash culture for the Dutch, and where Elvira's American friend, Nancy, also a long-committed Cash fan, joined the group. Sun Studio is a thriving tourist business by day and still a going concern as a recording studio by night. It also charts the appropriation of black music culture by whites, beginning with Sam Phillips's efforts at building the studio around the work of Mississippi bluesmen like Howlin' Wolf, only to find that unworkable, then shifting emphasis to the emergence of rockabilly and the recordings of Elvis, Carl Perkins, Jerry Lee Lewis, and Cash.[1]

A rockabilly hipster conducted the tour with studied cool, alternatively straight and snarky. The tour was punctuated with bits of songs. When the tourists reached the actual recording studio, the hipster guide explained where people had stood, and what was original in the space (avowedly, the microphone and the black Xs on the floor where people recorded). Everyone took turns posing in front of the microphone. Then Theunis picked up the guitar and started playing and singing. It was surreal to watch this young fan of rockabilly, a thorough convert if a relatively recent one, play in the studio where it all began; then Elvira walked to a stand-up bass and started playing too. Theunis was taken with the moment: "It's a dream come true. I think Sun Studio is very special."[2] In actually taking up the instruments at Sun, they had gone beyond what most tourists thought they could do in the studio; usually visitors content themselves with standing at the mike, but to play there represented an irresistible temptation. As with Barry, the moment of performance was necessary to confirm themselves as not only fans, but fans who were committed to the perpetuation of the music by playing it as well as listening to it.

It is not wrong to question whether Elvis or Cash actually used the microphone that Theunis mugged with, or how long those black Xs had been on the floor. The belief was as good as the reality, which would take some effort to verify. There are two basic definitions of authenticity: one is a type of trueness to yourself and the second is a recreation of an original (Crawford 2001). The Sun experience was likely a bit of both—a sense that what tourists wanted was at once real and a recreation. Elvira and Theunis performing in the place of their heroes felt real; Sun Studio was special anyway. In contrast to Barry's pleasure in performing, which was a matter of design, this was

Theunis Lourens, lead singer of the Black Suspenders, with a guitar at Sun Studios in Memphis, Tennessee.

spontaneous, but no less pleasurable for that. If Barry were writing a kind of life text with his show at the Storytellers and felt fulfilled, the Dutch could just feel lucky.

Dyess was their next Cash destination, which they found by a combination of American and Dutch GPS. After a run of highway, they landed on a complex of dirt roads near town. A post office truck slowed to ask them where they were going. Unwilling to give up on the adventure of navigating dirt roads in an unfamiliar land, Elvira said that they were just driving around. (When forced to give a zip code at gas station terminals and other credit card locations, Elvira blithely gave 90210, the zip code turned teen television show. The real postal code in the Netherlands would not have worked; it was a digit short.) The postman was amused and gestured at the car's California plates. He knew they were tourists and likely Cash fans. Even though he gave them directions to the town center, the group persisted with the GPS, but the postman's remark was spot on: a visit to this remote point of Arkansas could only be because of Cash fandom. The group arrived in the old town center, which has been transformed through refurbishment in the last decade, likely because of the marketing potential of Cash fandom. It has been developed by Arkansas State University at Jonesboro into a recognizable historic site, with an enormous visitor center and museum.

The group chatted with Tim Jones, who ran the visitor center. Then the former mayor of Dyess, Larry Sims, came by to drive them by shuttle bus to the house. On a previous visit by Silverman, over ten years ago, it was still privately owned, and there was a sign asking for money for each photograph.[3] Now the house had been meticulously restored, and the tourists wore blue protective galoshes to protect the redone floors. The house was interesting even without the context of Cash; the exhibition recreated a 1930s small farm home, with the furniture, decorations, and even foodstuffs from the era, some of it from the Cash estate. Within this context, it seemed most interesting because of the distance Cash had traveled between this house and international stardom. That seemed to be an unintended outcome of the video playing in the visitor center that documented the refurbishment project, which stressed Cash's star power as the motive for the restoration, including testimony from members of the Cash family.

Like others in the universe of Cash fandom, Sims was highly engaged but just outside the main sphere of the family, and happy in that role. He noted that like many who worked at the visitor center, he did not live in

Elvira van Poelgeest holds Johnny Cash's boot in Bill Miller's office at the Johnny Cash Museum in Nashville, Tennessee.

Dyess but in Memphis, an hour away. He had hosted visitors from more than fifty-eight countries at the house. "There is not a week that goes by that we don't have an international visitor," he said. "People come from all over the world." Despite its remoteness, the town is accommodating to Cash fans from across the world because it has to be. There are thousands of different music fandom reasons for seeing Memphis but only one for going to Dyess, so the postman was doing his bit for the local economy, as well as just being sociable.

The remoteness is also vital in measuring Cash fandom; Dyess is proof of how far Cash came, but it is also proof of how far people are prepared to travel to engage with Cash's history. More remarkable is that this development is relatively recent; Cash fans are laying the tracks for what will be a much more thoroughly developed (but less fan specific) tourism in the future. The world is still waking up to Johnny Cash in the twenty-first century, and more avidly than ever before.

There was a couple from Dubuque, Iowa, on the shuttle bus. Meeting the Dutch, one said, "That's a long plane ride." While the group was sitting on the porch, a car with Virginia plates stopped, someone took some pictures, and the car drove off. Visiting the site was part of a completionist project engaged by many Johnny Cash fans, who wanted to see all the places associated with him, but for some, it was enough to glimpse it without leaving the car. All the members of the Dutch group were interested in Dyess; they were really experiencing rural America, and there was enough larger context for anyone, even those who were not Cash fans.

Since the trip to Sun Studio, race had been absent as an explicit context; there was no mention of it at Dyess either, although it did provide a clearly defined portrait of rural poverty and the struggle to overcome it. Back in Memphis at the Stax Museum of American Soul Music, devoted to the famous rhythm and blues label Stax, however, the Dutch tourists were immersed in it. After a well-produced video introduction, an extensive timeline indicated the reasons for the label's decline, directly addressing the racial strife after the assassination of Martin Luther King Jr. in Memphis and the cheating of the label's African American coowner, Al Bell, by CBS. When CBS refused to honor the terms of a contract the label had to distribute the company's records, it drove the label into bankruptcy (Danois 2018). The group's members read through everything carefully, though sometimes it felt like homework as much as it did tourism. Yet this was a reminder of how music was serious business in this part of the world; its legacy was necessarily intertwined with problems of racial division and discrimination. The subtext: Al Bell was easier to cheat because he was black; by the same brutal logic, it was easier for Johnny Cash to rise up out of Dyess because he was white.

They went for a drink by the Mississippi. The group remarked on a man driving around the area in a golf cart, passing every few minutes with a drink in his hand. Back in Groningen, Elvira had remarked that nobody was really poor in the Netherlands; now Yte, the tall Dutchman, commented that "everyone in America is rich or poor." From a country as securely middle class as the Netherlands, it was astonishing to see a place where that middle did not appear to exist. In Clarksdale, there were thriving businesses next to derelict lots; in Dyess, there was a pristine visitor's center and a direly disheveled gas station. To Dutch eyes, there was no in between, although other Europeans might have viewed it differently. Learning the geography of the Mississippi also meant learning the terms of an alien economy. Barry's group had designed a trip in which this mostly could be viewed peripherally, but the Dutch were seeing it directly. Traditionally, European Cash fans tend to come from its most well-protected zones in the north, where jobs and welfare enjoy considerable protection. Seeing such demonstrations of inequality must have been shocking, but also part of the reverse glamour of the United States.

This necessarily sharpened their experience of Cash's residences around the city, such as one on Tutwiler Drive, where the Dutch perhaps overreacted to the sight of trash on the street and in one resident's doorway. It was unkempt, but it was not a slum. The day before, they had been to Graceland, which was close to the hotel and full of contrasts to Dyess. It was also very American—something Elvira was determined to enjoy, insisting that they park closer to the entrance, even if the parking spot was in the sun: "We're in America, and I don't want to walk," she said. In Europe, this would have been an embarrassing thing to proclaim; in America, she was immersed in the fantasy of leaving that behind.

Graceland basically assumes that you know something about Elvis before visiting—perhaps a safer assumption ten or twenty or thirty years ago. There was hardly anything that explained Elvis's life directly. Visitors could see he got married, had children, consorted with famous friends, shot his guns, played racquetball, drove a golf cart, watched TV, and was buried there, but there was precious little about his inner life or even his career. The Dyess complex was not comprehensive either, but it was not supposed to be the end or ultimate Cash journey. It was just one of the stops in learning to understand Cash, an out-of-the way trip to see where he grew up. Graceland was supposed to be the ultimate Elvis experience, but it was curiously insubstantial and had removed anything that got in the way of easy consumption. In some ways, ten minutes at Sun Studio revealed more about Elvis, or at least his musical career, than Graceland did. Elvis at Sun was part of a creative collectivity, incorporating Perkins, Lewis, and Cash; he was also seen, however briefly, as a phenomenon of social change.

Hinds visited Graceland on a snowy day in November 2018, and because it was so empty, with only himself and a friend, some Scottish tourists, and a self-identified gay man on the way back from planning a Dollywood wedding doing the rounds, everybody had time to talk. Everyone visiting was white; everyone working there was black. One young guide called out loudly to his colleague on the stairs of the mansion, "I mean, who wants to go and see Elvis's house? Who's going to learn about Elvis in class?" The answer would have to be white people.

For a European Cash fan traveling extensively in the South, the value of thinking about Cash in the geographical and historical contexts of race is clear: race relations has been the dominant social issue in American history and culture, and thinking about Cash as being outside that context limits any understanding of him. The Dutch did not think about whiteness as a default state; this was understandable, given the political divisions centering on issues of race and immigration that had emerged recently in the Netherlands and other European countries. America is not a place to come to if you want to leave an awareness of racial problems behind. Elvira's group was largely repeating the same path as Barry's, and they were enjoying the kind of fan experience that being middle class and European can afford, both in terms of time and money, but they were also giving themselves a lesson. As they were moving around the map, they would also be mindful of how such mobility was denied to others on the same landscape.

Back with the Dutch, the group visited Elvis's gravesite, one of the few places that demanded quiet and care, though people still took photos. After visiting, Theunis approached Silverman with tears in his eyes, telling him how emotional it was for him. Graceland, even in its name, is a type of shrine, and visitors are in effect pilgrims, though as Chris Gibson and John Connell note, "the 'holiness' of Graceland stems more from the attitudes, behavior and actions of fans rather than any intrinsic merit in the life of Elvis" (2005, 202). That said, its white statuary in the memorial garden is entirely reminiscent of what is found in Catholic shrines in Europe and elsewhere; its pilgrim kitsch is partly by design.

Graceland was designed for pilgrims, as Karal Ann Marling notes: "Pilgrims in search of Elvis instinctively believe there is something to be learned from the costumes and the rooms he planned in apparent defiance of the canons of good taste, for these were the aspects of his life over which he exerted the most direct aesthetic control. The management of Graceland takes it as an article of faith that 'this place is Elvis'" (1993, 103).[4] Elvira and the Dutch were not interested in so specific a purpose. The group all averred that they liked Graceland but found it a bit exhausting without being as comprehensive they would have liked. This is a classic case of museum fatigue, identified in 1916 by Benjamin Ives Gilman as what happens when museums preserve things rather than show them: "In some proportion of the objects put on public view in every museum the qualities for which they are shown are rendered wholly invisible by the way in which they are shown." By comparison, Walter's museum in Austria seemed vibrant, but that was because it was a celebration of Walter's love for Cash, and the lengths to which it had taken him. Fandom animated the whole place rather than Cash himself.

Elvira and others were not quite as visibly moved as Theunis. After lunch, they visited the other exhibits, one by one. There was the car exhibit, with many of the different cars Elvis owned, accompanied by a well-done and often intentionally hilarious montage of Elvis in cars in movies and television. It proved that Elvis was far more of a born actor than Cash, who rarely had more than a moment of genuine ease in front of the camera. Comparisons to the "One Piece at a Time" exhibit at Bon Aqua also came to mind, which inventively and wittily brought the ingenuity of Cash's conception to life. Elvis's cars were more simply a demonstration of glamour. Yet above all what Graceland missed about Elvis were the very things worth recalling: his historical complexity, but also his sexiness.

Deep into the trip, they visited the National Civil Rights Museum, constructed out of the Lorraine Motel, where James Earl Ray had assassinated Martin Luther King Jr. As they had at Stax, the group went through the museum conscientiously, in keeping with its thoughtful design, focusing on the period between 1950 and 1975, with contextual material before and after. The emotional apex was the carefully preserved hotel room where King spent his last moments. Across the street was an exhibit about the search for King's killer, including the place from where James Earl Ray might have taken the shots (though not exactly).

Theunis felt everything sorely again: "It was very emotional. When I got to Martin Luther King's room, I started crying." What did it mean to cry at the grave of Elvis and the memorialized room of King? One died before his time in the context of a permissive culture that seemed to enable his worst behaviors, and the other died at the hand of a racist who presumably could not handle the changing culture. Perhaps it was just a general sense of empathy for those who died too soon; both King and the King certainly needed to be mourned. Theunis was the fan who enjoyed performing old country classics by Ernest Tubb and Hank Williams better than anyone; he was the most attuned to its rhythms and nostalgic tendencies. Here that capacity for empathy had taken him somewhere else—somewhere more tragic and more implicating. He had not cried for Cash yet, though that seemed sure to come.

Yte had already spoken about class, and now he addressed race directly, commenting on the terror white Americans committed against African Americans. When asked what a civil rights museum in the Netherlands might look like, he said it would probably not be much different, focusing on the immigrant/migrant population now and the legacy of slavery and the Dutch East India Company. Although the tourists had listened to the blues in Clarksdale, race had not come up much in any of the Cash contexts outside of the city. Now, however, they were in downtown Memphis, which was much more racially mixed than in Nashville, and engaging with it was a matter of everyday urgency.[5]

Memphis seemed to be struggling in a way Nashville was not. As David Smith (2018) notes in an article about the fiftieth anniversary of King's assassination, the Lorraine "represents a psychic scar for the city, the south and America. It was here that, amid seething racial tensions half a century ago, Martin Luther King was gunned down by a white drifter. It is a scar that modern Memphis—a majority black city with places of pilgrimage for music lovers such as Graceland, Beale Street, Sun Studio and the Stax Museum—is still struggling to heal." Quoted in the article is Tami Sawyer, who notes that the legacy of the assassination still haunts the city: "It's a large part of our identity. We are constantly referred to as the city where Dr. King died. Memphis died with Dr. King, in a way." There is contrast between the easy symbolism of a martyr and the complexity of a city altered by the assassination. This legacy was clearly affecting the Dutch.

U2's "Pride (in the Name of Love)" contributed to this sense, with lyrics that seem to martyrize King. In the wake of the Stax Museum and especially this one, the song seemed inadequate. "Shot rings out in the Memphis sky" seems to be a way of minimizing the racist intent of the gunman by intimating the shot's agency; taking a life, not "your pride," seems to consign King to martyrdom despite King's consistently evolving approach to fighting injustice. U2 has significant history as international Cash fans, recording a portion of their *Rattle and Hum* album at Sun Studio in 1988, and inviting Cash to sing "The Wanderer" on their album *Zooropa* (Island Records, 1993), an invitation that prefigured the American Recordings project, for which Cash would record U2's "One." In a supreme inversion, however, while Cash's cultural capital is on the rise, U2's has fallen, and all that remains of their once iconic Windmill Lane Studios is its graffiti wall where U2 worshippers once made their mark. Bono's keening version of spiritual wisdom has been culturally displaced by Cash's grit.

The Civil Rights Museum seemed like a larger contextual mission for Elvira. Perhaps not coincidentally, the first Google search result for "Johnny Cash Martin Luther King" is actually a post by her through the Johnny Cash Infocenter about Larry Murray's song "Six White Horses," first taken to prominence by Tommy Cash in 1969. Elvira posted it on Martin Luther King Jr. Day in 2014: "Here's Johnny's beautiful acoustic version of 'Six White Horses,' and refers to a funeral procession, specifically those belonging to John F. Kennedy, Robert Kennedy and Martin Luther King. Brother Tommy Cash recorded this song in 1969 and is still singing it in his shows. Goodbye Martin." The lines in the song about King focus on preaching "black" and "white," "wrong" and "right," "love" and "fight," ending with "Takes every kind to make that world go round takes one to gun you down/Goodbye Martin six white horses come to take you home." Arguably, the song does not seem to do much civil rights work; it presents a type of reporting and pleading for tolerance that seems to allow someone to be against killing in general without any precise commitment to fight racism. It should be said that Johnny Cash added the first line about the preaching of "black" and "white" to Tommy Cash's version, which made it more relevant to King's actual mission.

The song bolsters the opinion that country music avoids dealing with race, as LZ Granderson (2011) notes,

But I will also tell you I am disappointed that so few artists will sing about the one glaring aspect of life in the country that greatly defines how many Americans view the genre—and that is race. Scan the singles released over recent decades and it's as if race doesn't exist as an issue despite the South, the home of country music, being the backdrop for the beginning of the civil rights movement.

Yet the fact that the Dutch were here and at Stax suggested that their priorities were not those of country music fans or the industry. Most of them would not identify themselves as country fans anyway, even if Elvira's interests only went up to 1975.

The following day took them to the Johnny Cash Museum in Nashville, where Cash's story was told chronologically as well as thematically; it was thoughtful and well done, the exhibit about Cash's film career especially so. Nevertheless, Nancy, Elvira, and Silverman all found a few things either off or missing, and some dates were wrong. There are also layers of revelation and truth; the museum did not seem to take pleasure in its revelation of his more sordid history. The purpose was only to give fans context, to round out their listening history, to give their movie watching some depth. It could not hope to compete with an ardent fan and scholar's depth of knowledge. Yet the fan nevertheless must go, to visit all sites associated with Cash, to see all the Cash things, but also to see how Cash is being received by the cultural mainstream.

Observing how Cash was represented had a critical appeal for such fans, it was in many ways their most active area of concern and contention. Afterward, the group was brought by museum staff to meet with Bill Miller, who ran the museum. He first met Johnny Cash when he was a child, and he has been collecting memorabilia ever since, finally bringing enough together for the stocking of an actual museum. His wife, Shannon, brought out a box of costumes, including one from Johnny Cash's video of "Chicken in Black," a silly novelty song he recorded in 1984. Elvira clearly had a close networking relationship with Bill, and this was evidence of how she had accessed a high-level fan network that even Barry had yet to reach. Andy Bennett and Richard A. Peterson might call this network a "virtual scene," for these scenes have online components that are especially "devoted to the needs and interests of fans" (2004, 11).

Like Elvira, Nancy was also highly connected. Their friendship was not coincidental; Elvira had commonly organized her American travels so she could engage with American fans, and they had met through arranged rooming in a Cash cruise. Elvira was really part of a hybrid scene, one that involved the translocal with the virtual, with Friesland, the Infocenter, and foreign travel all part of the package (Bennett and Peterson 2004). Whatever it was called, it was real and powerful. Elvira and Nancy had talked about this network at Jerry Lee Lewis's restaurant in Memphis, and it was hard to know what or who was most important within it, but Bill was clearly crucial. He had had a podcast, he was collecting materials, he ran the museum, and most importantly, he seemed to be committed to openly connecting with fans. He represented how a fan could convert their fandom into a business, which was not what Elvira and other superfans exactly wanted. Yet the further they went into Cash fandom, the more the realities of the fan market became impossible to ignore. Networking and arranging meetings with key potential partners is exactly what people conventionally do to progress and grow within a business culture; the critical difference for Elvira was the absence of a financial motive.

Bill Miller seems to know everyone in Cash fandom, and he was unhappy with Walter's claim that Bill had validated the guitar he had bought and put on show in the Austrian museum as Johnny Cash's: "That story is bullshit." He showed the emails (though not their specific content) that had gone back and forth between the two. After the visit in his office, Bill showed the group his new project, a restaurant and bar featuring magic. As he walked, he talked about the museum and restaurant, and he noted that someone had offered him the opportunity to buy the place on Tutwiler Drive that the group had seen a few days ago. Someone suggested he buy it and turn it into a Cash-themed Airbnb. He seemed to consider this seriously. He left them with a gift of free admission into the Patsy Cline museum.

When Bill left, Elvira said: "Everyone has an agenda . . . except me." That was not altogether accurate; rather, her agenda was very clear, as it was with the Infocenter. She was looking to communicate personally with fellow Cash lovers, to bring them together, yet she was also clearly curious about how far fandom could take a person. She had asked Silverman, "Are you with us or following us?" and had asked to see his notes more than once, probably joking. Upon being told that it was no secret that work was being done on a book, she secured the last word: "So you're following us, then."

This frankness matched an openness to the American experience that was practically unbounded; the possibility of watching the Sounds, Nashville's minor-league baseball team, was mentioned. So they dropped off their stuff and started walking toward the stadium. There were some complaints about the walk, but they made it there. It was throwback night, with throwback prices ($2 a beer) to match. Silverman introduced the Dutch to the koozie, the foam protective cover designed to keep beer cold, and the Dutch took the drinking from there. The group left before the game was over (the Sounds won 12–7).

On the way back, a freight train had stopped on the tracks, and they were forced to climb over it, with Johan going first and then filming the rest of the group as they clambered over. Out of their preparedness to go forth, the Dutch had been rewarded with a staple moment of American adventure. They were temporarily allowed to play the American game of Huck Finn or hoboism and had accidentally converged again on a part of Johnny Cash's imaginative world—that of the train blues.

The next morning was planned as a roundup of Cash sites in the vicinity, led by Lisa Horngren, a Cash intimate who had played and toured with his ex-bandmate. The goal of the day was to visit a number of Cash sites and end with a jam session at Lisa's house. This was an example of the kind of people Elvira could access, and it further confirmed that she had emerged as a significant Cash liaison between the United States and Europe.

The first stop was the apartment complex in Nashville where Waylon Jennings and Cash briefly lived in 1967, then Mother Maybelle Carter's old residence, where Cash courted June back before the Folsom Prison concert. They were also shown the bowling alley that Mother Maybelle used to attend, which led to a daylong flurry of jokes (all in good taste) about all the different places she liked to visit. Johan was not taken with these stops: "I like the music, but I don't need to go into all the places a person lived. It's not important to me." He had a point, but this was a day for confirmed Cash fans, those ready for the quest to experience wherever Cash went. At this level of detail, fandom can be alienating; Johan had Cash fatigue. The graveyard in Hendersonville came next, where Johnny, June, and other Carter and Cash family members are interred. Now Theunis cried for Cash, but there was no time to dwell in the moment, as they went on to the old House of Cash, famous from the "Hurt" video, which had now become a real estate office. Annoyed workers ducked around them as they looked at a few Cash murals.

The next stop was Mama Cash's house in Hendersonville, which had been purchased by Brian Oxley (the co-owner of the Storytellers). As part of the welcome, he explained that the room they were in was unusual: it contained pieces of Colonel Tom Parker's house, which Brian had dismantled after the property was sold. He explained the Parker house's historic value; Elvis had spent considerable time there, and Brian showed photos with Elvis in front of wallpaper and paneling, then pointed to the same piece of wallpaper and paneling. The impulse to derive value from this deconstructed house was important to Brian, as was the story he told about it. He mentioned that a short documentary he made about it was going to play at the Nashville Film Festival. He had been unsuccessful in trying to get Graceland to purchase the house because the Presley estate did not like Tom Parker, who was reported to have taken an outrageously high cut of Elvis's royalties as his manager. There must have been anxiety that in the world of fan commodities, the dismantled house of an unbeloved figure might prove hard to move.

They walked into the kitchen, where the really interesting part of the experience for Cash fans started. Brian told the group that Cash and June Carter had spent the last six months of their lives living here, because their house across the street was challenging to navigate with their infirmities. Moreover, Brian said that not only did Cash live here, but he also recorded *American Recordings V* (American Recordings, 1994) here, which was released after his death. He showed the recording logs and a set list to prove he was telling the truth.

Thomas Gabriel, Cash's grandson, was sitting in the living room. Earlier that week, someone from the Dutch contingent had played a cover of "Hurt" by Gabriel, and admittedly, it sounded more like Cash than any other tribute. Brian asked Gabriel to play it, which he did, and he played his own composition as well. It was unclear why Gabriel was there—whether he had been asked to come through the Cash fan network or had visited of his own volition. He took orders willingly, though there was something underneath the willingness that was hard to put a finger on. It felt like something was at stake. Then Brian directed Gabriel to play "Hurt" with Theunis, with Theunis playing an old guitar of Johnny Cash's. Theunis did fine, though late Cash was definitely not his specialty. Nerves played a part; he had been noticeably emotional on the trip.

Brian then made an apparently outrageous suggestion that might have been his intention all along: to have the Dutch government purchase the Tom Parker house. Parker was a Dutch immigrant, and Elvis is popular in Europe. Elvira did not say no, and even seemed willing to go along with the scheme, which seemed surprising, although she may simply have been reluctant to disappoint him. She had created or at least curated a network of relatively prominent Cash-related people, though most were outside the actual Cash family, all of whom knew her to be an influential person in international Cash fandom. If she could organize Cash fans, she could bend the ear of her country's ministry of culture. What was remarkable was the power that Brian attributed to her—a gesture of respect as much as necessity. Elvira the manager of a publishing firm might not have enough respectability to query a government, but Elvira the power fan might.

In return, Brian offered the Dutch a place to sleep at the Cash farm, Bon Aqua, after they visited the Storytellers Museum. So Elvira could sleep in the same room Cash did, and the sudden proof of how she was being treated as a person of diplomatic consequence in the Cashworld was immediately apparent. The upstairs of Graceland, where Elvis's bedroom was located, is inaccessible to visitors, but Elvira could have Cash's bed if she wanted. As if that might not be enough to seal the deal, the Dutch were invited to try on some of June and Johnny's clothes. What would other fans have made of this opportunity? Charlie Taggart or Marco Rockmilhaud might have laughed it off; Barry Winters would try on all he could; Walter Ringhofer would attempt to procure the clothes for his displays (he already had one of June Carter's dresses on show in the museum). Yet the chances were that these other superfans would not be offered this opportunity.

After dinner at Lisa's house, the Dutch went into the jam room, full of instruments. Silverman sat as the tourists and Lisa played Johnny Cash. Then she insisted on setting up Silverman with an electric keyboard, and he was terrible. He could pick out the chord structures, but he had forgotten how to accompany other musicians, and his band experience was with New Wavers in the early 1980s. He finally managed to pick out and play the trumpet part of "Ring of Fire"; Lisa figured out how to make the synthesizer sound like a trumpet. No mistake about it, they were all having fun.

Above all, fun remained central to Elvira's fandom. She had visited the United States before, and this time she enjoyed introducing others to the musical culture of the South. She also clearly enjoyed the way she was party to the politics of Cash fandom and its nascent industry, the world of Bill Miller and the Oxleys. In one sense she was just a Dutch woman on vacation, but in the particular world of Cash fandom, she was a prominent citizen, highly visible and highly respected, and it was not yet clear what that might lead to.

Even as the trip had conscientiously invested in acculturation, attempting to draw on the history of the South in terms of race and class, it had ended up engaging with the privileged few of Cash fandom, the small percentage who extract a substantial profit from it. It was unclear whether those people saw Elvira as a competitor, a partner, or as a potential agent. It was also unclear what she had anticipated from the trip—but an invitation to sleep in Cash's bedroom, or to wear his wife's coat, had not been part of the plan.

13 CASH BOMBING

Finding Fandom in Portugal, June 2018

The sophisticated programming of the international superfans represented one compelling version of Cash fandom, yet gestures of Cash fandom kept emerging unanticipatedly from another world of Cash attachment that bore little relationship to the one Barry Winters and Elvira van Poelgeest moved through. The T-shirt in Charlottesville and the man with OCD in Nijmegen spoke of a more chaotic domain where Cash became important for people, but in much more disorderly ways. To tease out such responses from the ground up, Hinds undertook fieldwork by insinuation, to encourage varieties of Cash fandom to reveal themselves. Instead of seizing on Cash fans who announced themselves as such, what would result from introducing the subject of Johnny Cash in a particular environment? Silverman's experience of teaching Cash in Norway had led to the extraordinary revelation of the tattooed leg of the boy in Tomb, amounting to a kind of speech without words that turned out to be a kind of gesture shared internationally by all sorts of body parts.

Hinds visited a foreign country that had not been discussed thus far in the study and delivered a seminar on Cash and Cash fandom, then observed the unfolding of the discourse as he also let people know this was why he was in town. That would also involve instigating talk wherever possible about

Johnny Cash, whether in the university, a café, or a street corner—in other words, Cash bombing. This concept came from former Sex Pistol John Lydon, whose *Anger Is an Energy: My Life Uncensored* (2016) recounts nights from his London childhood where his Irish immigrant parents would invite people to their home and play selections from "their enormous record collection" (38). Music was for dancing, but it was also for creating mischief to see what their guests were made of: "'A Boy Named Sue' by Johnny Cash was the kind of record my mum and dad would like to hear, to challenge their friends and see what their reaction would be" (38). When Johnny Cash gets played, it has a litmus effect, engineering a powerful response from his audience, showing who they are. In the same way that you never know what you are going to get from someone hearing "A Boy Named Sue," it has proven to be impossible to entirely predict what Johnny Cash fans are like, or what they will be prepared to do in the name of following him. The definition of a Johnny Cash fan proves to be more open and fraught than ever, and this is magnified by Cash's international popularity.

The insinuation experiment could have been performed anywhere other than in the United States to see how Cash plays in a particular place for international fans, but the opportunity arose to do the work in the university city of Coimbra in Portugal. The experiment revealed the complex transgenerational love Cash inspires, as well as the remarkable way his presence is woven into the cultural life of a college town abroad. Cash also emerged as politically significant; one of his songs had been effectively weaponized in the early 1990s as an expression of license in a recently liberated country.

None of this was anticipated. Even if there were good reasons for going to Coimbra, there were also sources of discouragement, the main one being that Johnny Cash never played Portugal. This fact in itself might seem surprising, given his intensive touring, but it seems less so when Cash's itineraries are scrutinized closely. They indicate that his international marketing strategy was pragmatically conservative, favoring Ireland and the United Kingdom in particular, and rarely moving into Southern Europe. Johnny Cash on a European tour was a northern phenomenon. Cash fandom normally flourished where he had played abroad, and Portuguese fans had no such encouragement.

It is especially surprising that Cash did not come to Portugal in the years after its liberation from over forty years of rule under the fascist dictatorship of António de Oliveira Salazar. A young population then suddenly demanded as much foreign culture as they could get, especially culture from the United

States. While Salazarism had sought to enclose Portugal culturally, keeping it conservative and Catholic, pop culture had already become an active instrument of soft resistance. This found its ultimate expression on April 25, 1974, when the dictatorship was overthrown by the so-called carnation revolution, designed to take place while most of the country was watching the country's entry in the Eurovision Song Contest, "E Depois do Adeus" (After the farewell). The competition was won by an unknown band from Sweden called ABBA, singing "Waterloo," and so the softest of coups was set to the clamor of sing-along pop (Eurovision Times 2010).

Salazar fed the country a slumberous formula of nationalism and piety. Not much came into or out of Portugal, especially people in the entertainment industry. Salazarism cast a deeply repressive pall over the country from the 1930s to the mid-1970s, distancing its own version of fascism in a business suit from that of the overt militarism of Spain, Germany, and Italy, and using state media to generate a passive stupor.[1] Once TV became available there in the mid-1960s, it was heavily monitored and censored, so there was not much access to American performers, particularly those who evidently stood for values that could be seen as counter-Salazarist. Portugal was where you were supposed to think exclusively about Portugal, and where you did so in highly prescribed terms.

The culture of Salazarism is notoriously described as a trinity of *f*s, or *três efes*: Fatima, *futebol,* and *fado.* The first is the village in central Portugal made famous for its reported apparition of the Virgin Mary in 1917; the second is the nation's favorite sport, which is never off the television; and the last is a mode of Portuguese folk song whose modern history dates back to the early nineteenth century and is usually understood as having begun as the area around Lisbon underwent aggressive urbanization. *Fado* is a melancholic response to the pressures of modernity—a country music for the city. In this sense, it could be seen as a potential complement for Cash's music, whose version of country has always had urbanites hearkening to it.

The other place in Portugal that claims a particular relationship to *fado* is Coimbra, the venerable university city in the middle of the country that was Salazar's birthplace, and the site of the planned Cash bombing. It is a notable center for American studies scholars and has welcomed a series of celebrated American artists in the postrevolutionary years; Lou Reed performed there in July 2003. Students form a substantial portion of its population, and they are determinedly and intelligently conversant with American culture.

There is also an ambivalence about American cultural influence in Portugal that cannot be discounted. Salazarism was protected and supported by a succession of US governments during the Cold War, as maintaining its sleeperhold meant keeping the Communist Party of Portugal at bay. Yet emigration connects Portuguese people radically to Latin America and the United States, and instances of Portuguese culture can be found in unexpected places; 178 Inman Street in Cambridge, Massachusetts, is home to the Casa do Benfica do Nova Inglaterra, for example, a supporters' club for Portugal's most popular football club. Portugal is European, but right on its westward frontier, so it is no wonder it looks away to America.

This state of contradictions is exactly where Cash's music often seems to take hold. In the Portuguese case, it is also as if people are catching up with music that they would only have been able to encounter with great difficulty during the Cold War years when it was made; sailors on the ships that came and went out of Lisbon or Porto would have sometimes brought records with them (as they did to other great port and music cities like Liverpool and Hamburg). Or he could just appeal to the Portuguese version of hipsterism that is found elsewhere, where middle-class kids affect beards and brilliantined haircuts, listening to music from the 1950s on technology from the 1950s while sipping a locally made ale. Both explanations express a wish for a past that was cooler than Salazar's culture of compulsory boredom.

The seminar was hosted by Professor Stephen Wilson at the Institute of American Studies, who had conducted a preliminary consultation with the seminar students as part of his master's course on film and music. From what they said there, Cash meant three things: *Walk the Line,* "Ring of Fire," and *At San Quentin.* Significantly, none of the Rubin-era material featured on this list; yet once the seminar began, practically all the students cited the video for "Hurt" as their first encounter with Cash's work.

The religious side of Cash was of no apparent interest whatsoever. Then again, post-Salazarist Portugal has become a determinedly secular state, with the Catholic Church having to accept a minor role in the composition of society after its years of collusion and compliance with the dictatorship. So it is not only that religious music is less hip but also that it is practically off-limits. These preferences were not just about degrees of cool; rather, they indicated that the perception of cool was in itself highly politicized for these students. Cash the eternal rebel, endlessly raging against the dying of the light, was practically whom they had been educated to like. Perhaps it was unsurprising that the late-stage Cash, who conformed at least superficially to the idea and iconicity of a contemporary rock star (despite his age and his religiosity), was the one who had registered most with the students.

Then there was the black. Traditionally, Coimbra students wear a black cloak called a *capa* throughout the years of their undergraduate studies, a garment that (by repute) remains unwashed as a badge of honor. Typically, however, this story turns out only to be a story; few Coimbra students can be seen in a cloak bearing four years' worth of dirt. It had been introduced into the seminar to attempt a segue into talking about Cash's own stage outfit—and his demythologization of it in his autobiography, where he advances the explanation that wearing a black suit was more a matter of happenstance and less of a political statement: "I didn't own a suit, or even a tie—but each of us did have a black shirt and a pair of blue jeans . . . and since . . . musicians are deeply superstitious—if they tell you otherwise, don't believe them—I suggested we stick with the black" (1997, 69). This is a remythologization by Cash of himself as a road warrior, whose black garb is defined by the hard work of being a self-employed worker of the culture industry rather than outsiderdom. The students entirely rejected both readings; they declared the legend of their own institution's *capa* as bizarre and disgusting. They were modern, confident, and skeptical, with little time for legends.

The group was entirely female and consisted of seven participants: Eduarda, Orlessia, Maria Anna, Sylvia, Alexandra, Daniella, and Leonore. The class was organized around a slideshow that laid out the development of the Cash fandom project and talked about the difficulty of turning disparate anecdotal material into a cohesive whole. Simultaneously, it argued that this disparateness was explorable productively, making a polyphony of perspectives and experiences around Cash. The slideshow presentation consisted of forty-three slides, and the class was slated to last three hours, an allocated time that is not usually used up entirely. But after that time had elapsed, the group was still talking, asking questions and offering anecdotes of their own. So Leonore reported how she had in fact come across Cash, not through his music or image story but rather as a simile. First was an episode of *Hannah Montana* (2006–11), where the eponymous heroine has lost her voice and is agonizing over how she can perform on stage, a dilemma resolved when her father tells her to speak her lyrics "just like Johnny Cash." Leonore then cited the Good Charlotte song, "All Black," which also proclaims being "Like Johnny Cash" to be a way of situating yourself in the lineage of rock 'n' roll melancholia.

The students were particularly taken with the scenario of Charlie Taggart in his shop, not least because it seemed as though he had evolved a way of living and working for himself within his pleasure. As such, he appeared to have fulfilled Marx's aspiration for productively demolishing the line between leisure and work, in that Charlie achieved freedom in work rather than seeking freedom from it. While at work, he was always still enjoying his fandom.[2] This had utopian appeal for these educated people in their early twenties, still figuring out how to make a living out of their culturedness. It also has peculiar pertinence with an economy as stressed as Portugal's, where making the most of limited resources is an existential necessity.[3] Charlie's apparently hermetic world was in fact a model for a particular kind of specialized economy in which these arts graduates felt they might have a chance of surviving. Maybe not so perversely, for all the low-tech aspects of his business and his fandom, Charlie appeared almost hipsterish in his ability to create a work world in which he could listen to Johnny all day, every day, if he wanted.

When a slide showed the list of European contributions to the Johnny Cash Project website, the response was hilarious. Laughing in chorus, students pointed out that of the two places in Portugal noted on the list of Johnny Cash Project contributions, one was the capital city, Lisbon, but the other was a village, Ferreira do Alentejo, that they thought might be just about the smallest in Portugal (and also reputedly the hottest).

Maria Anna immediately took to googling and announced that its population was 8,200. If it is not then the smallest town in Portugal, it nevertheless had an impact on the students; it had not occurred to them that anybody from that town would be interested in anything. This proved that Cash fandom has a formidable reach, but it also showed the students were not above a bit of intellectual snobbery.

The next image was of a Brazilian posting of the "Hurt" video on YouTube; none of the students remarked that it had been posted from Brazil until they were told. Even once they were told, they did not find much to comment on. They said that they just did not think about where such posts originated. Asked the question of how American they thought Cash to be, they said with unanimity that they thought of Cash as international.

The same analysis was extended when the next slide showed Takahiro Saito performing "I Walk the Line" on *The Johnny Cash Show* in January 1971. The obvious way for an Americanist to approach this video is to worry aloud about its symbolism of cultural imperialism, with the Japanese tribute singer indicating deference to American power. These were students at an American studies institute, but they were not particularly interested in the power play of national identities. Instead, they homed in on the immediately remarkable thing in Saito's performance: how he begins singing in English with a fairly high baritone, but when he switches to Japanese, he drops significantly lower, his voice becoming far more Cashlike.

This "dropping-low," as Wilson described it, was what the class had spoken of beforehand as the single most remarkable thing about Cash in performance: a quality of voice that called attention to itself and signaled the genotext, to use Julia Kristeva's (1969) term for how a song communicates through the physical apprehension of the volume and fabric of vocal performance rather than its significations in terms of intellectual interpretation, or ways in which a subject might be conventionally constructed. Roland Barthes (1977) renames this "the grain of the voice" (181), which is what cannot be reduced to mere interpretation or explanation. Saito only dropped low in Japanese, as if getting that little bit closer to the grain of Cash were a private matter for him rather than something for the American TV audience to share, yet the audience intimately understood what Saito was doing.

The class in turn signaled their appreciation that this was a good imitation of Cash, an apt tribute, one based on a sense of musical connectivity rather than a cruder politics of domination. It also provided a spur for a further discussion about the cultural influence of the US servicemen on various places across the world in the post–World War II period, although Portugal had not become a vital part of such cultural exchange.

The class explicitly addressed the issue of race, echoing questions that had been emerging throughout the study about the hegemonic whiteness of Cash fandom, notwithstanding his exemplary outspokenness on behalf of some oppressed or forgotten American minorities. The students were less familiar with this activist aspect of Cash's work and seemed favorably surprised; the inference that could be made from this was that they also had formed a construction of Cash based on whiteness. The student who had googled Ferreira do Alentejo was Portuguese African, and she had said in anticipation of the Cash seminar, "The thing about Johnny Cash, the Man in Black . . . is that he's not black." This was irrefutable and was well worth talking about.

The class had viewed the celebrity-populated video for "God's Gonna Cut You Down" earlier in the session and had remarked just how many African

American performers had taken part in it, including Chris Rock and Kanye West, something they had not noticed previously. This was compared with the YouTube video "50 Johnny Cash Tattoos for Men," in which all fifty bodies are apparently white or certainly nonblack (Next Luxury 2017). This discussion subsequently took particular shape around two texts, one literary and the other visual. First, the class looked at Mark Greif's "What Was the Hipster?" (2017), a twenty-first-century response to Anatole Broyard's foundational work on the ur-hipsterism of the 1940s, which he saw as an expression of stylish resistance to white convention, "developed from a sense that minorities in America were subject to decisions made about their lives by conspiracies of power they could never possibly know" (214). Greif observes a turn in the new hipsterism, a kind of cooler than thou, defanged as a mode of resistance, instead an arch mode of self-assertion entirely arrogated to whiteness—the very thing that original hipsterism had queried: "The new young strangers acted, as people said then, 'hipper than thou.' . . . But these hipsters were white, and singularly unmoved by race and racial integration" (214). Greif moves into a list of cultural artifacts and phenomena that might be attached with the rise of this unapologetic whiteness:

> Indeed, the White Hipster—the style that suddenly emerged in 1999— inverted Broyard's model to particularly unpleasant effect. Let me recall a string of keywords: trucker hats; undershirts called "wife beaters," worn alone; the aesthetic of basement-rec-room pornography, flash-lit Polaroids and fake-wood paneling; Pabst Blue Ribbon; "porno" or "pedophile" mustaches; aviator glasses; Americana T-shirts from church socials and pig roasts; tube socks; the late albums of Johnny Cash. (2017, 214–15)

In this context, a liking for late Cash becomes part of a chain of signification that could be said to relate directly to the Trump presidency, the Proud Boys, and Charlottesville. It poses a difficult question for people who like the late albums of Johnny Cash and would advocate a pluralist and progressive agenda, which is a view that appears to be what Cash himself endorsed, to some degree. Can you prevent a person whose political beliefs you abhor from liking an artist? This question came into immediate focus with a slide featuring images of the Charlottesville shirt. The students had not been aware of the controversy and knew nothing of the Cash family's prompt efforts to distance themselves and their father's legacy from the carnage in Virginia.

Yet as one student pointed out, the T-shirt-wearing Nazi was part of the legacy too. The class was moving to a depressing conclusion. In the fundamentalisms of twenty-first-century identity politics, the whiteness of Cash was not so much the issue; rather, it was the whiteness of those who may proclaim various degrees of affection for him. On the other hand, if Johnny Cash's name was jeopardized by association with racist thugs, then it was only an example of how other things, like bodies and values, were in far greater jeopardy. The family had done the right thing, because they had put an emphasis on their disgust with the politics of the man in the T-shirt rather than only seeking to preserve the sanctity of Johnny's memory.

So in this city, so alive to how culture was thoroughly political, it is not surprising that the city should have produced subcultures that were dedicated to creative dissent. A prime example is the rockabilly scene, which has persisted since the late twentieth century in Coimbra and which now centers on the roots music and craft beer bar, the Academico, run by Pedro Serra, aka Portuguese Pedro, who doubles as a recording artist and DJ. Pedro also broadcasts via a podcast, *Portuguese Pedro Radio Show* (https:// portuguesepedroradioshow.blogpost.com), usually curating shows around particular influences on his own career and work. The meeting with Pedro took place in the Academico directly after the seminar at the university.

The Coimbra scene generated originally in the late 1980s and 1990s with the psychobilly band the Tédio Boys, led by Paolo Furtado (still performing as the Legendary Tigerman),[4] an outfit that created social spectacle and disruption to match their sonic distortion.[5] Everyone in Coimbra, across generations, referred to the band as notorious, with a combination of rue and awe. They got one kind of notoriety by playing naked at the university's celebrated annual festival, the Queima das Fitas, spattered with blood, with rubber chickens (sort of) covering their genitalia. If they were looking to achieve any kind of fame, this alone sealed it; thirty years on, it was still the first thing people referred to in relation to them. More significantly, one of the songs through which the band announced themselves to the world (or Coimbra at least) was a cover of "Folsom Prison Blues."

Tédio is the Portuguese word for boredom, a term with a peculiar politics in Portugal, where under Salazar it had practically been state ideology. Pedro was introduced to Hinds by Paulo Anjel, a pioneering sociologist and activist,

Portuguese Pedro's rockabilly ale.

and an intensely knowledgeable interpreter of Portuguese life; he endorsed the view that rockabilly (and precisely the psychobilly of the Tédio Boys) had become intensely popular in Coimbra because it was a response to Salazar's fascism, a noisy reinvention and reclamation of the past. Even more than with a conventional punk statement, the Tédio Boys were giving a shock treatment to what their record label describes as "an amorphous city," getting it to feel and think again, from feet to spine to brain (music available at Bandcamp at porkabilly-psychosis). Pedro had gotten into the Ramones and psychobilly in the wave generated by the Tédio Boys (who themselves became punkishly canonized by being invited to play at Joey Ramone's birthday). He formed bands, learned to play, and above all thought about how to live for independence. The first Johnny Cash song he encountered was "Folsom Prison Blues," and he heard it through the peculiarly distorted rendering of the Tédio Boys. In their cover, first released on the 1994 album *Porkabilly Psychosis* (Rastilho Records), they play a classic slow–fast game, singing the opening verse as if in the drunk tank, with an accompanying backdrop of hiccups, then accelerating drastically into head-rush mode. They enact being in jail, but they also make you feel as if you are busting out of it.

As soon as sixteen-year-old Pedro heard it, he learned how to play it, and thus began a retrospective journey into the roots and causes of rockabilly. Now he performs with name recognition in the international world of rockabilly at festivals across Europe and in the United States. In 2018, his album *The Full Enchilada* was released on Sleazy Records—confirmation of his redoubtable verve but also a vindication of his recent decision to live through his fandom full time. He was a graduate of the University of Coimbra and had worked as a civil engineer for years, traveling all over Portugal, depending on where his governmental employers sent him. In 2015, he decided on a radical change: he opened his bar in Coimbra's Praca de Republica, at the foot of the steps leading to the university. He wanted his place to have an identity, counter to what he said was the conventional Portuguese wisdom about opening a bar, which is to make the place as anonymous and blandly conventional as pos-sible—more cultural Salazarism. Pedro went the other way, shouting aloud his fandom, expressing it through music, decor, and even the menu (you can buy a veggie burger in Pedro's bar, practically unheard of in Portuguese bar cuisine). Like Charlie Taggart, Pedro had apparently managed the discovery of freedom in work. His life was not without concerns, however; his phone kept ringing because his son was sick at home, and he remarked lugubriously when congratulated on the success of his business, "If this bar was in Lisbon, I'd be a fucking millionaire." Then he commanded that Cash be played on the jukebox.

Pedro was a combination of elements that are also identifiable in Cash; he had an appetite for the kind of insubordination and antisocial mischief that the right music can generate (as Pedro said, "Cash was the punk rocker of the 1950s"), but he was also a good father, a good businessman and impresario, yet someone with a palpable sense of social responsibility. Having worked for so long to build social infrastructure, Pedro's life and work project could also be seen as having an aspect of social engineering, an ambition to transform Portuguese life through good music and beer. This was obviously good fun, but he also seemed exhausted.

Enjoying the role of proprietor, bottles of Portuguese Pedro American Pale Ale were ordered, and—telephonic interventions apart—discussion moved into consideration of Johnny Cash, family, and *futebol* (the World Cup was a week away). At dinner later with Steve Wilson and friends, yet more sons of Coimbra appeared with opinions and substantial knowledge about Cash (including Miguel, who had read Reinhard Kleist's *I See a Darkness* [2009], a graphic biography of Cash, as part of his enthusiasm for graphic novels), and talk with them turned to the same things. Arguably, the Salazarist trinity of *f*s was still intact in some aspects, yet the displacement of Fatima with fandom, an alternative mode of faith, proved palpably liberating. For these Portuguese at least, for some of whom Jerry Lee Lewis was referred to in almost deific terms, Cash and rockabilly exemplified a hedonism that was not a mode of escaping reality but rather one of meeting it head on. The Johnny Cash of "Hurt" was cited again and again as well, in terms of proving how to live a life and knowing how to end it.

The Charlottesville T-shirt excited a lot of comment in Pedro's bar. He was clear about what had happened there; reactionary forces might try to claim the energy that Cash generates, as well as the integrity of his persona, but this demanded resistance, not acceptance or resignation. In this he was practically echoing the Cash family. In answer to the suggestion that you could not stop fascists or racists from liking Johnny Cash if they wanted, Pedro made the countersuggestion that you could. He told of how he had confronted Hells Angels and right-wing skinheads who had come to a festival, and that when they said, "We like rockabilly," he retorted, "No you don't." For him, music like Cash's was also an assertion of a right to live, a fierce tolerance that could take a form of apparent intolerance. He similarly denounced the knee-jerk anti-Muslim views that had acquired a presence in Portugal, just as they had in other countries: "How can anyone be anti-Muslim in this country? Look at us, most of us don't know whether we have Muslim genes or not!"

When he spoke of a favorite performance by Cash, summoning it on his phone, he cited Cash playing the doubly antic game of impersonating an Elvis impersonator on local television in 1959 (*Town Hall Party*), showing at the same time a formidable aptitude for looking and sounding wild. This wildness was not inconsistent with the fundamental common sense of what Pedro said about ethnicity; the impulse for fun that Pedro kept referencing was also an impulse for sanity, a corrective to the boring nonsense that Portugal had experienced for decades before.

A documentary made about the Tédio Boys is entitled *Filhos de Tédio* (Rita Alcaire and Rodrigo Lacreda, 2008). As sons of tedium, the band had done the situational groundwork of instituting revolution. As with any revolution, the problem is what to do afterward; as the son of the sons of tedium, Pedro was doing vital work of the next day, infiltrating and altering the rhythms of everyday life.

Alexandra from Steve Wilson's seminar group came around to his office the next day, where the conversation about Cash continued. Alexandra was the one student who was a self-declared Cash fan and was planning to write her dissertation on *Walk the Line*. She apologized for missing the last twenty minutes of the seminar, as she had to go to work, but she wanted to follow up on it. This was not only a matter of academic interest for Alexandra. When she was talking about Cash aging, and the pain of that aging being so visible in the "Hurt" video, she began to cry.

She said that she considered herself part of the "Hurt" generation— those who came to Cash through that extraordinary performance—but she quickly demonstrated a knowledge that showed how she had engaged with the range of his work. Before the class, Steve had said that Alexandra had declared some weeks earlier that "Ring of Fire" was the soundtrack to her life, but now she did not recall that. At the beginning of the seminar, she had said that "Cocaine Blues" was the first Cash song to come to her mind. Today, however, she launched into a remarkable interpretive riff on "Cry, Cry, Cry," talking about how well Cash communicated as a woman to a woman (something he also did in "Ring of Fire"). From this, Alexandra theorized that Cash is empathizing with Vivian Liberto's experience, and as such is exposing the fictive demonization that was visited on her by Mangold's *Walk the Line* (demonstrating a sympathy with Liberto that Elvira van Poelgeest had also expressed). She also spoke about the peculiar musicality of Cash, summoning the idea of his voice's grain, and she argued that his lyrical content is only of secondary interest: "Cash is like Nina Simone; they are so good sonorically that you do not care too much about what they are singing." This might have been news to Simone.

Alexandra's passion for Cash was such that she was equally passionate about sharing it. For her father's recent birthday, she had given him a best of Cash collection (what would Half Man Half Biscuit think!), but he was not "very keen," complaining that it "was old music from America" and that "Johnny Cash was that old American from the television." Her father was from the pre-1974 generations of Portuguese people who were simply not able to listen to Johnny Cash—or more importantly to experience the freedoms that he exemplified. Salazar did not ban American music (he reserved that privilege for art and culture in the Portuguese language, which was considered to be dangerously un-Portuguese), but that still did not mean it was obtainable other than through practically impossible channels. For most Portuguese, they had to sit tight and consume what the state sold and broadcasted—and that was not anything produced by Johnny Cash.

Working in the FNAC record store in Coimbra, Alexandra said that she had observed many people buying Cash albums and usually engaged with those who did so. She told the story of a young man who said that he was buying Cash for his parents, and that his own taste was for heavier and harder music. Alexandra's take on this was twofold; first, she suspected that he was really buying the album for himself, or that he was buying it for his parents because he really liked it and wanted to share it. She had given a best of Cash collection to her father as a present because she thought he would like it because it came from his youth, the 1950s and 1960s.

Stories of parents (and especially fathers) passing on a love for Cash to their children kept emerging; this had been Marco's story too. Yet in Portugal, the opposite appeared to be the case; one explanation was that this could be explained by the younger generation's sense that their parents had missed out on what was a hypervibrant musical culture in the 1950s and 1960s. The children were anxious to compensate their parents for what the Salazar sleepwalk had made them miss.

Cash also manifested a rebelliousness that Portuguese teenagers had not been able to enjoy in public until the 1970s. This had been a key point for Pedro; when he began with music, he started with punk, then found a particular home for himself within the psychobilly of the Cramps and the Tédio Boys. The point in liking rockabilly, Jerry Lee, and Cash was not so much that it and they were American; rather, it was a matter of being un-Portuguese according to the monotonous fiction of nationality that had been imposed on everyone in the recent past.

Four days in Coimbra had been a sustained experiment in listening to varieties of love story. Alexandra's was the most extravagantly impassioned, but the most restrained one was no less informative. The story came from a friend of Steve Wilson's named Hugh, a recently retired professor of chemistry at the university, highly esteemed and influential in his field. He was an

Englishman from Worthing in Sussex, where he had formed an early interest in American music, courtesy of his uncle owning a secondhand record shop where he could get privileged (if not free) access to imported records. So at the key fandom formation period of his teenage years, he got prompt access to New Orleans jazz and Mississippi blues, and along with that came bundles of records from Sam Phillips's Sun label.

Out of this, he became a member of the English chapter of the Jerry Lee Lewis fan club, and a lifelong interest in American music began. Music was a constant point of reference for Hugh, something he shared with friends and family through trips to concerts or pilgrimages to the Southern United States after retirement. Steve, an Ezra Pound scholar by trade, had much to share with Hugh in this regard, having been brought up in the cultural vibrancy of the early 1960s in Birkenhead (home to Half Man Half Biscuit), just across the river Mersey from Liverpool (the kind of port city that saw imported records moving through it all the time, to the benefit of the Beatles).

Meeting for lunch in a café behind the university every day, the conversation between Steve and Hugh became a constantly rolling flow of anecdote and query centering on music as life text, the thing that provided all present with an opportunity for sharing experiences between lives that otherwise had few points of connection. The esteemed chemist and the Ezra Pound professor do not thrive on comparing notes on the uses of potassium and "In a Station of the Metro"; on a bad day, they might talk about grading schemes or grant allocations. Yet they could commune in a Memphis of the imagination, which could quickly shift to anecdotes from London in the 1960s or Ireland in the 1970s, as long as the subject was popular music, and the things that a love for it will lead you into.

A fact of life in a place as determinedly academic as Coimbra is that many people you meet are knowledgeable like Hugh; as Wilson said, "It's a place where you can find twenty people in the phone book to offer private tuition in Sanskrit but only two to fix your plumbing." It was more surprising that so many of these intelligent people should share a specialized knowledge in American music of the 1950s. But apart from Steve, none of them knew one another or had ever spoken to one another. They did not necessarily think about their passion for music as a phenomenon of commonality.

What came out of these various conversations was Steve undertaking to introduce Pedro to Hugh, and Alexandra to Pedro. It was odd to think that so many people had expressed degrees of connection to Cash, but that they did not necessarily know each other and had not spoken about this connection to one another. There was an invisible network connecting them despite that. This network was the complex of Cash himself and the relationships he generates. These fans did not really need each other as such; their fandom would have remained as sharply realized had they never met each other. Yet the experiment showed that at least in this place in Portugal, if you started to talk about Cash, people would listen. More importantly, they would join in.

14 SPIKE PRISON BLUES

*Reuniting and Networking at a
Cash Concert, June 2018*

At the beginning of the yearlong cycle of fieldwork in Groningen, there had been informal talk with Elvira van Poelgeest and Barry Winters about collaborating on a concert. It would provide a reason for further communications between the book project and the activities of Barry and Elvira, who were already establishing a pattern of collaboration anyway. The day after the meeting in Groningen, Barry had played with the Black Suspenders at a festival in rural Holland, and they clearly had established mutual respect as performers and fans.

Gradually, plans emerged for the Black Suspenders to visit Ireland in the summer, to play both by themselves and then along with Barry's Strictly Cash at a celebration of the fiftieth anniversary of Cash's 1968 *At Folsom Prison*, held on Spike Island, the site of an abandoned military prison not far from the city of Cork on the southern coast of Ireland.

This was a concluding event in the year of Cash fandom; it was also a chance to see the inexhaustibility of these fan protagonists. These were not the only Cash fans in the world—they were everywhere—but they also were unusually dedicated to moving beyond conventional limits and incorporating degrees of risk into their fan activity. The events on Spike

Island also showed their powerful sense of occasion as well as the way fandom should always be looking for new opportunities to find expression. Whether it was how budget airlines created an unprecedented capability for cheap and fast travel, or how a Facebook post might create potential meetings or connections, they were ready to capitalize on it with their minds and bodies. A book project about people like themselves was another such opportunity, and it lent a meta aspect to their behavior. Barry had mentioned closure in relation to his traveling to the United States; now a version of it would be performed.[1]

Beyond this, the concert also opened up another community of Cash fans, those who came to the gigs; talking to them provided the real sense of an ending to the activities of Elvira and Barry, a confirmation that their fan work was not only for their own pleasure. At first it was not entirely clear to what degree there would be an actual on-stage collaboration. Barry had steered Elvira and the Black Suspenders toward Richie Cotter, a leading figure in the rockabilly scene in Ireland, for help with bookings. Originally their tour was modest in conception and geographical reach. They were booked to play three nights in Ireland, two in different bars in the town of Enniscorthy in County Wexford (best known as the site of a catastrophic military defeat against the English in 1798) with a night in the medieval city of Kilkenny in between. There would be limited driving between venues—desirable because the band would already have undertaken a ten-hour drive from the east of Holland to the port of Cherbourg in Normandy, from where they would take a twenty-hour car ferry to Ireland.

Things altered dramatically with Barry's invitation to the Black Suspenders to join Strictly Cash on the bill at Spike Island. The first concert sold out in thirty minutes, buoyed especially through ticket buying by the staff there, according to Michele Cronin, a senior tour guide. Two more concerts quickly sold out, and the Black Suspenders canceled their second Enniscorthy gig so that they could play Spike Island instead.

Barry's commitment to acting out his fandom was incessant, his enthusiasm unrelenting, his planning phenomenal. He also monitored the project via Facebook, not missing any opportunities for Cash talk and commenting on the fan work of others. When Silverman posted a list of five favorite songs on Facebook for some requested meme, Barry, writing as the Johnny Cash Tribute, wondered why there was no Johnny Cash listed. When Hinds posted a photo of the track selection on the jukebox in Portuguese Pedro's bar in

Coimbra, through his Johnny Cash Tribute Facebook ID, Barry identified the Cash songs on it as the items that made the jukebox "okay."

Expressions of international fandom had become hard to avoid. When visiting Winnipeg for a conference, Silverman met with another fan/tribute artist, AR Cash, fronted by Aaron Prociuk. Aaron had also performed at the Storytellers Museum with Tommy Cash and claimed tribute artistry because of his meticulous approach to recording and performance, as well as instrument instruction. He had won a Josie, an independent music award, and seemed to be on the same path as Elvira and Barry in trying to find the places and ideas that would constitute finding the real Cash and walking in his footsteps. Aaron would likely recognize his type of fandom in how Barry and Elvira followed Cash through degrees of performance.

Cashdom made itself visible in other ways too; on the way to dinner with his mother and nephew in Toronto, Silverman saw a man playing "Ring of Fire" on the street, and a few weeks later in Ireland, he heard someone singing an emotionally wrought cover of "Hurt."[2] A woman spoke powerfully to Hinds of how her father's love for Johnny Cash was an unforgettable and valuable part of her childhood, not least because she associated it with his alcoholism; he would fall asleep on the living room couch with a Cash album on for a kind of lullaby.

A month before that, when cycling to work, he had seen an elderly man, drunk, wearing little but boots and an American Recordings T-shirt, weaving through traffic and hurling abuse at all comers. A horse called Folsom Blue ran fourth in the Irish Grand National steeplechase; it had previously been a stablemate of a horse called Empire of Dirt. A man in a Cash "Bird" shirt shoved past him in IKEA. A prizewinning stud dog in Norway was called Lovinda's Johnny Cash, a Dalmatian.

And now the Black Suspenders were in Ireland. Their show in Kilkenny was at Ryan's Bar (officially called Andrew Ryan, which appeared on the outside), famous for its music. It had posters for a wide scope of Kilkenny music festivals and other rock memorabilia: posters, tickets, and other art from some Irish but mostly American bands and artists like Bob Dylan, John Hiatt, and Jimi Hendrix. There was a large portion of the low (medieval) ceiling devoted to Polaroid shots of women's cleavage, as well as an entire wall of the same behind the bar.

The band was setting up in a small area at the front of the bar, effectively in the front window that looked out onto the street. Elvira provided updates on how things were going in her network, saying she had some updates about the Colonel Parker/Oxley project that she could only allude to, such was their sensitivity. So she had taken the offer seriously after all. She offered a fuller account of trying on Johnny and June's clothing, without drawing too many conclusions beyond the fact that it had been "fun" but "weird." They talked about the nature of how Cash fandom differed from Elvis fandom, to some degree because of its relative structural newness; Elvis has been dead for forty years and Cash less than half that. That said, Elvira pointed out something else too. Elvis operated in a relatively small network of family and fellow musicians, all of which was circumscribed by Tom Parker, and was relatively closed off to the world. Elvira encapsulated Parker's philosophy simply: "Let the people ask for more."

Johnny Cash had multiple networks, even if his bad behavior in the 1950s and 1960s led to strains in them. He lived in Arkansas, Memphis, California, and Nashville; operated in at least three major genres in the form of country, rockabilly, and folk; had four record companies; had two families; had a son-in-law in Nick Lowe, which led him to connect with modern musicians; had five legendary producers (Sam Phillips, Don Law, Bob Johnston, Jack Clement, and Rick Rubin), all of whom had their own connections as well as musical styles; and was a working and performing musician in six decades, touring the world for almost all of them. Cash also was hyperconscious of his place in popular culture; the decision to record the prison albums, host a network television show, produce a biblical epic for the cinema, make cameos on *The Simpsons* (1989–) and on U2's "The Wanderer"—all of this shows a man unafraid to engage with the world. That phenomenal mobility now extends to the networks that include fans of all ages who are adept at sharing and often creating content on YouTube, Facebook, and Twitter and other media. He wrote two autobiographies and had recently been rebranded as a poet, with the posthumous publication in 2016 by Random House of *Forever Words: The Unknown Poems,* edited by Paul Muldoon, and through that getting a quick pass into literary canonicity.

Such paths led to multiple ways for fans to come into the Johnny Cash orbit: an enormous catalog for media producers to mine for content, six decades of film and video performances, and multiple locales, unsecured by a single cultural authority. Elvira and the Dutch trying on clothes was a result of not having one holder of Cashanalia but at least four: the family, the Oxleys, Bill Miller, and Rick Rubin, plus combinations of those people.

Elvira also described divides within the family: some do not engage with the fan community while some do, such as his daughter, Kathy Cash; his sister, Joanne Cash Yates; and his brother, Tommy.

"They want to keep the legacy alive," Elvira said. The Cash family sold both the farm and Mama Cash's house without taking everything out of it, which led to that Friday in the Oxleys' home, where Theunis had access to Johnny Cash's guitar, then got to sing with Johnny Cash's grandson, and then wore the jacket of the Man in Black, all documented and now all on Facebook. "It was special," Theunis said; he also said the clothing fit was big. Such acts are part of Elvira's quest to learn more about Cash, one that cannot be completed, and to develop a network, which also does not have a finishing point. Forget closure.

Her answer was typically and comically pragmatic about the clothing. She didn't make a particularly big deal about it, instead talking about the quirks of intellectual property that had allowed them such access to what in other hands would have been untouchable heirlooms. What really commanded her interest was the people she encountered in Cashworld: "My agenda is to meet people, especially Cash people," she said. The networks allowed her to learn about "the man Cash. I want to know what he did," she said. "I find it more valuable than having albums." This suggested a change in her orientation from what had got her into setting up the Infocenter. If she had originally looked to exchange recordings, now it was to share experiences. As Elvira put it, "Not everyone sleeps in Johnny Cash's bedroom." She knew that she had benefited from being a representative fan who facilitates a huge network, and she knew that this was naturally something the Oxleys wanted to cultivate good relationships with. She had become an agent of exchange, trading her experiences as an intrepid Cash fan, an organizer, and a voyager, someone who had done this to such an extent that it seemed valuable to others.

Her networking had also led to this gig in Ireland. The time commitment involved for all concerned came up in conversation, providing a reminder about how fandom expression can be intimately connected to issues of class—at least if that is defined by income. Some of the band members had been able to plan for multiple trips during the year and still have time for a conventional summer holiday; for others, this was their annual holiday. Albert the guitarist was going to be back at work the morning after they arrived back in Holland.

Barry had only been able to become an intrepid Cash traveler owing to his retirement and his children being grown (his wife would say on Spike Island that her public-sector job did not afford her anywhere near enough days to accompany him everywhere). The wealthier people in this group (at least in terms of time and money) were also the ones who were most conspicuous in their fandom consumption, with more stuff about them and more stuff to talk about. Theunis, young and unmarried with a decent government wage, had entirely outfitted himself and his house in vintage stuff from the American 1940s and 1950s. He was enamored with Ireland, which he compared favorably to the United States. "I really like it here. I feel like home here." Of Americans, he said, "They like to talk about themselves. Here they are more interested in you." He sipped a Guinness and gazed up at the ceiling.

It turned out the small venue was appropriate for the Black Suspenders, who focus on rockabilly and country music, not all of it known to their audience. The bar's front held twenty-five to thirty-five people, which was basically the attendance for most of the evening, and it felt crowded, though not so crowded that people could not dance, which people started to do as the show got going.

There were only white people in the bar; more than 92 percent of Ireland identifies as white and just over 1 percent identify as black, so it was unremarkable that the crowd was not diverse in terms of race (Central Statistics Office 2016). It was diverse in other ways, however: there were audience members of many different age groups, and the gender breakdown was about equal. Many turned out to be language students from other European countries.

The Black Suspenders play a mix of familiar rockabilly and early country music, so they incorporate Elvis Presley's "That's All Right" and Hank Williams's "Hey Good Lookin'" in their sets as well as about a half dozen Cash songs, but they also play quite a few songs that are not immediately recognizable, from Ernest Tubb and Jimmy Rodgers.

Theunis always gives the crowd the song title and the date of the song, confirming the band's sense of historicism. Even if the song is not immediately recognizable, the genre conventions are: a small combo playing short songs at an upbeat tempo, with three to four verses and two guitar solos per song for Albert. Rhythms are precise and tight: the Black Suspenders produce rockabilly like what they promise in their promotional literature: "Pumpin, steady, ours!" The genre's relatively small range means that even

Theunis Lourens waves his hat on the ferry to Spike Island prison in Cork, Republic of Ireland, while Barry Winters rests his eyes.

when listeners do not know a particular song, they feel familiar with it. Still, within this range of familiarity, listeners knew Cash songs better and responded to them with more enthusiasm than other songs.

After the show, a man named Liam Ellis agreed he was a Cash fan, and of all the many different phases of Cash's music, entering through "Forty Shades of Green." Cotter, who was lodging the band, came over and talked about Cash's power coming from his miserable early life, growing up with nothing: "He came from that." (For the record, Cash does not really talk about impoverishment in his own storytelling; it is implied through readers' perception of stories he told as well as those about him.)

Come Sunday, the day of the Spike Island concert, Barry was waiting at the harbor, dressed for the unusually intense heat: a pair of mirror shades and a baseball cap from a police department, a plaid shirt, and shorts. They joked about them being his stage clothes. Then the Black Suspenders came up the quayside, already suited up and Stetsoned.

On the boat to the island, a man overheard Silverman's American accent and asked him where he was from. As the conversation ensued, the man (Michael Bradley) was surprised that a Cash concert was happening on the island. The facility had only ever been used for one musical event before, so it had little local profile as anything other than a museum. This again suggested that as a promoter, Barry had been unusually alert to see the potential of the island as a venue. Bradley said he was a Bruce Springsteen fan, one of many Irish people who find themselves similarly committed (that is another story), but he had a friend who gathered his friends together to sing a few songs from *At Folsom Prison* every year. Bradley was on an excursion to see the jail with his local choir group, and indeed most of these passengers were only there for the tour of the prison. The concertgoers would not arrive until considerably later.

When they disembarked, they saw the enormous structure of the prison up a hill. It was made of imposing gray stone and looked ageless and forbidding. Theunis looked like he was struggling. It turned out that his cowboy boots were not cut out for uphill walking, and he had no other footwear with him. In fact, cowboy boots were all that he owned, ten pairs in total. What we thought was his costume turned out to be his everyday clothes.

Elvira indicated where the concert would be held, at the end of the quad, in the former officer's quarters. (The cells were completely derelict, burned out in a fire several years before.) The room had a community center feel, with a small stage and enormous posters with images of Johnny Cash and his band from the Folsom Prison concert, specially made to advertise the event, contributed by the venue when they realized the extent of the ticket sales.

Barry's family had come over on the same boat: his wife, Hilda, his daughter Katie, his sister-in-law, Margaret Cotter, and Margaret's daughter, Jenny. They spoke about the traveling Barry had done in the past year. His American trip had been a sixtieth birthday present, a momentous trip of trips that in itself had taken a lot of organization, much like the current concerts. Hilda told them that Barry was a perfectionist and that he would not be anxious about the concert, but that he would nevertheless want it to be well received. She also divulged that Barry had a longer tribute performance history that was previously undisclosed; at one point, he had worked on a cruise boat to Bermuda, playing Cash and the Irish traditional music based on jigs and ballads known vernacularly as diddley-eye. It was not quite clear how this had coincided with his police work. She confirmed that he was a Cash obsessive, even measuring Katie's size at birth in Cash tapes, which summoned the memory of Charlie Taggart's son's being born to the strains of Cash's "Lost on the Desert." She also said that in her recollection, Barry began as primarily an Elvis fan; he insisted that they get married on Elvis's wedding anniversary. Barry shared some of the same origin story as Elvira, who had said in Groningen that Elvis was her entry into Cashdom. Barry demurred later on, when asked about this early preference, saying that was not how he remembered it.

Hilda spoke about his campaign to promote the concert through the internet, newspapers (both local and national), and radio stations. She called the concert "an opportunity to him," as his band could relaunch itself, but also that he regarded it as an opportunity for Cork to see both the potential of Spike Island and the vibrancy of the city's musical culture. He had been disappointed by the response of young people involved in a local video collective, who had not expressed much interest in his suggestion that they film the shows. A subsequent curiosity of the concert was that only Hinds and Silverman appeared to shoot any video of the performances, at least in terms of what was posted on Facebook or YouTube. Their footage ended up on the social media pages of both bands. The people at the shows were there to have a good experience but were not anxious about preserving that memory.

Barry later confirmed that the concert on Spike Island was a genuine triumph for him, the culmination of a year's heroic traveling and entrepreneurial activity. He had identified an opportunity for staging a prison show at Spike Island, and he had demonstrated a potential use for the facility that had previously been unexplored. Barry was interested in giving his band, Strictly Cash, a renewed profile, which surely had been some motivation for him ever since he had heard about our book project, but his overarching ambitions did not seem to center on self-promotion but rather two things: making what he regarded as apt tribute to Cash, and using that to cultivate relationships with his own community—motivations comparable to those of Elvira, Marco, Walter, and Charlie.

The Black Suspenders: Kees van der Lay, Albert Visser, Elvira van Poelgeest, and Theunis Lourens. Courtesy of Elvira van Poelgeest.

After the collapse of the Celtic Tiger, Barry had been in Cash exile, and Strictly Cash had not played for eight years. Now, in just the past year, he had been to Holland, Germany, and Austria as well as the Southern states of the United States. Now this twenty-first-century Odysseus had managed to get hundreds of people from his hometown onto boats to see him pay homage to Cash, an act that also promised to be one of renewal.

Cork is a city that enjoys the role of righteous underdog and contrarian, so it should not be a surprise that so many of its inhabitants might relate powerfully to the music of Johnny Cash. In conversation on the boat ride back to Cobh harbor after the gig, John McCullough from Cork gave a thorough indication of this connection. John had brought along his wife and six-year-old son, the youngest person at the concert. He said, "Johnny Cash is like Bob Marley. He is the working man. He went through his own phases. It's the flaws." This list of attributes could almost make Cash an honorary citizen of Cork. In the surveys, the poet-activist Dave Lordan (from Clonakilty in County Cork) said he thought of Cash in the terms of "an outlaw and a rebel and a preacher" if he had to think of him as an American. He said he liked Cash more "because he wouldn't shut up," and that he would describe him as "courageous, eloquent, witty, committed." Vicky Seaman from Cork city explained her love for Cash thus: "Because he speaks up for the underdog, and that deep voice carries so much emotion."

A colleague of Hinds later told an anecdote about another ferryboat in County Cork, going from the port of Schull to Cape Clear Island, where the pilot of the boat always sings "Forty Shades of Green" when the boat makes its return trip. Someone else had weighed in with the question, "Is that eejit still singing that bloody song on that boat?" The first colleague then took issue with the accuracy of Cash's observations in "Forty Shades of Green," claiming that there could not be fishing boats at Skibbereen (as Cash claimed) because it is a riverside and not a seaport. That is not actually what the song says, but it is what the colleague said, and he is from Cork, where they will not shut up.

Barry spoke of how his previous work in logistics for the police helped the organization of the concert: "Absolutely . . . 100 percent. We plan for every eventuality." In a Facebook message that he sent the next day in response to a video of the performance, he expanded fulsomely on this subject, indicating a desire to communicate the weight of his knowledge and experience. He threw in nice narrative touches, as when he compared the greetings that would be offered by different social classes on his beat as a policeman, which connected the poshest part of Dublin to one of the poorest:

I may have told you, but while I started out on the beat at the now closed Kill of the Grange (part of my beat was Foxrock "Good evening Officer" and Sallynoggin "Hey, Mister") I transferred into the Telecommunications Section, where one of our responsibilities was installation and maintenance of communications equipment. Planning for a special event, e.g. big matches, EU meetings, we would have to have everything covered, 2-way radios, spare batteries, emergency channels, back-up power supply and more, with contingency plans and standby equipment, in place.

He said this concert was different than it had been playing in front of actual prisoners at Mountjoy prison in Dublin: "There was tension in the prison, where we had no control." In a follow-up email, he wrote about the stark contrast between being a prisoner and performer:

> As we were leaving in the minibus, I watched a young lad, in the company of a uniformed figure of either a Garda or a prison officer, standing at the main gate. The small door opened, and the lad was ushered inside, and the door closed. It was like a curtain coming down at the end of a real life show and I could imagine it fading to black and the credits rolling, as we headed to our homes, and he was going to his new home for however long.

Barry has a powerful visual memory, as his memory of Cash's performance of "These Hands" showed; here it extended into a compassionate and poetic portrayal in which he extended his own sense of theatricality onto the drama of a life observed.

When the Black Suspenders played, the crowd was enthusiastic, especially some family and friends that had also traveled from the Netherlands. The group did not play any Cash songs, as presumably they did not want to duplicate Barry's repertoire. However, through their mix of early country and rockabilly, they did a good job giving a context for Cash's music and getting the crowd lit. They sang along raucously to Hank Williams's "Hey Good Lookin'," and Theunis proved that he had a fully evolved second life as a performer, venturing out into the crowd and dipping his hips. Kees was a brilliantly unfussy drummer, and Albert was in his studied groove. Elvira the indefatigable played a full set with the Suspenders and then also with Strictly Cash, whose regular bassist was indisposed.

Barry began with songs from *At Folsom Prison*, really hitting his stride as the set progressed. He took requests, which in itself ensured a local compact with the crowd—a sure sign that Barry was performing with them, not just in front of them. (Theunis had done the opposite, archly raising his eyebrows and being as suggestive as he could possibly be with his material.) Early in the show, Barry reiterated that his act was an expression of fandom, not impersonation: "I've been a fan for fifty years. I would never pretend to be him, but I could pay tribute to him forever."

The crowd sang along with a special enthusiasm for (inevitably) "Forty Shades of Green," "Ring of Fire," and "Thing Called Love," which never would have received the same response in the United States. The construction of

Cash being generated by Barry was as much informed by the history of that Irish reception as Barry's own preference. He was cleverly reminding an Irish audience of how they had always loved Johnny Cash. He invited a female singer up on stage to sing June Carter's parts, and then the Black Suspenders joined them for a final few songs, including a medley with another version of "Ring of Fire," "I've Been Everywhere" (performed particularly well by Barry) and, like many Cash concerts, a cover of the Carter Family's "Will the Circle Be Unbroken," which also implicitly referenced Barry's own appearance at the Carter Family Fold.

On the way back to the mainland, the crowd and the performers were buoyant. Barry had reestablished himself in his own community as the Man who Loves the Man in Black (and who wants to share the love). He did not want financial reward but rather an audience and a community. It was also a striking moment for the work on this book project, because we had originally planned that we would finish our fieldwork by organizing a concert such as this ourselves. However, the need for this had been obviated by the sheer will of Barry and the drive of Elvira.

The book had begun in the north of Ireland with Charlie, one type of Cash superfan who had no apparent need to connect to others such as himself, content with what Cash's work continued to give him, above all as a listener. Now it was concluding in the deep south of the same country with other superfans who were irrepressible and extroverted in their sense of mission, determined to meet other fans of Johnny Cash and even to turn the uninitiated into fans, doing what the man himself had always done.

AFTERWORD

The Fandom Stops for No One

Strictly Cash and Barry Winters played yet another prison concert at Spike Island in 2019, this time to celebrate the fiftieth anniversary of the San Quentin album. We were not there; Cash fandom has gone on without us. The Black Suspenders were not in attendance either, and the Infocenter has not returned to being fully operational. But the Facebook page has more than 96,000 likes, 92,000 followers, and continues to regularly post material.

While our year of following Cash fans happened mostly in person, we never stopped looking for material, and we stumbled on yet another international response of note from when Cash died in 2003. There were many tributes to him then that emphasized his support for the state of Israel and his long-term commitment to touring and working there; perhaps more surprising was a testimonial essay by Yusuf Agha (2003), which begins with a scenario of formative listening that has become familiar among Cash fans. He relocated to the United States as an adult, far from Pakistan, where he first heard Cash: "My predominant memory is of a group of teens huddled around a 45 rpm record ten thousand miles away from Nashville, listening to that commanding baritone voice and the guitar that 'played the boogie in the strangest kind of way.'" The essay veers away from nostalgia into an elegy for America. Agha sees Cash as a metonym for a complex of human values that he regards as thoroughly American. Yet Cash's death also means that America died with him: "When the Man in Black ruled the airwaves, America meant more to the world today than the image of The Terminator it has become."

As the image of Cash's America fades, new horrors come into view, and Agha (2003) identifies the rise of mutual brutalities in both of the places he has called home, the United States and Pakistan: "That America had exported the sights and sounds of freedom. It was a time when an American trotting the globe would end up as a guest at your dinner table instead of ending up headless like Daniel Pearl, when President Johnson could stop on the street amidst a thrilled crowd and invite a Pakistani camel driver to accompany him to Washington." Cash inspires powerful rhetoric from Agha, but he does something more interesting again halfway through the article, as if to offset any criticism that he was exploiting the memory of Cash only for the making of a political point. In a gesture that must be read within the context of the fan scholarship at which our subjects have excelled, Agha moves into quoting verses from a selection of Cash songs, then describing how their content offers a rebuke to a contemporary injustice. Beginning with reference to "Matthew Twenty-Four," then "The Ballad of Ira Hayes" and "The Man in Black," Cash is shown to be someone who speaks with particular authority about war and how it brutalizes soldier and citizen alike.

Agha (2003) talks about the peculiar capacity of Cash to allow listeners to process (and perhaps make sense of) their suffering: "Cash meant many things to many people, each hearing his words filter like light rays through prisms of their own anguish." Agha progressively focuses on the predicament of Palestinians as the essay comes to a conclusion, finding resonance in yet more Cash performances from across all of his career. Cash's version of the Eagles' "Desperado" leads to thoughts of the activist Rachel Corrie: "Above the notes of his music, I hear the scream of Rachel Corrie—a true portrait in American courage—crushed by an Israeli bulldozer as she firmly stands her ground, defending the rights of the downtrodden, and protecting, with frail body and outstretched hand, the house of a Palestinian family." Whether Cash himself was a supporter of Israel is beside the point, because Agha hears a fundamental expression of justice in his performance that transcends such a concern. What he loves about Cash's music is what also drives him to speak out about the other things that passionately concern him. He uses Cash's example as a means of examining himself and his relationship to the world; the point is not to duplicate Cash's politics but to refer to them as a way to get readers to understand his.

In a sense, to love Cash is to use him as a way of thinking about your own place in the world, and when thinking about the world, Cash serves as a portal to understanding what his fans value. Cash gives his fans the space to remain themselves, as the subjects of our study have shown; yet at the same time their fandom exists in porous and dynamic negotiation with the rest of the world. Charlie uses Cash to swat away the divisions of his society, while online commentators debate life, love, and death; Pedro tells racists they cannot like rockabilly even as a neo-Nazi slips into his Cash T-shirt at Charlottesville. The Cash family wanted to distance their father from that man's fandom, but they could only really question the rightness of his fandom, rather than his right to it. The whole question of what a fan is, and who that fan is, is the inevitable outcome of these concerns.

In this book, we spend a lot of time in the material world of fandom, but the way the world transacts much of its business is through the digital, and accordingly, the digital realm undergirds the way we came to and approached our subjects. Agha's 2003 article appears via an online search of "Johnny Cash and Palestine," a search that followed our discovery of Hip Hughes putting on his Cash T-shirt to explain the politics of the Middle East. "Searching for Johnny Cash (Online)" could well be the book's subtitle; it would not just apply to us but to the subjects, who of course have done their own googling. Fandom adapts to the latest technological advances in ways that are obvious (Facebook groups versus newsletters) and less so (GPS and travel search engines). Whatever tool is front of Cash fans, they will use: clicking on a YouTube video to write a comment, posting to YouTube their band's cover of "Ring of Fire," or arranging for themselves to perform live with Johnny Cash's brother.

If technology in this way makes the Cashworld smaller and threatens to flatten its fandom into a globalized sameness, Cash fan behaviors nevertheless remain sui generis. One could probably not play publicly with Elvis's relatives, as Barry did with Tommy Cash, or wear Bruce Springsteen's clothing in a house he bought for his mother. Cash remains in play, and people remain excited and excitable about him everywhere. Portugal proved how young people are drawn to Cash, who perceive him as universal and present, rather than only part of the American past.

The contributor to the online Johnny Cash Project who identified herself as Deborah from Nowhere sums up the problem of trying to overcategorize fans. There is a resonant lonesomeness in this that seems very Cashlike; it also revives the problem of trying to map voices in cyberspace to physical reality, and whether it matters. Deborah's nowhereness is both a state of freedom and homelessness, an existential zone where you are as rooted or deracinated as you might want to be.

Yet this project has established that it still matters where people come from, and if Deborah says she is from Nowhere, that too has to be regarded as a place, the same as Tomb, Omagh, or Coimbra. The desire to see and feel and hear other countries may actually be increasing by virtual fandom. It certainly allows for networks of the interested and committed to emerge, and they let each other know that there are worlds beyond screens. The range of geographical participation in the Johnny Cash project, and in Johnny Cash fandom altogether, allows for an understanding of the world as friendlier than it might seem through the headlines.

If Cash is now only another thing to pass through cyberspace, a matter of virtual reality, then why did people from dozens of countries visit a small town in Arkansas to see Johnny Cash's boyhood home? In a world increasingly without digital borders, physical ones still mean something. Cash enabled these people to enjoy the particular pleasure that comes from crossing a border, to leave their communities behind; yet they also went home, bringing something back, bound by wild desire.

APPENDIX

The How, Where, and Why of Cash Fandom

Theory and Methodology

This book began with the idea of studying Johnny Cash's international fandom as a cultural phenomenon that is based on a shared experience of encountering Johnny Cash fans in divergent ways. The initial project morphed into a series of hybrid processes: a qualitative survey; ethnographic/journalistic accounts of meeting fans; close readings of photographs, YouTube videos, and comments; and analysis of texts, both visual and literary. Marcia J. Bates (1989) calls the method of using evolving multiple methods "berrypicking." In berrypicking, "end users may begin with just one feature of a broader topic, or just one relevant reference, and move through a variety of sources. Each new piece of information they encounter gives them new ideas and directions to follow and, consequently, a new conception of the query."

Thinking about what they had discovered through a survey and their initial experiences, we decided to begin interviewing fans, in particular Elvira van Poelgeest, the head of the Johnny Cash Infocenter, whom we interviewed in her residence in Groningen, the Netherlands. That experience led to a series of interviews and immersive experiences that ended up constituting the book. As Daniel Cavicchi notes in his study of Bruce Springsteen fans, there is a complexity of impulses that inform fan experience, and by implication fan study: "Fandom is not a bounded entity to be discovered and commented on, or a problem to be questioned and answered; it is a complex, private yet shared, ongoing experience" (1998, 18). Studies of fandom frequently come up against the sheer diversity of modes of behavior and identification that may relate to it; as Mark Duffett writes, "Fandom can indeed involve different experiences, concern different practices and mean different things in various contexts" (2013, 19). In other words, berrypicking falls within the range of normal fandom investigations.

Consequently, interviewing and observing fans, and interpreting their behavior is in the tradition of many fan studies, including Henry Jenkins' *Textual Poachers* (1992; rev ed. 2002) and Janice Radway's *Reading the Romance* ([1984] 1991). Radway's work is on readers of romance fiction, fans by another name, and although the theoretical contexts were different when she was writing, her basic semiotic theory about everything being a text is useful for thinking through the singularity of international Cash fans: "If reading varied spatially and temporally, and one did wish to use literature in an effort to reconstruct culture, it would be necessary to connect particular texts with the communities that produced and consumed them and to make some effort to specify how the individuals involved actually constructed those texts as meaningful semiotic structures" (3; see also Lewis 1992). Engaging with fans directly means that fans also begin to generate events and discussion out of that engagement, providing material for analysis but also selecting what kind of content they think will be productive for the study.

Our goal was to put into context these fan behaviors over time and place, attempting what Lucy Bennett calls a "re-centering of ethnographical observations and the voice of fans." Bennett writes, "Within contemporary fan studies scholarship may be timely and useful—asking them to articulate their understandings of these different platforms, and how they negotiate digital technologies and relations with texts and producers, may move us toward a more comprehensive methodological approach more suited for today's media landscape and the uncharted research terrains" (2014). Gray et al. also align themselves with the idea behind the third wave of fandom studies, one that focuses on "the individual motivations, enjoyment, and pleasures of fans" (2007, 5). Morimoto notes, "By way of shifting the focus of transnational fan studies to actual fan activities and understandings, recent work . . . argues that any nuanced discussion of the fandoms that grow up around transnationally circulating media must account for how and why such media circulates outside its own industrial or national context" (2017).

The answer to the question of international Cash fandom could of course lie in the intrinsic appeal of Johnny Cash himself, but it also needs to be considered in terms of the peculiar cultural circumstances that might have brought fans to him. It was interesting to see how Johnny Cash addressed Norway or Ireland, but also to see how they addressed him.

As Morimoto notes, one of the issues regarding international fandom is that of maintaining agency when encountering corporations who could "effectively create a homogenous global culture distinguished by one-way flows from first to third world nations, the erosion of indigenous cultures in favor of a universal culture of mass consumption, and the consolidation of power into the hands of the few" (2017). The complexity of fan behaviors that we discovered during this project, however, was mostly outside of commercial concerns and was only tangentially engaged in American corporate capitalism. The variety of digital and technological levels of engagement that we encountered suggests that many fans have at best a metacognitive engagement with corporate capitalism (they are happy to stay in chain hotels, eat mediocre American pseudo fast food, watch American blockbusters, and drink mediocre American beer), but they find their own ways through engagement with Cash.

Europeans chug Starbucks beverages and eat Subway sandwiches at home, but they do not think of Johnny Cash as belonging to that particular cultural flow. Our work suggests that American cultural hegemony, the soft power of cultural domination, is not directly engaged by Cash fans. Rather, highly engaged fans are interested in what is available, both in commercial and underground markets. As Duffett notes, consumption in fandom has to be read discriminatingly, not least because conventional consumers are so often regarded as all too easily manipulated by the forces of capital, and fans like to think that they know what they are doing with their money: "Both fans and academics have rejected 'the consumer' as a shameful identity" (2013, 23). This project found people willing to commit huge resources not only to acquire objects but also to foster relationships. If they must be described in economic terms, such fans are more aptly described as investors rather than consumers.

Not only that, but Cash cultural products are created by fans themselves, and thus far, the Cash estate seems inclined to empower fans to do so. As Lincoln Geraghty notes in discussing the Star Trek franchise, fandom studies has encouraged people to study not only the text itself (Johnny Cash) but also what fans create in participating in fandom about Johnny Cash, such as the YouTube covers of "Ring of Fire" we study: "So, rather than studying *Star Trek* as a cult text, we might study fan-produced videos on YouTube as important texts of fan activity that carry inherent meaning and significant in and of themselves" (2015, 1).

In a way, focusing on fan engagement and empowerment is more logical because of this emphasis on text rather than institution and national identity. What seems more important are the degree and mediums associated with fandom rather than national identity, which Morimoto (2017) calls transcultural fandom. C. Lee Harrington and Denise D. Bielby note that "given rapid advances in technological distribution and evolving formal trade agreements, fan studies scholars have recently turned from the study of imported media to the notion of global media texts and internationally dispersed audiences" (2007, 180). There are tensions between producers and consumers, however, and in Cash fandom, this centered on issues that Elvira and Marco both expressed as the inadequacy of conventional media in representing people like them. This also implies that their voices are at least as authoritative as those of the conventional media experts drawn from the music press, or for that matter academia. As Henry Jenkins notes, "Media consumers want to become media producers, while media producers want to maintain their traditional dominance over media content" (2006, 554). The internet has allowed fans on all levels to participate in the making of meaning, as Jenkins notes: "The Net opened up new space for public discussions of media content and the web became an important showcase for grassroots cultural production" (555). Our study shows that Cash fandom has become a particularly dynamic zone of such production.

Our own scholarly and national differences from one another could be called transcultural as well as transnational; both as music fans steeped in American cultural production and as academics, we have plenty in common. At the same time, differences necessarily emerged during the writing of the book, and in particular over the degree of culture-specific explanation that was necessary to showing how Cash fandom emerged in a particular place. To understand the political significance of a Portuguese cover of "Folsom Prison Blues" requires contextualization, as does the language peculiar to the East End of London if fans connected to there are communicating with one another in slang. What was self-explanatory to one of us was not necessarily so to the other; this of course could extend to considerations of Cash, who was not necessarily popular to the same degree (and at the same time) in different parts of the world.

The work took place between Europe and America in a tumultuous political context, with the rolling news stories of the Trump presidency, Brexit, and the rise of various extremisms across the world constantly casting a shadow over discourse. Johnny Cash leads people to think about politics, reflecting critically on their own situation and that of others, not necessarily what might be said of other American recording artists. The Charlottesville incident also demonstrates the value of Cash as a political agent, as he was claimed by opposing ideologies. More than ever, Cash appears as a model American but also as a model person and citizen, to the degree that it is a vital part of his mythology. If people could vote for him, they would.

Johnny Cash has also always been a musician whose work seems simpler than it really is. He and his promoters designed it that way, especially in the eras of Bob Johnston (producer of the prison albums) and Rick Rubin (American Recordings producer), with a focus on perceived simplicity in constructing his persona, his songwriting, and the methods of production. Yet Cash's work now has a radically active life online. That shift in culture has affected his fandom and how we study it. As Paul Booth and Peter Kelly (2013) note, "As the internet has widened the scope of fan practices, so too has it allowed fan researchers to engage in new methods of analysis." Cavicchi has addressed a consequent problem, however, particularly in how periodicity in fandom has altered through the relationship of fans to media: "Today's fans are seen as the result of social media and 'narrowcasting,' yesterday's, by default, should be seen as the result of the culture industry and 'broadcasting.'" This in turn creates a difficulty for engaging with fandom in all of its historicity, and Cavicchi stresses how "the challenge is exacerbated by contemporary disciplinarity, which tends to limit scholars' perspectives" (2014, 53). This study has attempted to suggest that such perspectives currently not only coexist but also contribute to one another. The web led Elvira and the Irish tribute singer Barry Winters to meet, and within a year, they had both led fan odysseys to the United States and performed Cash's music across borders, both independently and together. The narrowcast became a broadcast.

Fans can gravitate toward one another, whether virtually or in person, and what they have done together as fans is an essential part of what fan studies scholars assess. Fans may operate independently; their identities are necessarily fused with others. At the same time, as Booth and Kelly (2013) note, "fandom as an identity necessarily entails duality: one is oneself, but also one is part of a larger group. That group today may be augmented by digital technology, but it has not been supplanted by it. Far from limiting relationships, technology today seems to help strengthen and build them—as fans have always done." It should be added that this plays out for fandom studies too; many of its most urgent debates manifest in blogs and other web forums.[1]

In terms of identity, fans' self-identification in terms of gender, race, and class is harder to explore. In terms of gender, in our work we did not find much evidence in Cash fandom of the "gender-related subjectivities of Beatles fans," as noted by Christine Scodari (2007, 49), but it should be conceded that this is because it was not what we were looking for, and it is not what these particular fan subjects sought to talk about. However, it is instructive to look at Elvira's experiences running the online Johnny Cash Infocenter; her pioneering work in new media as a communicator of Cash's legacy would lead her into encounters with power structures within the business of Cash fandom that were predictably male in practice and profile. Yet a brief exchange with her indicated that she did not think that she had a negative incident related to gender in her work as a Cash fan: "I haven't heard any positive or negative things about it. Only people who are enthusiastic once I tell them about it and then have a nice conversation going about why I like Cash and started the whole thing. More genuine interest" (pers. comm., J.S., September 14, 2018).

Like Elvira, subjects in this study characteristically did not foreground issues of gender politics, at least in terms of struggle. Yet in talking with both Walter Ringhofer and Charlie Taggart, they volunteered answers that indicated how Cash had become part of the fabric of their marriage, and Charlie had his wife come to both of the interviews we conducted with him. Cash was "the other man" in their marriage, yet it seemed a contented form of cohabitation. In this way, the politics of reproduction did intervene in the story, as it showed the abiding power of the family unit for not only these fans but also their cultural context. Bringing family into their fandom may be read as evidence of a desire to make their fandom socially respectable, to seem like a less self-driven endeavor. Cash fandom became an extra offspring.[2]

Issues of race in Cash fandom inevitably center on its long association with whiteness, though Cash's appeal is broader in terms of genre than most country artists. It is surely significant that Cash plays big in Ireland and

Norway, relatively monoracial cultures until recently. Yet as the afterword shows, Cash reached teenagers in Pakistan, and his music has been appropriated and sampled by reggae and hip-hop artists to a degree that confirms both his worth and exchangeability as cultural capital. Yet the incidents in Charlottesville also indicate a countertendency that wants to claim Cash for whiteness, leading to yet another counterblast from the Cash family. Cash fans are predominantly white, and they come from prosperous countries with predominantly white populations; however, in practice, Cash fans necessarily engage with race, not least because of how Cash writes about it in diverse ways, and with particular focus on the Native American experience. Once a European fan travels to Arkansas or Tennessee, the Cash trail is also a journey through a geopolitical landscape that projects racial politics in a way that they have never seen back home. As such, whether consciously or subconsciously, they see the vestiges of the cotton economy out of which Cash emerged, and that inevitably leads back to slavery.[3]

Another factor that must be acknowledged is class. New technologies mean that music and video can be accessed with remarkable facility, but this is the case only if you can afford or have access to an internet connection. The other manifestations of fandom involve potentially massive expenditures: fan tourism, travel and tickets to shows, sourcing and bidding for rare materials, investing in instruments and music lessons (for those who opt to emulate Cash through performance), not to mention looking the part.[4] A T-shirt is a pretty democratic fan artifact, but a Nashville-sourced pair of cowboy boots might not be. When looking at responses to the international fan surveys, the most engaged countries were also the richest countries, with Northern Europe featuring strongly. This does not necessarily imply that people from wealthier countries like Cash more than others, but it definitely suggests that they have more resources to commit to express that like.

However the cost of fannish activity is measured, every Cash fan has his or her own story to tell. To conceive of how these stories come together, they can be seen as performing the kind of historical narrative that Georg Lukács describes as "not the re-telling of great historical events but the poetic awakening of the people who figured in those events" (1983, 42). So a narrative like Tolstoy's 1869 classic *War and Peace* does not omit Napoleon but pushes him to the margins, shifting the focus instead to how the lives of ordinary people are affected by larger forces, moving them one way or the other. They are the true markers of history, even if they are not credited as its makers.

These Cash fans and their stories combine to prove the impact of Johnny Cash, but also to show how they were simultaneously affected by both him and the forces of history. It is no surprise that these protagonists should be drawn to Cash fandom: Cash himself often sang about such people, characters he brought into significance by showing how they were at the wrong or right end of circumstance. Just as Cash evokes a world in which people live through dilemmas and intensities of experience, international Cash fans live for the pleasure of following Cash, and we know that they do so with their own peculiar integrity.

NOTES

Introduction

1. The amount of biographical work on Johnny Cash is rapidly expanding. The best place to start is Johnny Cash's own autobiography: *Johnny Cash: The Autobiography* (New York: HarperCollins, 1997); it is funny and weird and unexpectedly revealing for those who think they know him through his popular portrayals. Leigh Edwards's *Johnny Cash and the Paradox of American Identity* (Bloomington: Indiana University Press, 2009) is an excellent scholarly review of his life. Robert Hilburn's *Johnny Cash: A Life* (New York: Little, Brown, 2013) is a thoughtful, thorough biography. There are many books by former band mates, friends, and family members, all of which have their merits. One other book worth noting is Michael Streissguth's *Johnny Cash at Folsom Prison* (Boston: Da Capo Press, 2005); it reveals a great deal about Cash in his heyday in the 1960s, as does Robert Elfstrom's documentary, *The Man, His World, His Music* (1969). Christopher S. Wren's *Winners Got Scars Too: The Life of Johnny Cash* (1971) got there first, did not overexplain, and left an honest record of Cash's life.

2. Video addresses are available through searching posters' names; they are also listed in our bibliography. The ephemeral nature of YouTube posting is well established. These videos were available at press time unless otherwise noted. Research on them was done in the summer of 2018. All our communications with our subjects that were in person are cited journalistically—in other words, they are quoted in context. We include web addresses or sites of the various entities that have a specific web presence—for example, we listed the Johnny Cash Infocenter website because it is a cultural marker in itself. Anything else may be found either in our bibliography or through a web search.

Chapter 1

1. In 1980, Big Tom resorted to crossing the Atlantic by ship in order to fulfill his ambition of recording in Nashville.

2. According to the Johnny Cash Infocenter (http://www.johnny-cash-info-center.com/), Cash played the following venues in Norway: Mommen (November 4, 1983), Stavanger (April 4, 1986), Oslo (August 26, 1987; April 4, 1992; August 30, 1992; April 12, 1997), Kristiansand (August 27, 1987), and Bergen (April 3, 1997).

Chapter 2

1. The statement was communicated via Rosanne Cash's Facebook page and was entitled "A Message from the Children of Johnny Cash." It received extensive press coverage. The hot response of the Cash children could be compared to the diffidence of Donald Trump's words ("There are good people on both sides") about the protests, which led to the death of one antifascist protestor, killed after a neo-Nazi ran over her with his car. The message begins: "We were alerted to a video of a young man in Charlottesville, a self-proclaimed neo-Nazi, spewing hatred and bile. He was wearing a T-shirt emblazoned with the name of Johnny Cash, our father. We were sickened by the association" (Cash 2017).

2. It does not come as a surprise to find someone online from Los Angeles describing himself as Johnny Cash; see Johnny Cash Zee Barber (http://www.instapuma.com/johnnycasshh).

Chapter 3

1. All forum postings are reproduced verbatim.

2. There are endless essays about how defining "American" is problematic. Many American studies scholars consider the term itself a problem, though without much movement to change it.

3. Anderson ([1983] 2006) discusses the nature of what constitutes a country.

Chapter 4

1. There may be more. Although the Country Music Hall of Fame's archive is excellent, it doesn't have everything—for example, it has limited archives of *Strictly Cash* and does not have *The Johnny Cash Fanzine*.

2. As we will see, another Barry—Barry Winters—calls his band Strictly Cash. In looking at a Dutch fan club newsletter at the Country Music Hall of Fame and Library, Silverman found that Jan and Elvira Flederus ran the Johnny Cash

Friends: European Fanclub out of Dalfsen, Netherlands, with a newsletter date for number 56 of August–September 1978.

Chapter 5

1. In Scotland and Wales, he played Glasgow and Cardiff, cities also celebrated for their peculiar grit.

2. Leigh Edwards (2009) discusses this trope. See Fox (2004) and Ellison (1995) for this phenomenon in general.

3. In a 1987 interview with *Woman's Own* magazine, Thatcher famously said, "There's no such thing as society."

4. This has been attributed to Wilde, although no proper source for it appears to exist.

5. Winstone's tough-guy filmography includes *Scum* (1980), *Sexy Beast* (2001), *The Proposition* (2005), and *Beowulf* (2007).

6. Homeless Paul is clearly something of a local celebrity around the University of Manchester; he appears in several YouTube videos, including one for "Cocaine Blues," posted by John Mannion on May 19, 2016. This YouTube video, shot at night on a phone, features Homeless Paul reciting "Cocaine Blues" perfectly and rhythmically. Mannion posts the description: "Paul is a homeless man from Bolton on the streets of Manchester." He also manages a few lines of "A Thing Called Love."

Chapter 6

1. A good indication of this can be derived from looking at the items listed on the *International Fan Club Newsletter*'s Trading Post section; more than thirty of those items were available on eBay as of July 2018.

2. It turns out that Plato is in fact a chain of independent record stores across the Netherlands—proof of the abiding popularity of traditional trends of music consumption in the country—but Plato also runs an online store. The Cash people in Groningen whom we talked to knew of the store but did not seem to shop there very often.

3. Cash and Carter feature on the passenger side, along with a smaller image of Cash smiling with a guitar. The driver's side bears an image of the later Cash perched on his guitar; next to it is a smaller image of Cash on an American flag. The transport-bed side has an image of Johnny Cash at San Quentin on one side

and an album-type image of the Highwaymen (the supergroup of Cash, Merle Haggard, Willie Nelson, and Kris Kristofferson) on the other side. Topping it off is the image of Johnny Cash giving the bird to the crowd at San Quentin on the back of the cab—an image that would not likely be visible with a payload.

Chapter 7

1. It is thus not surprising, for example, that the texts often referred to by You-Tube commenters in saying how they came to know Cash's song "The Man Comes Around" are two movie blockbusters: *Logan* and *Dawn of the Dead*.

2. Several schoolteachers indicated to us the educational usefulness, for all age groups, of Cash in the course of this project.

3. For a discussion of fans who create videos to evoke emotional responses, see Pennington (2016).

4. We think the most frequently watched YouTube video of Cash performing is JohnnyCashRingofFire (February 24, 2009), which had twenty-six million views as of August 28, 2018, although Demonicgrinch's (YouTube, April 15, 2007) emoji version boasts thirty-one million views.

5. Wikipedia lists the following participants in the video: David Allan Coe, Patricia Arquette, Travis Barker, Peter Blake, Bono, Sheryl Crow, Johnny Depp, the Dixie Chicks, Flea, Billy Gibbons, Whoopi Goldberg, Woody Harrelson, Dennis Hopper, Terrence Howard, Jay-Z, Mick Jones, Kid Rock, Anthony Kiedis, Kris Kristofferson, Amy Lee, Adam Levine, Shelby Lynne, Chris Martin, Kate Moss, Graham Nash, Busy Philipps, Iggy Pop, Lisa Marie Presley, Q-Tip, Corinne Bailey Rae, Keith Richards, Chris Rock, Rick Rubin, Patti Smith, Sharon Stone, Justin Timberlake, Kanye West, Brian Wilson, and Owen Wilson. The poster suggests that these celebrities are a form of diabolical chorus (with an Illuminati-style triangulation of hands at the video's end to support this), not seeking humility but merely stating their damnedness as a condition of their eliteness. Where Cash stands in relation to this appears almost irrelevant. The video is in fact too powerful for the song, given how insistently it makes you think about the globalized phenomenon of celebrity culture, which inevitably inspires distrust. Some of the participants in the video cry, some look to heaven, and some affect gestures of piety, yet every gesture is readable as hypocritical.

6. Žižek writes: "If anything, Cash's description evokes the well-known scene of people lined up for a brutal interrogation, and the informer pointing out those selected for torture: there is no mercy, no forgiveness of sins, no jubilation; we are all fixed in our roles: the just remain just and the filthy remain filthy. Even worse, in this divine proclamation, we are not simply judged in a just way; we are

informed from outside, as if learning about an arbitrary decision, that we were righteous or sinners, that we are saved or condemned—this decision has nothing to do with our inner qualities. And again, this dark excess of ruthless divine sadism—excess over the image of a severe, but nonetheless just, God—is a necessary negative, an underside, of the excess of Christian love over the Jewish Law: love which suspends the Law is necessarily accompanied by the arbitrary cruelty which also suspends the Law" (2006, 186–87).

Chapter 8

1. Carson (1986) provides a classical model for interpreting "Ring of Fire."
2. A segment on *The Johnny Cash Show* titled "The History of Country Music Part 2," broadcast on January 27, 1971.

Chapter 9

1. Camus's *L'Etranger* was first published by Gallimard in 1942, and the first English translation, by Stuart Gilbert, appeared in 1946. Camus actually rejects the connection between his novel and existentialism despite the remarks of others. See Raskin (2001).
2. For a history of the international impact of existentialism as both style and thought, see Blackwell (2016).

Chapter 10

1. For an explanation of how text tourism manifests itself in other media, see Reijnders et al. (2015).

Chapter 11

1. Although it is hard to photograph at Graceland, given that the visitor is also carrying around the iPad that is provided with the tour.

Chapter 12

1. "My conviction was that the world was missing out on not hearing what I heard as a child. Memphis was the inducement—I mean, going out and hearing a black man pick a guitar and pat his foot and put a wood box under his feet as he sings . . . I said 'I've just got to open me a little recording studio, where I can at

least experiment with some of this overlooked humanity." Sam Phillips quoted in Guralnick (2015, 63).

2. It is important to note here that while Theunis's English is excellent, it is not his first language, and sometimes his responses appear to be shorter and less complex than the thought behind them. He is always a willing subject, but it is also clear that he does not think in English in the ready way that Elvira does.

3. Silverman did not pay because he did not even knock on the door; he had gotten there just after dawn and was not going to disturb anyone.

4. For a discussion of the term "cultural pilgrim" as well as a discussion of Graceland as a pilgrimage site, see Margry (2008) and Doss (2008).

5. These discussions took place in front of the museum on May 9, 2018.

Chapter 13

1. In 1970, the *New York Times,* in its obituary of Salazar by Alden Whitman, gave a good sense of his infectious anticharisma: "An anomaly among modern dictators, Antonio de Oliveira Salazar exemplified the power of a negative personality. He was ascetic rather than exuberant; aloof rather than gregarious; professorial rather than demagogic; understated rather than ostentatious. Yet he held Portugal in thralldom for more than 40 years, a record of durability unmatched by Francisco Franco, Benito Mussolini or Adolf Hitler, his flashier Fascist counterparts and good friends."

2. This recalls Quentin Tarantino's using his time as a video store clerk as a way of educating himself about filmmaking (Kotb 2004).

3. After Greece, Portugal was the European country that was hardest hit in the financial crises of the twenty-first century. A fair account of its crisis can be found in Badkar (2013).

4. The Legendary Tigerman's 2003 album *Fuck Christmas, I Got the Blues* requires no explanation.

5. A brief discography includes the Tédio Boys's *Porkabilly Psychosis* (1994, https://rastilho.bandcamp.com/album/porkabilly-psychosis) (which contains "Folsom Prison Blues"), *Outer Space Shit* (1996), *Fuck the Beatles, Go Country!* (1997), *Bad Trip* (1998), and *Jungle* (1999).

Chapter 14

1. Ideas of closure and other psychoaffective aspects of fandom are effectively explored in Williams (2018, esp. 19–30).

2. "Hurt" is not a Johnny Cash original, but his arrangement is distinct from the Nine Inch Nails original. It is easy to tell the difference.

Appendix

1. There are too many online discussions of fandom to cite exhaustively, but the work of acafan Henry Jenkins in engaging with international fandom and related issues is useful to anyone looking to further contextualize their explorations. See Henry Jenkins's blog, "Confessions of an Aca-Fan" (https://henryjenkins.org/).

2. Useful scholarship on Cash and gender can be found in Edwards's (2009) exploration of masculinity, and there has also been scholarship done on Johnny Cash's status as a lesbian icon (Ortega 1995).

3. Pande's 2018 study was regrettably published too late to inform the practice of our research, but it provides multiple academic contexts for how it can be reinterpreted.

4. Marshall (2003) is helpful in exploring the collecting work that was Elvira van Poelgeest's pathway into a fuller exploration of Cash fandom. Doss (1999) remains canonical and vital in considering how and why fans build collections, and invites comparisons with the curation of Cash materials. In terms of tourism in fandom discourse, see Zubernis and Larsen (2018). Geraghty (2018) is also of direct relevance. See also Lundberg and Ziakas (2018, 203–13).

REFERENCES

Adorno, Theodor. 1959. "Words from Abroad." *Notes to Literature* 2 (2): 187–88.

Adorno, Theodor. 2002. *The Jargon of Authenticity*. London: RKP.

Agha, Yusuf. 2003. "Cry, Cry, Cry: Johnny Cash, America, Palestine." Yellow Times, September 15, 2003. http://www.axisoflogic.com/artman/publish/ Article_1550.shtml.

Anderson, Benedict. (1983) 2006. *Imagined Communities: Reflections on the Origin and Spread of Nationalism*. Rev. ed. New York: Verso.

Aprilgriffin. 2012. "Johnny." DeviantArt, August 16, 2012. https://www.deviantart .com/aprilgriffin/art/Johnny-321452531.

Badkar, Mamta. 2013. "How Portugal Became a Horrific Economic Mess." Business Insider, April 12, 2013. https://www.businessinsider.com/portugals-economic-crisis-overview-2013-4?IR=T.

Barthes, Roland. 1972. *Mythologies*. London: Fontana.

Barthes, Roland. 1977. "The Grain of the Voice." In *Image-Music-Text*, 179–89. Translated by Stephen Heath. London: Fontana Press.

Bates, Marcia J. 1989. "The Design of Browsing and Berrypicking Techniques for the Online Search Interface." Online Review 13 (5): 407–24.

Baym, Nancy K. 2018. *Playing to the Crowd: Musicians, Audiences, and the Intimate Work of Connection*. New York: New York University Press.

Benjamin, Walter. (1937) 1985. "Eduard Fuchs, Collector and Historian." In *One-Way Street and Other Writings*, 349–86. Translated by Edmund Jephcott and Kingsley Shorter. New York: Verso.

Bennett, Andy, and Richard A. Peterson, eds. 2004. "Introducing Music Scenes." In *Music Scenes: Local, Translocal, and Virtual*, 1–16. Nashville: Vanderbilt University Press.

Bennett, Lucy. 2014. "Tracing Textual Poachers: Reflections on the Development of Fan Studies and Digital Fandom." *Journal of Fandom Studies* 2 (1): 5–20.

Berger, Monica. 2008. "Scholarly Monographs on Rock Music: A Bibliography Essay." *Collection Building* 27 (1): 5–20.

Bishop, Josh, dir. *Made in Japan*. 2015.

Blackwell, Sarah. 2016. *At the Existentialist Café: Freedom, Being, and Apricot Cocktails*. New York: Knopf.

Blakemore, Erin. 2017. "Why Hate Groups Went After Johnny Cash in the 1960s." History.com, August 2, 2017. https://www.history.com/news/why-hate-groups-went-after-johnny-cash-in-the-1960s.

Bokula. 2009. "Johnny Cash: The Real RocknRolla." DeviantArt, December 27, 2009. https://www.deviantart.com/bokula/art/Johnny-Cash-148184026.

Booth, Paul. 2010. *Digital Fandom: New Media Studies*. New York: Peter Lang.

Booth, Paul, and Peter Kelly. 2013. "The Changing Faces of *Doctor Who* Fandom: New Fans, New Technologies, Old Practices?" *Participations* 10 (1): 56–72. https://www.participations.org/Volume%2010/Issue%201/5%20Booth%20&%20Kelly%2010.1.pdf.

Brickell, Katherine, and Ayona Datta. 2011. Introduction to *Translocal Geographies: Spaces, Places, Connections*, edited by Katherine Birckell and Ayona Datta, 3–22. London: Ashgate.

Butor, Michel. 1994. "Bricolage: An Interview with Michel Butor." Conducted by Noah Guynn. *Yale French Studies* 84: 17–26.

Caffeinegoddess. 2003. "Cash Man Johnny." DeviantArt, October 31, 2003. https://www.deviantart.com/caffeinegoddess/art/Cash-Man-Johnny-3657699.

Carson, Anne. 1986. *Eros the Bittersweet*. London: Dalkey Archive.

Cash, John Carter. 2011. *House of Cash: The Legacies of My Father, Johnny Cash*. San Rafael, CA: Insight Editions.

Cash, Johnny. 1997. *Johnny Cash: The Autobiography*. New York: HarperCollins.

Cash, Rosanne. 2017. "A Message from the Children of Johnny Cash." Facebook, August 16, 2017. https://www.facebook.com/RosanneCash/posts/a-message-from-the-children-of-johnny-cashwe-were-alerted-to-a-video-of-a-young-/10155413372345336/.

Cavicchi, Daniel. 1998. *Tramps Like Us: Music and Meaning among Springsteen Fans*. Oxford: Oxford University Press.

Cavicchi, Daniel. 2014. "Fandom before 'Fan': Shaping the History of Enthusiastic Audiences." *Reception* 6: 52–72.

Central Statistics Office. 2016. "Census of Population 2016—Profile 8 Irish Travellers, Ethnicity and Religion." Central Statistics Office. https://www.cso.ie/en/releasesandpublications/ep/p-cp8iter/p8iter/p8e/.

Chapman, Robert. 1990. "The 1960s Pirates: A Comparative Analysis of Radio London and Radio Caroline." *Popular Music* 9 (2): 165–78.

Chatty Mouth. 2006. "Johnny Cash's 'Ring of Fire' in Jamaican Music." Chatty Mouth: Reggae, Rants and Reasoning (forum), February 20, 2006. http://djgreedyg.proboards.com/thread/5345.

Chin, Bertha, and Lori Hitchcock Morimoto. 2013. "Towards a Theory of Transcultural Fandom." *Participations* 10 (1): 92–108. https://www.participations.org/Volume%2010/Issue%201/7%20Chin%20&%20Morimoto%2010.1.pdf.

City Jackdaw. 2016. "If a Drunken Donald Sutherland Did Johnny Cash." City Jackdaw: Notes on a Life, March 18, 2016. https://cityjackdaw.wordpress.com/2016/03/18/if-a-drunken-donald-sutherland-did-johnny-cash/.

Coates, Ben. 2015. *Why the Dutch Are Different*. London: Hachette UK.

Craig, R. Stephen. 1986. "The American Forces Network, Europe: A Case Study in Military Broadcasting." *Journalism of Broadcasting and Electronic Media* 30 (1): 30–46.

Crawford, Richard. 2001. *America's Musical Life: A History*. New York: Norton.

Crystal, David. 2012. *English as a Global Language*. Cambridge: Cambridge University Press.

Danois, Ericka Blount. 2018. "The Soul of Stax Records." WaxPoetics, September 12, 2018. http://www.waxpoetics.com/blog/features/articles/the-soul-of-stax/.

de Grazia, Victoria. 1989. "Mass Culture and Sovereignty: The American Challenge to European Cinemas, 1920–1960." *Journal of Modern History* 61 (1): 53–87.

Desert Island Discs. BBC Radio 4. January 2, 2015.

Doss, Erika. 1999. *Elvis Culture: Fans, Faith, and Image*. Lawrence: University of Kansas Press.

Doss, Erika. 2008. "Rock and Roll Pilgrims: Reflections on Ritual, Religiosity, and Race at Graceland." In *Shrines and Pilgrimage in the Modern World*, edited by Peter Jan Margry, 123–42. Amsterdam: Amsterdam University Press.

Duffett, Mark. 2012. "Boosting Elvis: A Content Analysis of Editorial Stories from One Fan Club Magazine." *Participations* 9 (2): 317–36. https://www.participations.org/Volume%209/Issue%202/18%20Duffett.pdf.

Duffett, Mark. 2013. *Understanding Fandom: An Introduction to the Study of Media Fan Culture*. London: Bloomsbury.

Duggan, Seamus. 2006. "The Johnny Cash Appreciation Society." Vapour Trails, June 2, 2006. http://theknockingshop.blogspot.com/2010/09/johnny-cash-appreciation-society.html.

"Edmond Rivero." n.d. Todo Tango. http://www.todotango.com/english/artists/info/300/Edmundo-Rivero.

Edwards, Leigh. 2009. *Johnny Cash and the Paradox of American Identity.* Bloomington: Indiana University Press.

Ellison, Curtis W. 1995. *Country Music Culture: From Hard Times to Heaven.* Oxford: University Press of Mississippi.

Eurovision Times. 2010. "ESC History: How a Eurovision Song Started a Revolution." Eurovision Times, October 11, 2010. https://eurovisiontimes .wordpress.com/2010/10/11/esc-histroy-how-a-eurovision-song-started-a-revolution/.

Fiedler, Leslie A. 1960. *No! In Thunder: Essays on Myth and Literature.* Boston: Beacon Press.

Fox, Aaron. 2004. *Real Country: Music and Language in Working-Class Culture.* Durham, NC: Duke University Press.

"Frank Chisum." n.d. Irish Showbands. https://www.irish-showbands.com/ images/dwane/ddxfrankchisum88.htm.

Fruoco, Jonathan. 2017. "Johnny Cash: Un Héros aux Mille et un Visages." Pop en Stock, August 27, 2017. http://www.academia.edu/34436579/Johnny_Cash_ un_h%C3%A9ros_aux_mille_et.un_visages.

Furmanovsky, Michael. 2008. "American Country Music in Japan: Lost Piece in the Popular Music History Puzzle." *Popular Music and Society* 31 (3): 357–72.

Geraghty, Lincoln. 2015. "Introduction: Fans and Paratexts." In *Popular Media Cultures: Fan, Audiences and Paratexts,* edited by Lincoln Geraghty, 1–14. London: Palgrave Macmillan.

Geraghty, Lincoln. 2018. "Passing Through: Popular Media Tourism, Pilgrimage and Narratives of Being a Fan." In *The Routledge Handbook on Popular Culture and Tourism,* edited by Christine Lundberg and Vassilios Ziakas, 203–13. London: Routledge.

Gibson, Chris, and John Connell. 2005. *Music and Tourism: On the Road Again.* Clevedon, UK: Channel View.

Gilman, Benjamin Ives. 1916. "Museum Fatigue." *Scientific Monthly* 2 (1): 62–74.

Giulianotti, Richard. 1999. *Football: A Sociology of the Global Game.* Oxford: Polity Press.

Gould, Jack. 1966. "A Voice That Europe Trusts." *New York Times,* April 17, 1966.

Granderson, L. Z. 2011. "Why Can't Country Music Deal with Race?" CNN, November 8, 2011.

Gray, Jonathan, Cornel Sandvoss, and C. Lee Harrington. 2007. "Introduction: Why Study Fans?" In *Fandom: Identities and Communities in a Mediated World,* edited by Jonathan Gray, Cornel Sandvoss, and C. Lee Harrington, 1–16. New York: New York University Press.

Greif, Mark. 2017. "What Was the Hipster?" In *Against Everything.* London: Verso.

Guardian. 2018. "Melania Trump Wears 'I Don't Care' Jacket en Route to Child
Detention Centre." *Guardian,* June 22, 2018. https://www.theguardian.com/us-
news/video/2018/jun/22/melania-trump-wears-i-dont-care-jacket-en-route-
to-child-detention-centre-video.

Guralnick, Peter. 2015. *Sam Phillips: The Man Who Invented Rock 'n' Roll.* London:
Weidenfeld and Nicholson.

Gussow, Adam. 2017. *Beyond the Crossroads: The Devil and the Blues Tradition.*
Chapel Hill: University of North Carolina Press.

Harrington, C. Lee, and Denise D. Bielby. 2007. "Global Fandom/Global Fan
Studies." In *Fandom: Identities and Communities in a Mediated World,* edited by
Jonathan Gray, Cornel Sandvoss, and C. Lee Harrington, 179–97. New York:
New York,.

Hills, Matt. 2013. "Fiske's 'Textual Productivity' and Digital Fandom: Web 2.0
Democratization Versus Fan Distinction?" *Participations* 10 (1): 130–53. https://
www.participations.org/Volume%2010/Issue%201/9%20Hills%2010.1.pdf.

Irish Times. 2018. "The Omagh Bombing: Key Events Before and After the Attacks."
Irish Times, August 12, 2018. https://www.irishtimes.com/news/ireland/irish-
news/omagh-bombing-key-events-before-and-after-the-attack-1.3593660.

Jenkins, Henry. (1972) 2002. *Textual Poachers: Television Fans and Participatory
Culture.* Rev. ed. New York: Routledge.

Jenkins, Henry. 2006. "Quentin Tarantino's Star Wars?" In *Media and Cultural
Studies: Keyworks,* rev. ed., edited by Meenakshi Gigi Durham and Douglas M.
Kellner, 549–76. Hoboken, NJ: Wiley-Blackwell.

Johnny Cash Channel. 2009.

King, Stephen A. 2004. "Blues Tourism in the Mississippi Delta: The Functions of
Blues Festivals." *Popular Society and Music* 27 (4): 455–75.

Kleist, Reinhard. 2009. *Johnny Cash: I See a Darkness.* New York: Abrams.

Kotb, Hoda. 2004. "From Video Store Clerk to Box Office Icon." Dateline NBC,
April 25, 2004. http://www.nbcnews.com/id/4817308/ns/dateline_nbc-
newsmakers/t/video-clerk-box-office-icon/#.XJ4hri3Mw64.

Kristeva, Julia. 1969. "L'engendrement de la formule." In *Semeiotike: Recherches
pour une sémanalyse,* 216–310. Paris: Seuil.

Lancashire Post. 2010. "Half Man Half Biscuit Turn Down the Tube." *Lancashire
Post,* November 12, 2010. https://www.lep.co.uk/whats-on/music/half-man-
half-biscuit-turn-down-the-tube1-2756797.

Legend. 1967. *The Legend.* Volume 1, January 1967. Johnny Cash Society, PO Box 95,
Oak View, CA, Country Music Hall of Fame and Library archives.

Legend. 1983. "Trading Post." *The Legend,* August 1983, 19. The Johnny & June
Carter Cash International Fan Club Yearbook, Country Music Hall of Fame and

Library archives.

Legend. 1984. *The Legend,* December 1984. The Johnny & June Carter Cash International Fan Club Yearbook, Country Music Hall of Fame and Library archives.

Legend. 1986. *The Legend,* December 1986. The Johnny & June Carter Cash International Fan Club Yearbook, Country Music Hall of Fame and Library archives.

Lewis, Lisa A. 1992. *The Adoring Audience: Fan Culture and Popular Media.* London: Routledge.

Lewry, Peter. 2001. *I've Been Everywhere: Johnny Cash Chronicle.* London: Helter Skelter Books.

Lukács, Georg. 1983. *The Historical Novel.* Translated by Hannah Mitchell and Stanley Mitchell. Preface by Fredric Jameson. Lincoln: University of Nebraska Press.

Lundberg, Christine, and Vassilios Ziakas, eds. 2018. *The Routledge Handbook of Popular Culture and Tourism.* London: Routledge.

Lydon, John. 2016. *Anger Is an Energy: My Life Uncensored.* New York: Dey Street.

Manc. 2016. " Drunk Guy Outside MMU." Facebook, March 18, 2016. https://www. facebook.com/themancuk/videos/1681666878759950/.

Mann, Geoff. 2008. "Why Does Country Music Sound White? Race and the Voice of Nostalgia." *Ethnic and Racial Studies* 31 (1): 73–100.

Mantione, Mariska, Martijn Figee, and Damiaan Denys. 2014. "A Case of Musical Preference for Johnny Cash Following Deep Brain Stimulation of the Nucleus Accumbens." *Frontiers in Behavioral Neuroscience* 2014 (8). https://www .frontiersin.org/articles/10.3389/fnbeh.2014.00152/full.

Margry, Peter Jan. 2008. "Secular Pilgrimage: A Contradiction in Terms?" In *Shrines and Pilgrimage in the Modern World,* edited by Peter Jan Margry, 1–16. Amsterdam: Amsterdam University Press.

Marling, Karal Ann. 1993. "Elvis Presley's Graceland, or the Aesthetic of Rock 'n' Roll Heaven." *American Art* 7 (4): 72–105.

Marshall, Lee. 2003. "For and Against the Record Industry: An Introduction to Bootleg Collectors and Tape Traders." *Popular Music* 22 (1): 57–72.

Martinsen, Svenn. 2013. "Norwegian Radio Days." Stella Maris, December 31, 2013. http://www.stellamaris.no/norwegianradiodays.htm.

Morimoto, Lori Hitchcock. 2017. "Transnational Media Fan Studies." In *The Routledge Companion to Media Fandom,* edited by Suzanne Scott and Melissa Click, 280–88. London: Routledge.

Motley, Clay. 2018. "'Life Gets Heavy': Blues Tourism in Clarksdale, Mississippi." *Southern Cultures* 24 (2): 78–97.

Mueller, Monika. 2013. "Johnny Cash and Bob Dylan Revisited: Musical

'Authenticity' and Transnational Adaptations of Country and Folk Music." In *The Transnationalism of American Culture: Literature, Film, and Music*, edited by Rocio G. David, 104–17. London: Routledge.

NME. 2016. "Soundtrack of My Life: Freddie Flintoff." NME Blog, July 15, 2016. https://www.nme.com/blogs/nme-blogs/soundtrack-of-my-life-freddie-flintoff-5680.

O'Connell, Kate. 2013. "Happy Birthday, Copy Machine! Happy Birthday, Copy Machine!" NPR, October 23, 2013. https://www.npr.org/2013/10/23/239241106/happy-birthday-copy-machine-happy-birthday-copy-machine?t=1530868654063.

OED. 2002. "New Words List June 2002." *Oxford English Dictionary*, June 13, 2002. https://public.oed.com/updates/new-words-list-june-2002/.

ORF. 2018. "Daheim in Österreich." Österreichischer Rundfunk (Austrian Broadcasting Corporation), September 3, 2018. https://tv.orf.at/gutenmorgen/stories/daheiminoesterreich/.

Ortega, Teresa. 1995. "'My Name Is Sue! How Do You Do?' Johnny Cash as Lesbian Icon." *South Atlantic Quarterly* 94: 259–72.

Our Kinda Cash. 1976. *Our Kinda Cash*, Fourth Quarter Journal, 1976. The Johnny & June Carter Cash International Fan Club, Country Music Hall of Fame and Library archives.

Our Kinda Cash. 1978. *Our Kinda Cash*, Fourth Quarter Journal, 1978. The Johnny & June Carter Cash International Fan Club, Country Music Hall of Fame and Library archives.

Our Kinda Cash. 1993a. "Pen Pals," *Our Kinda Cash*, Spring 1993, 16. The Johnny & June Carter Cash International Fan Club, Country Music Hall of Fame and Library archives.

Our Kinda Cash. 1993b. "Pen Pals." *Our Kinda Cash*, Summer 1993. The Johnny & June Carter Cash International Fan Club, Country Music Hall of Fame and Library archives.

Our Kinda Cash. 1996. "Pen Pals." *Our Kinda Cash*, Spring 1996, 9. The Johnny & June Carter Cash International Fan Club, Country Music Hall of Fame and Library archives.

Pande, Rukmini. 2018. *Squee from the Margins: Fandom and Race*. Iowa City: University of Iowa Press.

Pearson, Roberta. 2010. "Fandom in the Digital Era." *Popular Communication* 8 (1): 84–89.

Pennington, Diana Rasmussen. 2016. "'The Most Passionate Cover I've Seen': Emotional Information in Fan-Created U2 Music Videos." *Journal of Documentation* 72 (3): 569–90.

Pirate Radio Hall of Fame. n.d. "Spotlight on: 'Daffy' Don Allen," Offshore Radio. http://www.offshoreradio.co.uk/spotall.htm.

Pringle, Derek. 2006. "England Summon Ring of Fire to Ignite Triumph." *Telegraph,* March 23, 2006. https://www.telegraph.co.uk/sport/cricket/2334141/England-summon-Ring-of-Fire-to-ignite-triumph.html.

Radway, Janice. (1984) 1991. *Reading the Romance: Women, Patriarchy, and Popular Literature.* Chapel Hill: University of North Carolina Press.

Raskin, Richard. 2001. "Camus's Critique of Existentialism." *Minerva* 5: 156–65. http://www.minerva.mic.ul.ie/vol5/camus.pdf.

Rau, Nate. 2016. "Billboard Adds Americana Music to Charts." *Tennessean,* May 13, 2016.

"Ray-Ban Wayfarers." 2009. Stuff White People Like, December 22, 2009. https://stuffwhitepeoplelike.com/2009/?fbclid=IwAR3on3qJfo3NftK7OklGC4TMix1L1v wl1YxHMuJsqA2XVIox0AM-pXyloho.

Reijnders, Stijn, Leonieke Bolderman, Nicky Van Es, and Abby Waysdorf. 2015. "Locating Imagination: An Interdisciplinary Perspective on Literary, Film, and Music Tourism." *Tourism Analysis* 20 (2015): 333–39.

Rioux, Philippe. 2007. "Légion d'Honneur et Arts et Lettres: David Lynch Officier et Sting Chevalier." Ledepeche.ft, October 2, 2007. https://www .ladepeche.fr/article/2007/10/02/25058-legion-honneur-arts-lettres-david-lynch-officier-sting-chevalier.html.

Robinson, Mike, and David Picard. 2009. "Moments, Magic, and Memories: Photographing Tourists, Tourist Photographs and Making Worlds." In *The Framed World: Tourism, Tourists and Photographs,* edited by Mike Robinson and David Picard. Farnham, UK: Ashgate.

Scodari, Christine. 2007. "Yoko in Cyberspace with Beatles Fans: Gender and the Re-creation of Popular Mythology." In *Fandom: Identities and Communities in a Mediated World,* edited by Jonathan Gray, Cornel Sandvoss, and C. Lee Harrington, 48–59. New York: New York University Press.

Shriver, Jerry. 2009. "Grammys Will Be Putting Americana on the Map." *USA Today,* August 31, 2009.

SigmaOctanus. 2010. "Johnny Cash Undead." DeviantArt, August 23, 2010. https://www.deviantart.com/sigmaoctanus/art/Johnny-cash-undead-176559288.

Silverman, Jonathan. 2010. *Nine Choices: Johnny Cash and American Culture.* Amherst: University of Massachusetts Press.

Skinner, Frank. 2018. "Johnny Cash Started Me on the Rocky Road to Alcoholism." *Guardian,* April 24, 2018. https://www.theguardian.com/tv-and-radio/2018/apr/24/frank-skinner-johnny-cash-started-me-on-the-rocky-road-to-alcoholism-ostrich-attack.

Smith, David. 2018. "'Memphis Died with Dr. King'—Shadow of Civil Rights Leader Haunts City." *Guardian*, April 1, 2018. https://www.theguardian.com/us-news/2018/apr/01/martin-luther-king-memphis-mlk-50th-anniversary-death-lorraine-motel.

Sontag, Susan. 1997. *On Photography.* New York: Picador.

SOS. n.d. "SOS Children's Villages Mar del Plata." SOS Children's Villages International. https://www.sos-childrensvillages.org/where-we-help/americas/argentina/mar-del-plata.

Streissguth, Michael. 2005. *Johnny Cash at Folsom Prison.* Boston: Da Capo.

Strictly Cash. 1974. "Cash Country—Nashville." *Strictly Cash* 46 (1974): 3–9. The Official Johnny Cash Society, Country Music Hall of Fame and Library archives.

Strohler, Virginia. 1972. *The Legend,* 1972. The Johnny & June Carter Cash International Fan Club, Country Music Hall of Fame and Library archives.

Thanki, Juli. 2016. "Johnny Cash's 'Sanctuary' Opens to All." *Tennessean,* July 11, 2016. https://www.tennessean.com/story/entertainment/music/2016/07/11/johnny-cashs-sanctuary-opens-all/84235044/.

Thatcher, Margaret. 1987. Interview. *Women's Own,* September 23, 1987. https://www.margaretthatcher.org/document/106689.

Théberge, Paul. 2006. "Everyday Fandom: Fan Clubs, Blogging, and the Quotidian Rhythms of the Internet." *Canadian Journal of Communication* 30 (4). https://cjc-online.ca/index.php/journal/article/view/1673/1810.

Thompson, Clive. 2015. "How the Photocopier Changed the Way We Worked—And Played," *Smithsonian,* March 2015. https://www.smithsonianmag.com/history/duplication-nation-3D-printing-rise-180954332/#EGqJiMbFqIeB6L6a.99.

Thompson, Stephen I. 1992. "American Country Music in Japan." *Popular Music and Society* 16 (3): 357–72.

Tolson, Andrew. 2010. "A New Authenticity? Communicative Practices on YouTube." *Critical Discourse Studies* 7 (4): 285.

Vignoles, Julian. 1984. "What Is Irish Popular Music?" *Crane Bag* 8 (2): 70–72.

Whitman, Alden. 1970. "In Antonio Salazar: A Quiet Autocrat Who Held Power in Portugal for 40 Years." *New York Times,* July 28, 1970.

Wile, Rob. 2004. "The True Story of How McDonald's Conquered France." Business Insider, August 22, 2004. http://www.businessinsider.com/how-mcdonalds-conquered-france-2014-8?IR=T.

Williams, Rebecca. 2018. "Starting at the End." In *Everybody Hurts: Endings and Resurrections in Fan Cultures,* edited by Rebecca Williams, 19–30. Iowa City: University of Iowa Press.

Woolf, Nicky. 2014. "Man Develops Powerful Love of Johnny Cash Following Deep Brain Stimulation." *Guardian,* May 27, 2014. https://www.theguardian.com/music/2014/may/27/johnny-cash-deep-brain-stimulation-ur ge-listen.

Wren, Christopher S. 1971. *Winners Got Scars Too: The Life of Johnny Cash.* New York: Dial Press.

Žižek, Slavoj. 2006. *The Parallax View.* Cambridge, MA: MIT Press.

Zubernis, Lynn, and Kathy Larsen. 2018. "Make Space for Us! Fandom in the Real World." In *A Companion to Media Fandom and Fan Studies,* edited by Paul Booth, 145–60. Hoboken, NJ: Wiley-Blackwell.

INDEX

"Dub is My Occupation," 124

Dublin (Republic of Ireland), 9, 17, 23, 38, 40, 41, 109, 139

Duffett, Mark, 57, 63, 218, 219

Dutch East India Company, 175

Dyess, AR, 21, 142, 165, 169–72

Dylan, Bob, 39, 45, 92, 132, 201

Edwards, Leigh, 225n, 227n, 231n

Egypt, 121, 125–26

eight-track tapes, 16

Eindhoven (Netherlands), 41, 89

Elfstrom, Robert, 225n

Ellis, Liam, 205

Ellison, Curtis, 227n

Emo's (Austin, TX), 4

Engels, Friedrich, 65

England, 6, 18, 41, 53, 55, 62, 65–83, 196–97

English (language): Cash as singer in, 3, 103–104; and language of fans, 48–49, 62, 130, 157, 230n; as lingua franca, 52; of tribute performers, 117, 121, 127; slang, 71; in YouTube comments, 106, 107, 109, 112, 115

enka, 53

Enniscorthy (Republic of Ireland), 200

Ethiopians, the, 124

Europe: and Africa, 130–32; and American cultural influence, 42, 142, 219; Cash fan activity in, 36, 39, 56, 92, 98, 162, 188, 226–27n; Cash media profile in, 6; Cash and Northern Europe, 184, 223; Cash record releases in, 1, 45; Cash's tours in, 3, 23, 143, 184; country fandom in, 165; Elvis Presley's profile in, 180; as market for U.S. music tourism, 179; as political entity,

173, 186, 221, 230n; as site of tribute artists, 7, 193; travellers to U.S. from, 7, 143, 156, 159, 165, 172–73, 174. *See also* Brexit

European football championships, 76

European Johnny Cash Festival (Austria), 7, 98, 142, 143, 152, 158–62

Eurovision Song Contest, 185

Evening Herald, 94

existential, 37, 47, 67, 112, 132, 134, 188, 216, 229n

Facebook: as communications tool, 6, 7, 88, 129, 130, 131, 134, 135, 200, 202, 209, 226n; as media platform, 82, 87, 207; as a place to share experiences, 93, 153, 155, 156, 161, 162, 163, 203; as site for fan clubs, 6, 7, 63, 64, 87, 140, 213, 215

Falstaff, 81

Fan Club Johnny Cash France, 129, 131, 133

fan clubs, 5, 53, 54, 64, 91, 109

fandom: international collaboration within fandom, 5, 31, 34–36, 87–101, 199–211; international fandom conceptualized, 1–10, 217–24; superfans, 1, 8, 102, 130–31, 178, 181, 183, 187; transcultural, 5, 220; transgenerational, 4, 9, 13; translocal, 8, 35, 99, 178; transnational, 8, 16, 39, 46, 81, 99, 112, 116, 117–18, 218, 220. *See also* Cash, Johnny; fans of Johnny Cash; Johnny Cash Project; networks; YouTube

fans of Johnny Cash: artwork by, 32–37; as collaborator, 2, 5, 34–37, 88–89, 199–211; as collectors,

American South, 164–82, 197; as Johnny Cash related industry, 6, 8, 142–43, 150, 223; Johnny Cash tribute acts as tourist heuristic and, 124–25; participation aspect of, 120–21, 152, 167–68; through photography, 154–63; as pilgrimage, 7, 97, 143, 158, 173–74, 175, 197, 230n; and visiting Johnny Cash related sites, 6, 8, 59, 70, 74, 141–42, 145, 151, 155

Tranmere Rovers Football Club, 68

transcultural, 5, 220

translocal, 8, 35, 70–76, 99, 132, 178

transnational, 8, 16, 40, 46, 81, 99, 113, 116, 117, 118, 218, 220

Transylvania, 59

tribute artists, 1, 88, 92–93, 96, 147, 158, 180, 189, 200, 207, 210, 221; Cash tributes defined as, 95; categories of, 116–22; Elvis impersonators as, 15; fan perceptions of Cash tributes and, 24, 36, 77–78, 137, 147; as imitators of Joaquin Phoenix in *Walk the Line*, 95; popularity of 15, 88, 133, 136; on YouTube 104, 116–24

Troubles, Northern Irish, 16, 19

"True True True," 124

Trump, Donald, 16, 42, 110, 190, 221, 226n

Trump, Melania, 25

t-shirts: canon of Cash images on 29–30; Charlottesville controversy and, 4, 25, 31, 32, 70, 140, 183, 190–91, 194, 215, 226n; as fandom commodity, 31, 100, 150, 190, 201, 223; as signifier of affiliation, 5, 32, 35, 40, 130, 201; as signifier of

integrity, 31, 32, 215

Tubb, Ernest, 175, 204

The Tube (TV show), 68

U2, 73, 176, 202

Ulster-American Folk Park, 15

Unchained, 118

University of Coimbra, 193

Uppsala (Sweden), 41

USB device, 159. *See also* digital fan culture

Valencia (Spain), 41, 48, 49

van der Lay, Kees, 99, 208, 210

Venice (Italy), 33

video: as art project, 5, 31, 34–36; of Cash performances, 3, 6, 102–14, 177, 215, 227n; fan produced, 220; legacy of Cash on, 202; as tape, 55–56; travelogue, 125–26, 156–63; of tribute performances, 81–82, 115–28, 137, 207, 209, 227n, 228n. *See also* "God's Gonna Cut You Down"; "Hurt"; Johnny Cash Project; television; YouTube

Vietnam, 19, 21, 45

Vignoles, Julian, 15

Visser, Albert, 99, 203, 204, 208, 210

visual culture, 217; Johnny Cash as visual text, 29–37, 103, 190, 210; tribute performances and, 95; website as expression of, 133. *See also* movies; television; t-shirts; video; YouTube

The Voice, 115

Volbeat, 120

Walk the Line (2005): encountering Cash through, 2, 22, 29, 186; fan

FANDOM & CULTURE